FACES OF EDMONTON

SHAYNE WOODSMITH

Special thanks to Christina Sicoli and Christian Whitty for their design expertise and to all the people who bring Edmonton to life.

And to Megan: This book, this project wouldn't have been possible without your love and support. You gave Faces of Edmonton its name and encouraged me to pursue it. You are the behind-the-scenes inspiration for everything I do and often my first Faces of Edmonton photo of the day. Thank you. You're a beautiful person, and I can't imagine my life without you.

ISBN: 978-1511840071

First edition: June 2015

ABOUT

In the winter of 2014, my wife and I left our jobs, sold our house, donated many of our possessions, and then travelled to sixteen countries in four months. This was my sabbatical, my time to dismantle a daily routine that had made me feel stagnant and uninspired, my time to explore the world and rekindle my passion for storytelling.

While travelling, we tried to capture the essence of each city we visited, taking thousands of photos and writing accompanying descriptions, our words adding details that textured and complimented the photos. We posted many of our pictures and stories to a blog that became our travel journal. It's called Wandering Woodsmiths if you're interested in checking out some of the places we visited.

When we returned to Edmonton, we struggled to settle back into a normal life. It was hard to let go of the nomadic lifestyle, living out of backpacks, travelling to a new country every week. But we were back and suddenly very still. All that remained of our possessions fit snuggly inside a fifteen by seven storage locker, which we dipped into from time to time. The cats were staying with friends and seemed—in their dismissive, piss-in-your-shoes kind of way—happy to see us. We had no home, stayed with family, and looked for a place of our own.

I still felt like a tourist, as if Edmonton was just the next stop on our journey. I kept taking photos, kept seeing interesting and beautiful things that I wanted to capture. I also started talking to strangers, hearing their stories and taking their portraits.

I began to feel connected to Edmonton in a way that I never had before. I was getting to know new and interesting people, hearing stories of loss, pain, love, hope. Some stories made me laugh out loud while others brought tears to my eyes. These were the stories of Edmontonians, of being human, stories I thought everyone should hear to better understand and empathize with others, to feel less alone in the world.

I felt compelled to share the deeper connection with Edmonton and its inhabitants that I was cultivating for myself. I wanted to foster the curiosity most people have about strangers and help break down the barriers that keep us from getting to know each other. So with Megan's encouragement and knack for thinking up great names for things, I created a new blog, a hybrid between our storytelling travel journal and the humanity-capturing portraiture of Humans of New York.

Faces of Edmonton is a community-building project and photoblog that showcases Edmonton through the portraits and stories of the city's inhabitants. It is a forum where people can connect and share thoughts and feelings about the portraits and stories of strangers. It's a community where strangers become acquaintances and dear friends dearer. Faces of Edmonton has introduced me and many others to the beauty and diversity of Edmonton and the dynamic people who animate it.

Everybody has a story. Many of us define ourselves and understand others through our stories. Faces of Edmonton is a place where people can move seamlessly between the roles of teller and listener, and this book provides a glimpse into my year spent wandering the streets of Edmonton, meeting people and hearing their stories. This book captures and holds what it was like to be in Edmonton for one particular year, day by day, season by season.

To everyone who has stopped to chat with a camera-toting stranger, thank you. Thank you for the conversation and for letting me take your photo. I've enjoyed getting to know you a little bit. I often wonder how you're doing these days, what's changed in your life, and how our conversation would go if we were to meet on the street today. If you'd like, send me a message to facesofedmonton@gmail.com, I'd love to hear from you. I'd love to hear from anyone who has something they'd like to share with me. So drop me a line and tell me a story. While reading your message, I'll probably wish that I could have taken your photo while you were writing it.

Thank you to everyone who follows Faces of Edmonton. Your support and encouragement keeps me doing what I'm doing. This book is for you. I hope you enjoy it as much as I have enjoyed putting it together.

If you're in Edmonton, maybe we'll meet on the street one day. And who knows, maybe you'll even let me take your photo.

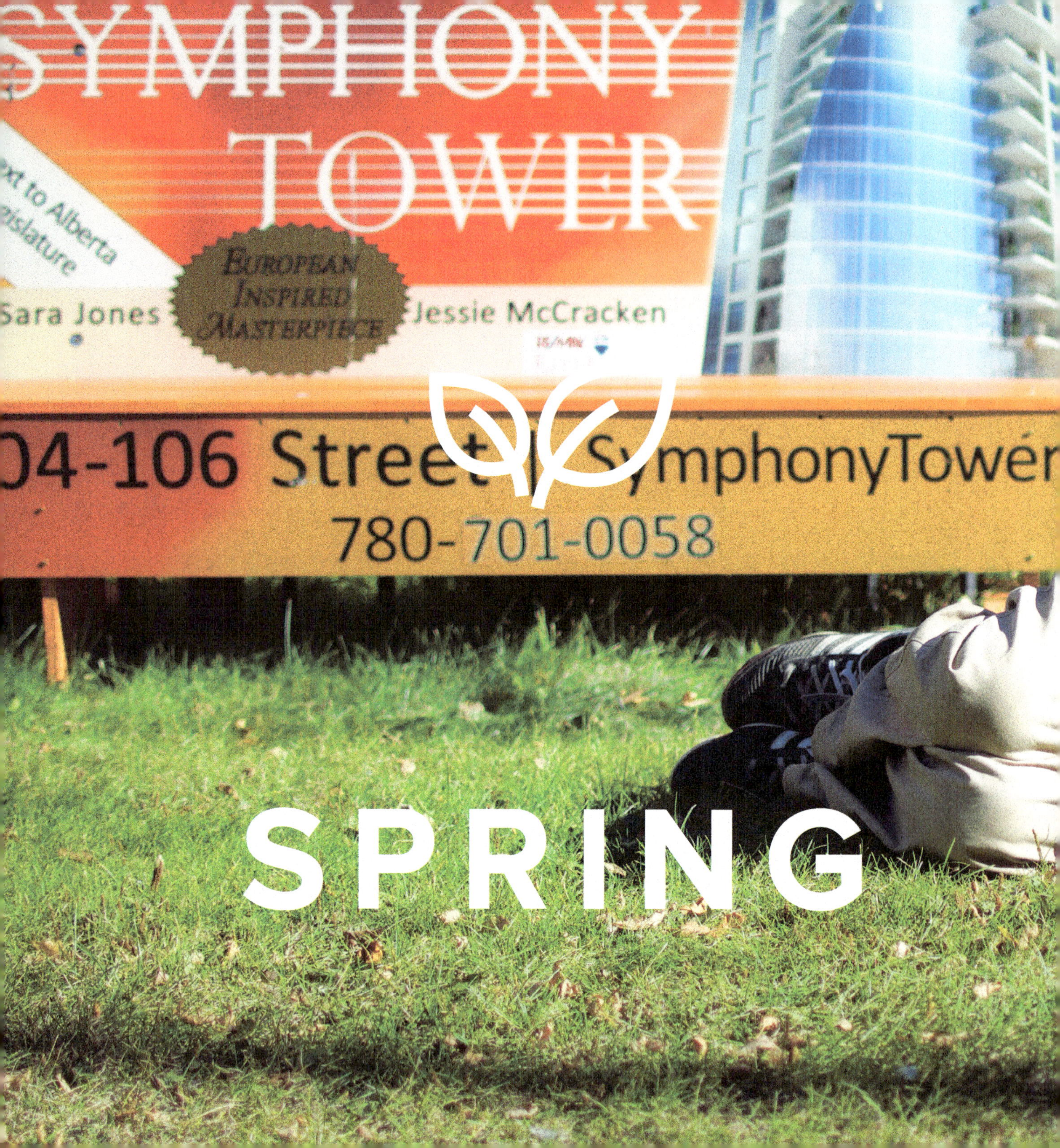
SYMPHONY
TOWER
European Inspired Masterpiece
Sara Jones
Jessie McCracken
04-106 Street | SymphonyTower
780-701-0058

SPRING

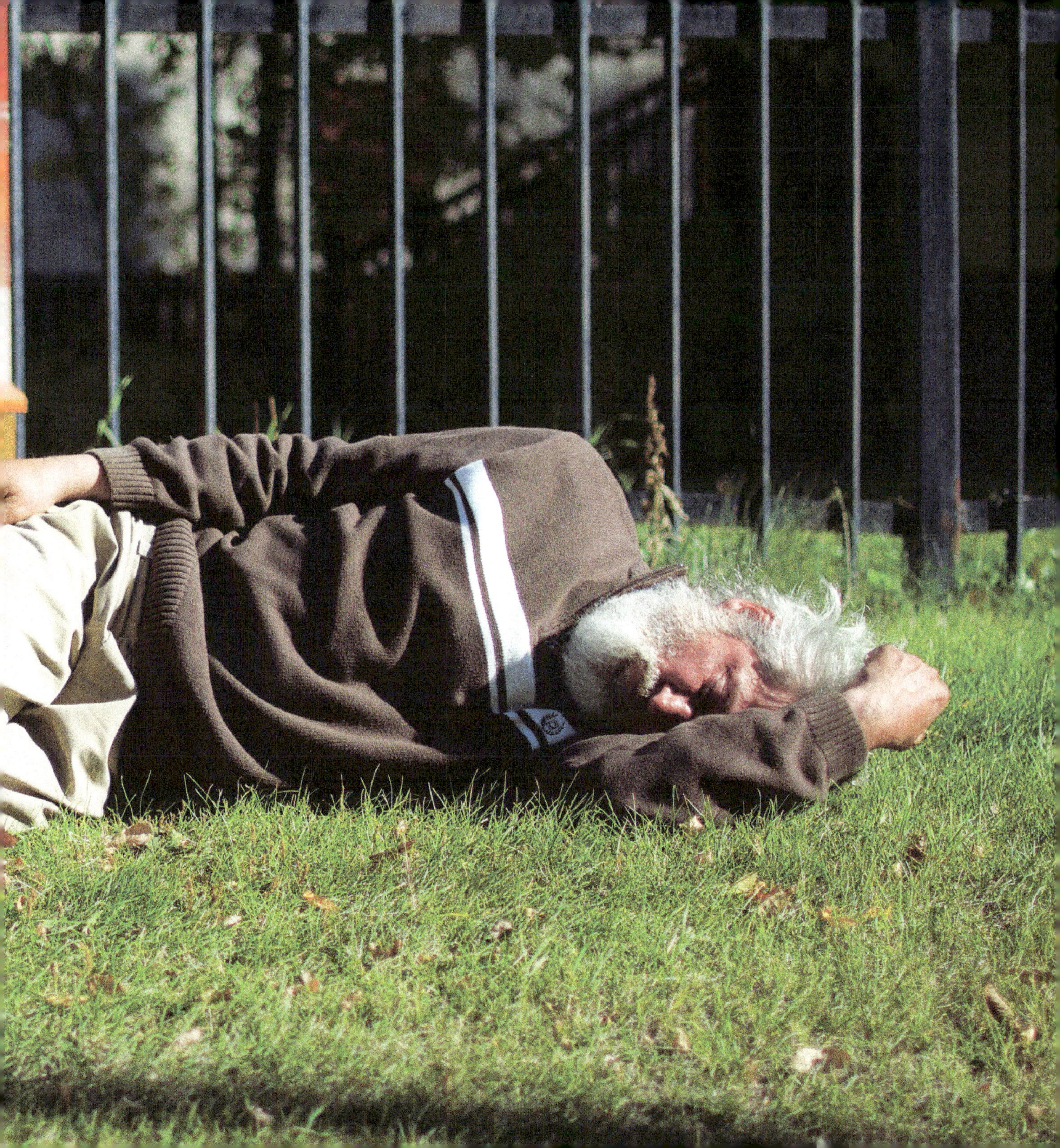

“My life has changed so much, and I just try to enjoy every day. Don’t take things too seriously.”

“Did you used to take things too seriously?”

“Oh yeah. I used to think that money or your position, that kind of stuff, would make you better, happier. It doesn’t. Happiness actually starts from within. It’s just the way you think and see things.”

“How long did it take you to realize that?”

“After I got divorced, I realized it was a problem with my expectations. Once I got that kind of mindset going, it was much better. But it took five years. I’m content. I find happiness more flighty. It works for me. And the thing I found is that it’s because I’m on my own. No one depends on me. So I don’t have to worry about who’s happy and who’s not happy. It’s much easier.”

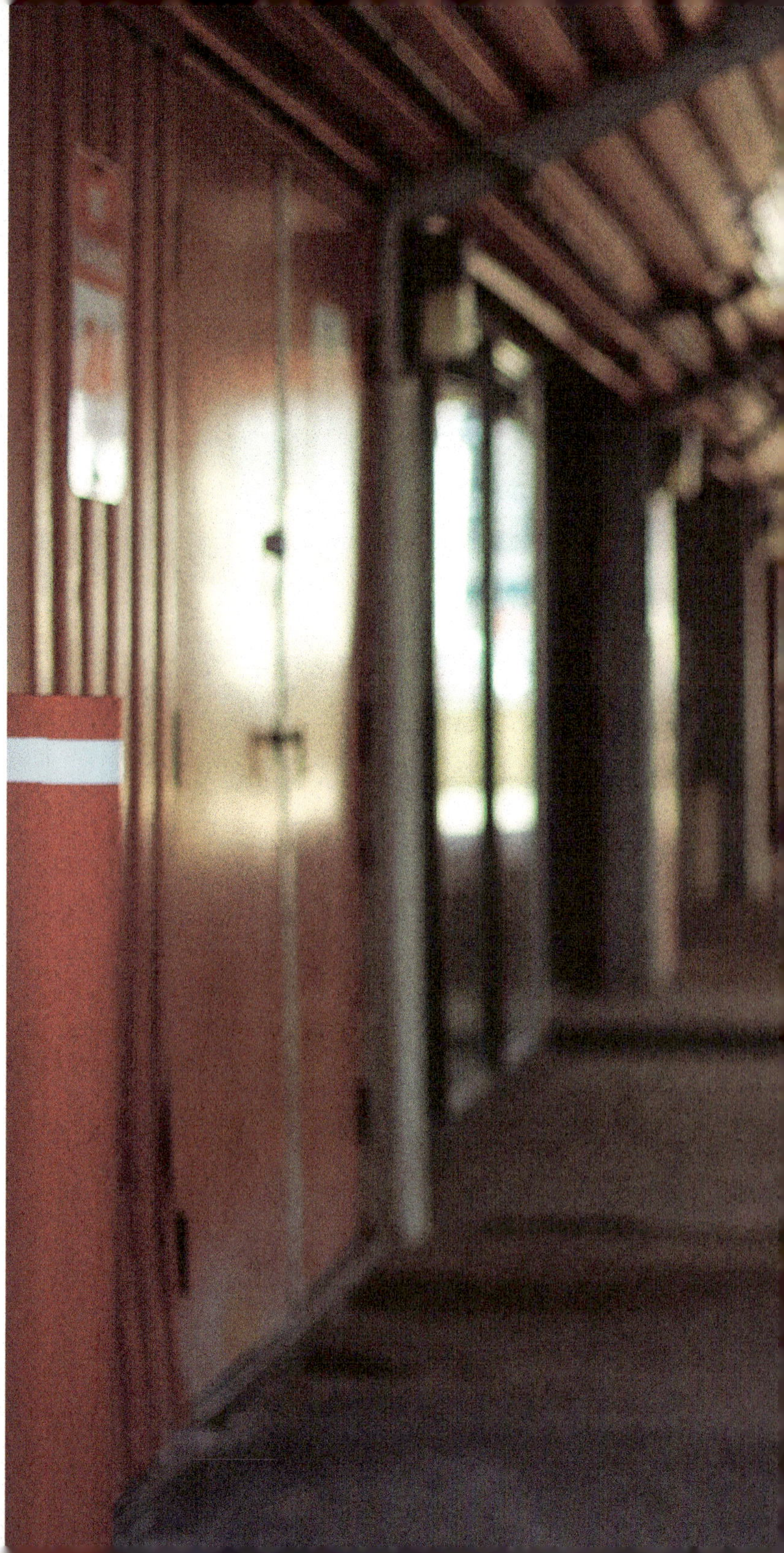

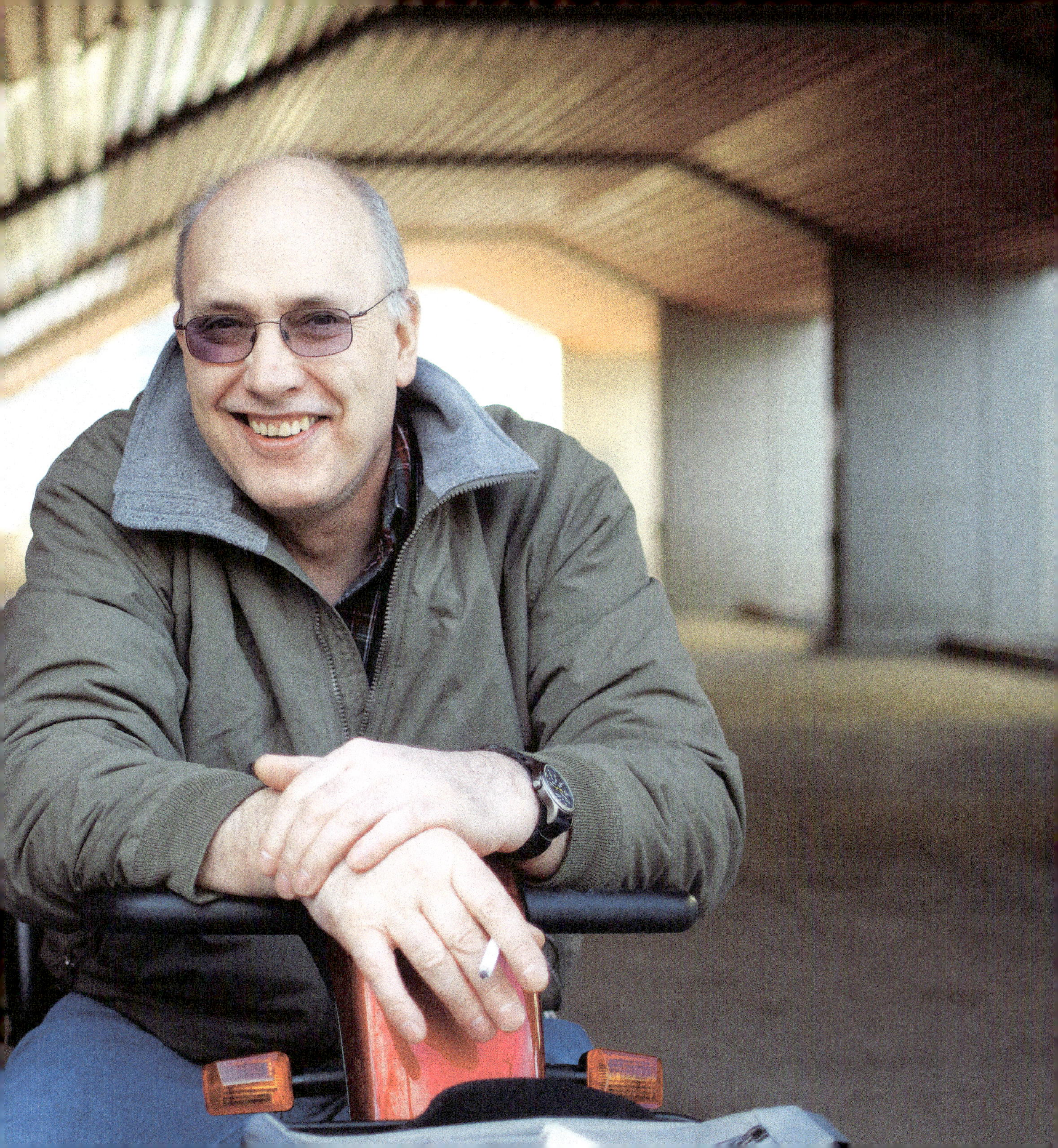

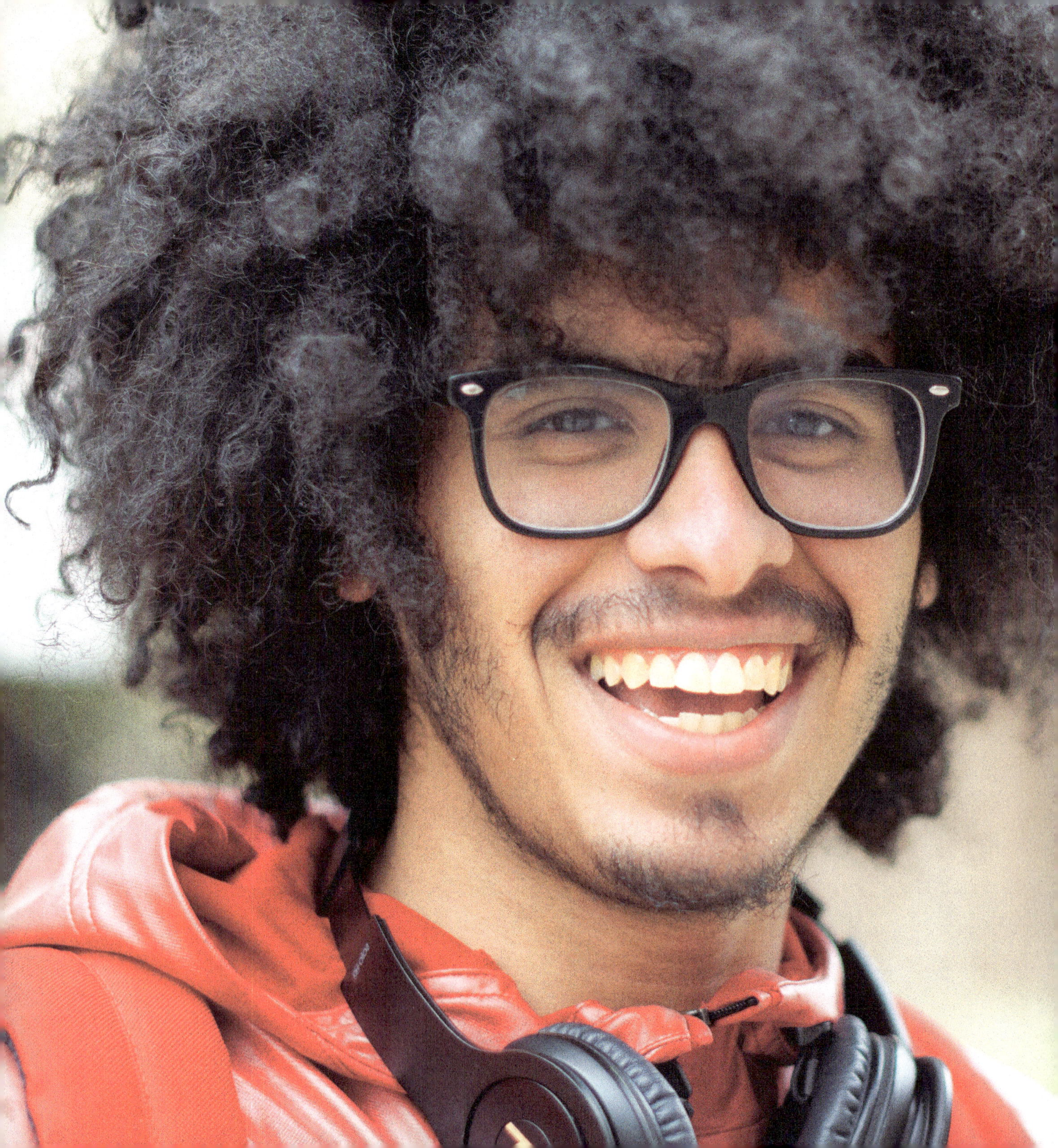

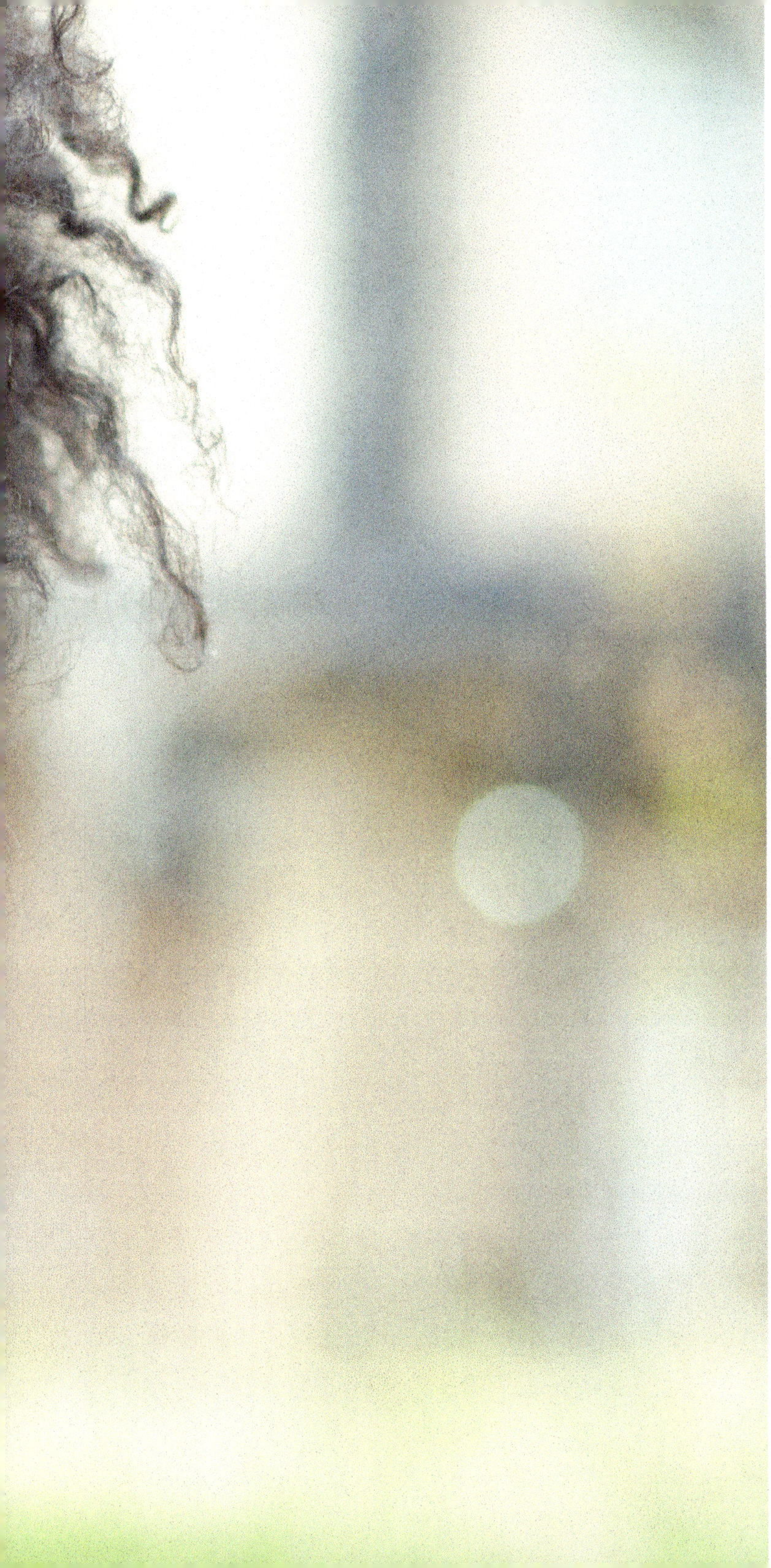

“What is your quest?”

“I actually have a lot of things. Yeah, man. I’m from Saudi Arabia and the purpose for coming here, studying English, was because English is one of the most important things in Saudi Arabia. If you want to get a job, the first question is, ‘Do you speak English?’ So yeah, I just came here to study English. Because our government pays for all things in university. So it’s for free, and I have a lot of choices.”

“What’s one of the biggest differences between Edmonton and Saudi Arabia?”

“Oh, a lot. The first thing is the weather, man. In Saudi Arabia it is extremely hot, like plus forty. Here it’s great. People here are very friendly, and freedom. Yeah, man. Freedom. In Saudi Arabia you cannot do a lot of things but here you can do it. For example, in Saudi Arabia, if you talk to a woman, it’s a problem. But here it’s okay.”

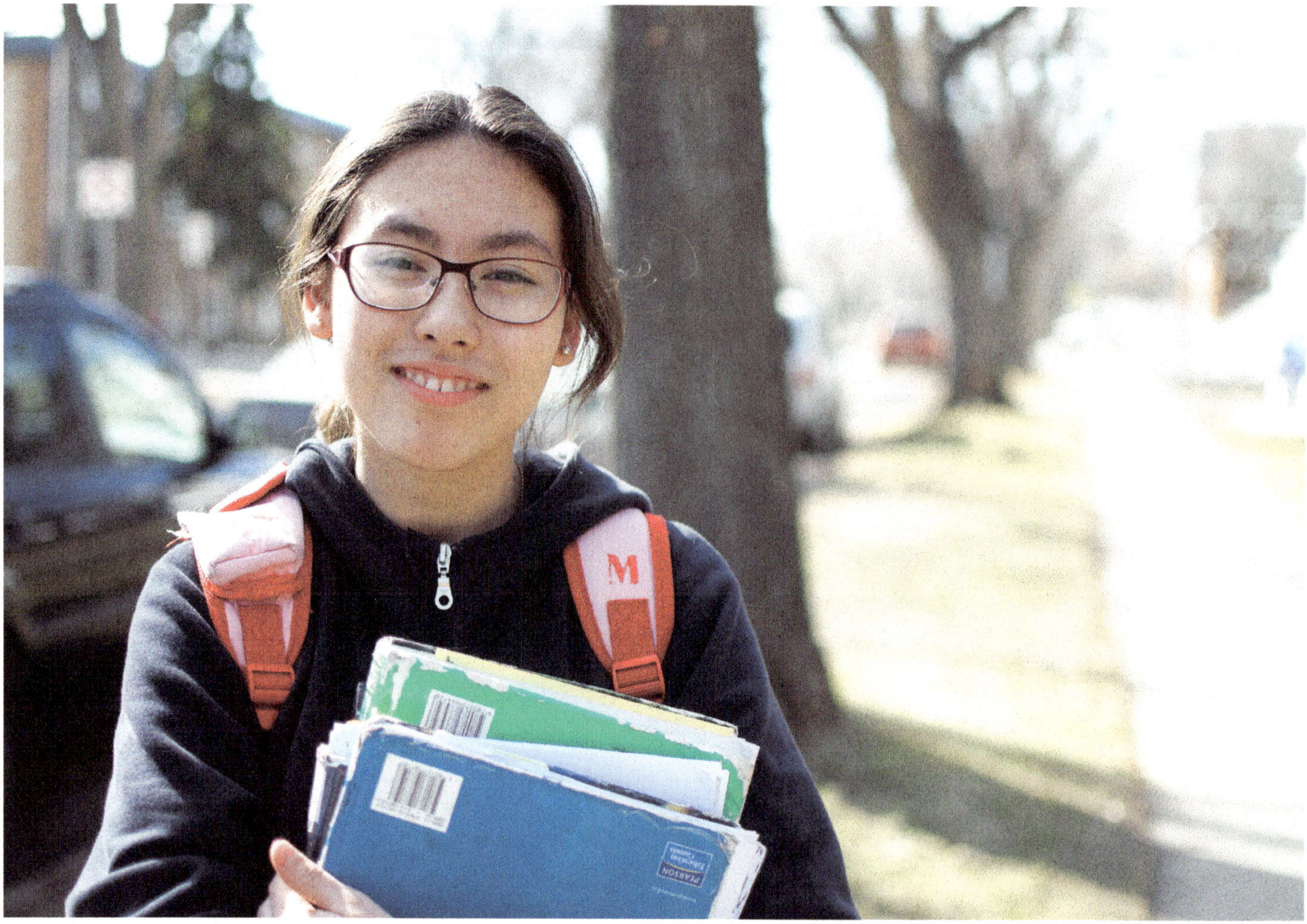

"I'm actually in an all-girls school, and we wear a uniform."

"Do you like wearing a uniform?"

"I do like the uniform. We all look united because of the uniform and most schools don't have that. It's all about drama and stuff, but it's not like that at our school. If we didn't have the uniform, we'd have a bunch a girls worrying about what they wear every morning, and it would actually get a little annoying. Just a little."

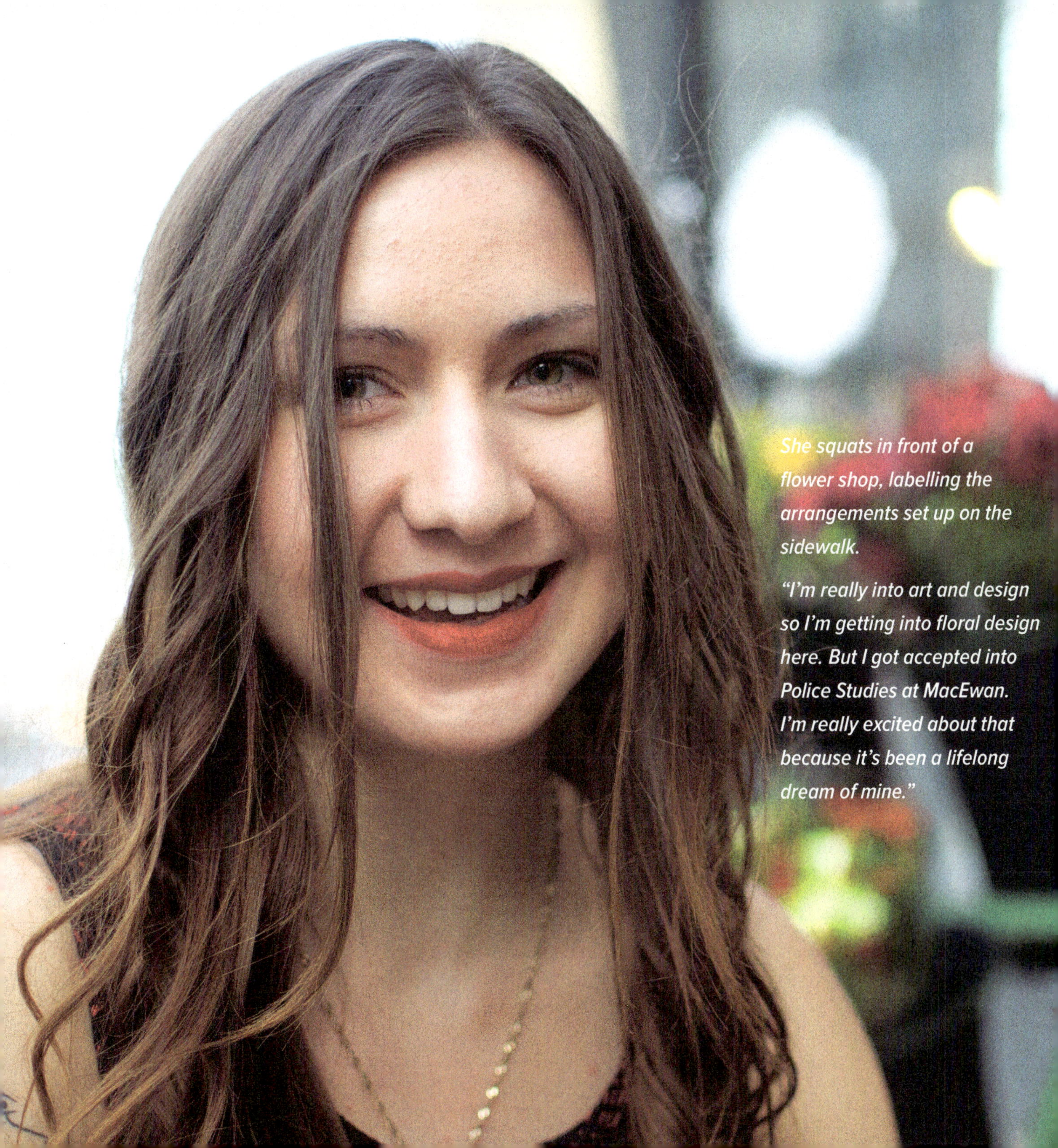

She squats in front of a flower shop, labelling the arrangements set up on the sidewalk.

"I'm really into art and design so I'm getting into floral design here. But I got accepted into Police Studies at MacEwan. I'm really excited about that because it's been a lifelong dream of mine."

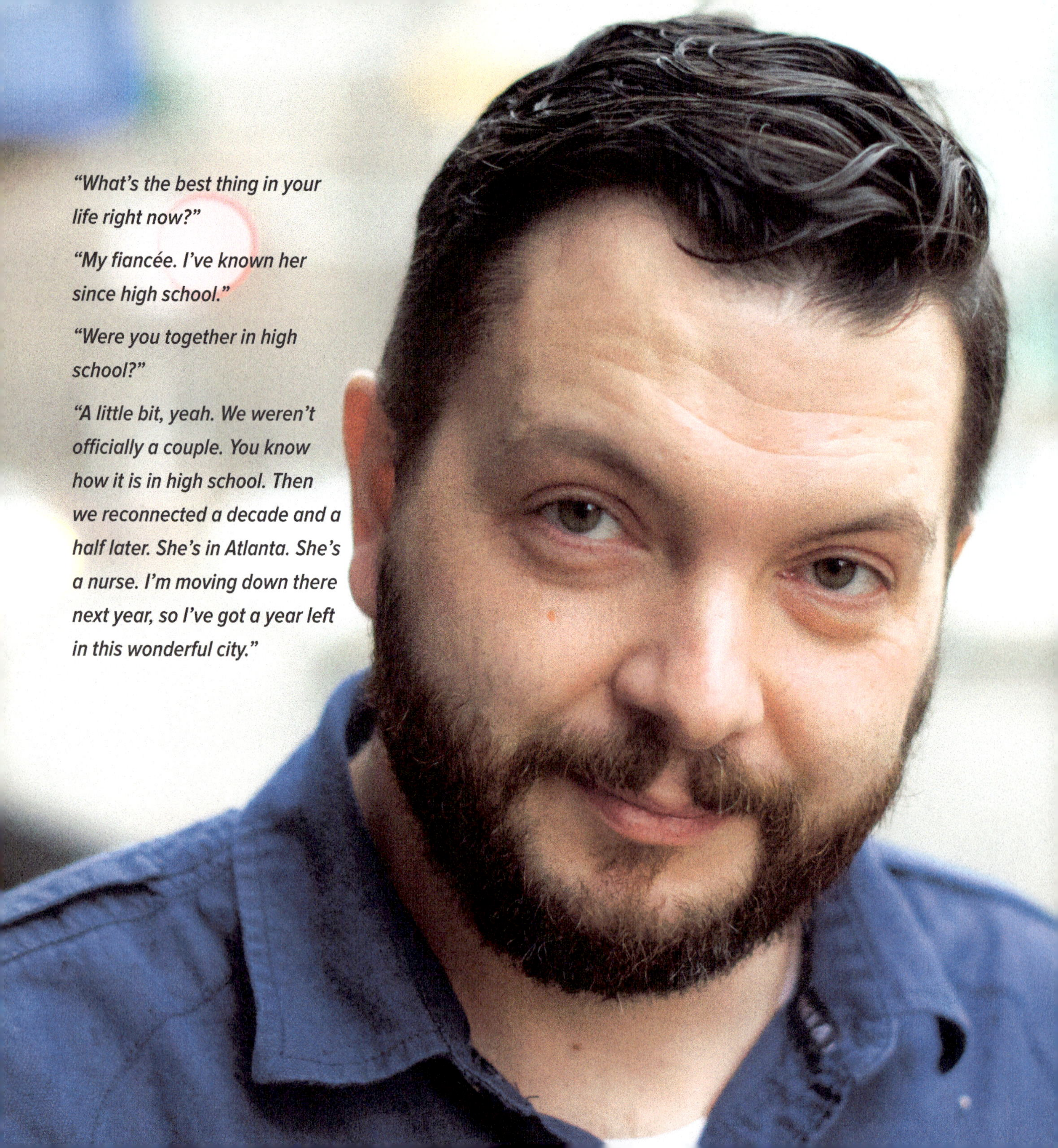

"What's the best thing in your life right now?"

"My fiancée. I've known her since high school."

"Were you together in high school?"

"A little bit, yeah. We weren't officially a couple. You know how it is in high school. Then we reconnected a decade and a half later. She's in Atlanta. She's a nurse. I'm moving down there next year, so I've got a year left in this wonderful city."

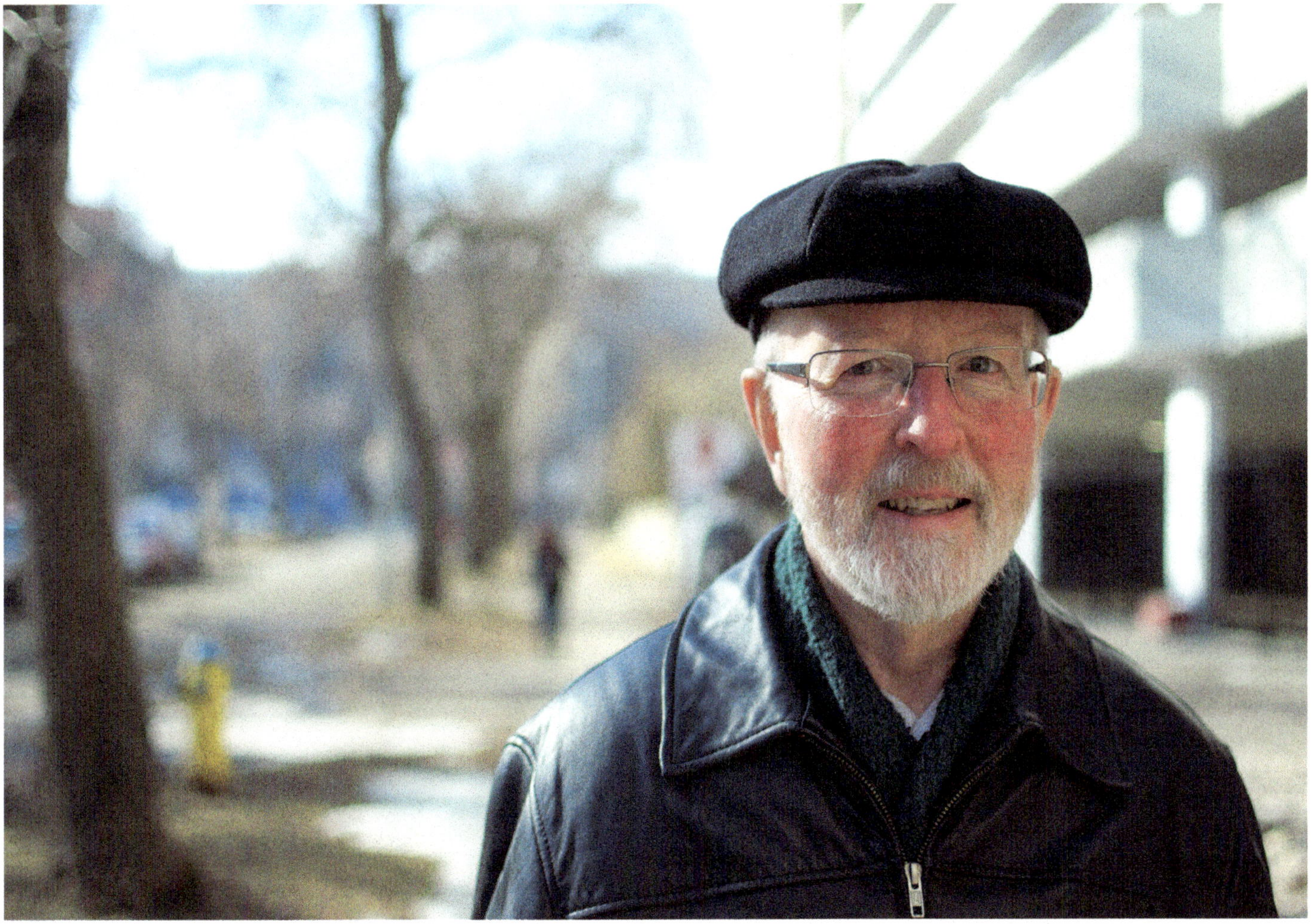

“What do you wish you knew when you were younger?”

“Lots of things.”

“What advice would you give your younger self?”

“Not to eat so much candy.”

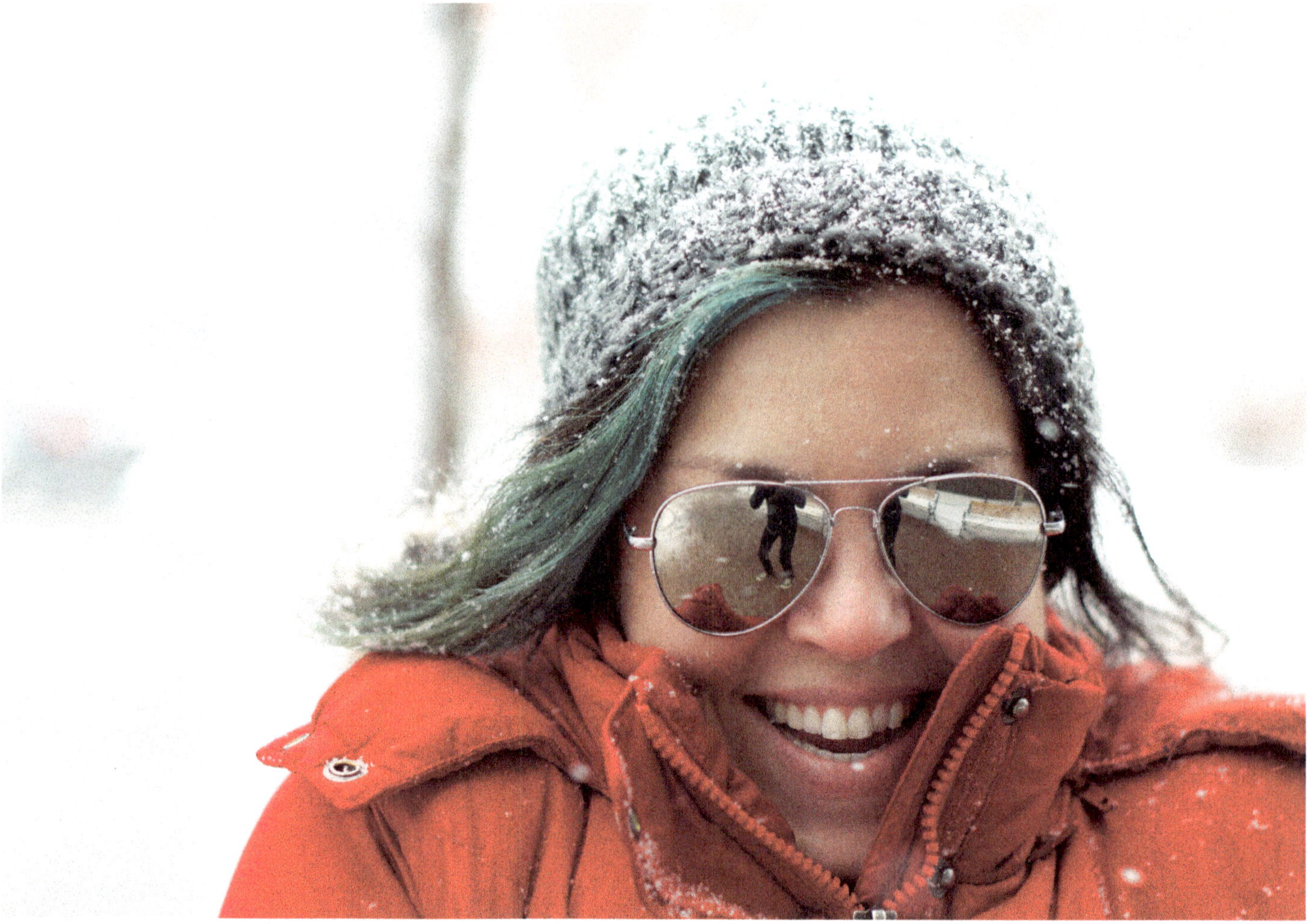

May 6, 2015: The day after the election. It snows. It snows a lot.

"How was last night?"

"Awesome. I freaked out. I am so pumped. It's sort of a shock. I couldn't believe it. I was like, 'Really?' I thought maybe a minority. Maybe."

"Do you have renewed hope in our political system?"

"Ah, yeah. I totally thought it was an exercise in futility for a long time. But the fact that it happened is crazy. I'm pretty excited. I'm excited about having an educated female in power that isn't a conservative. I'm super excited about that."

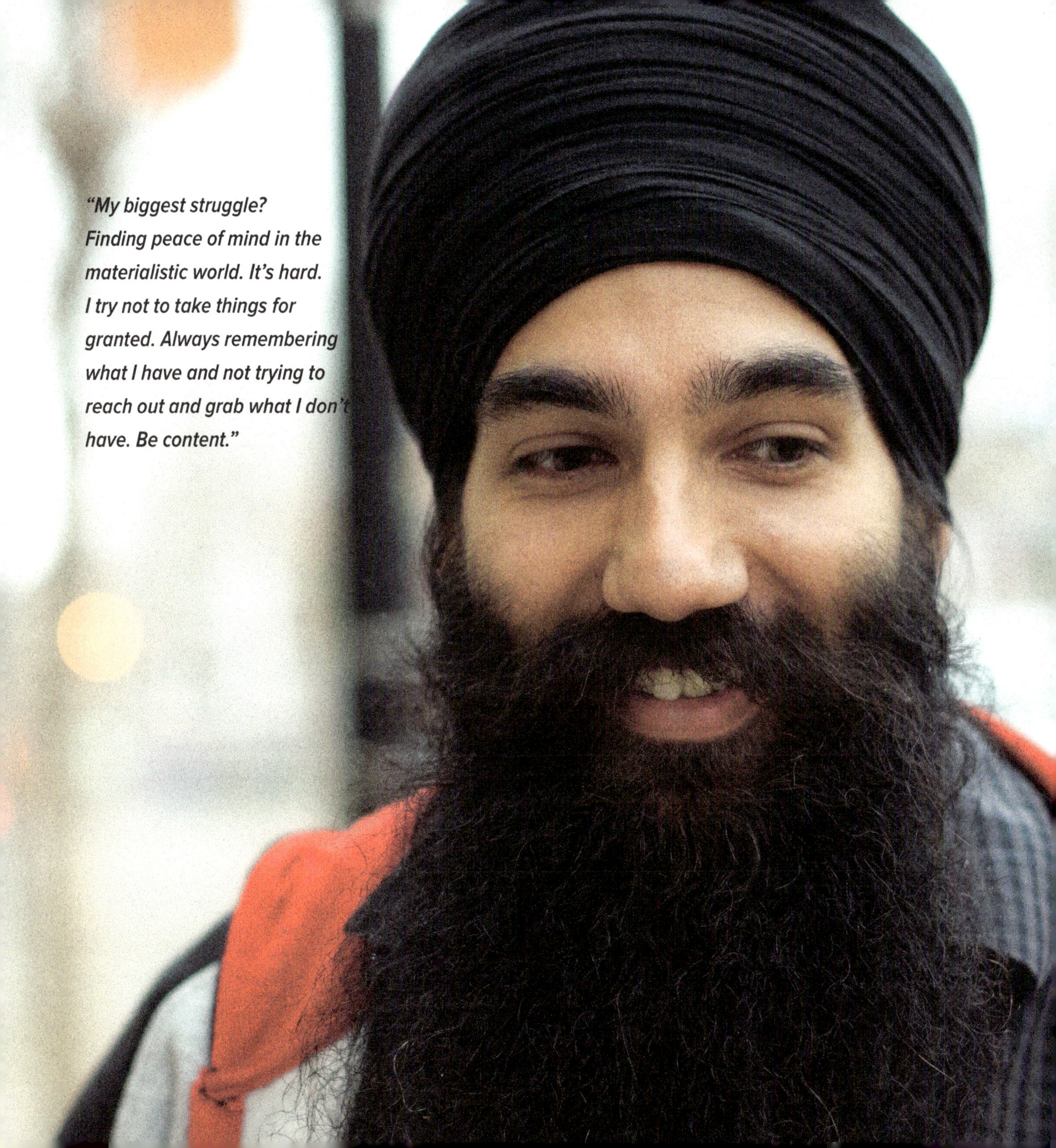

"My biggest struggle? Finding peace of mind in the materialistic world. It's hard. I try not to take things for granted. Always remembering what I have and not trying to reach out and grab what I don't have. Be content."

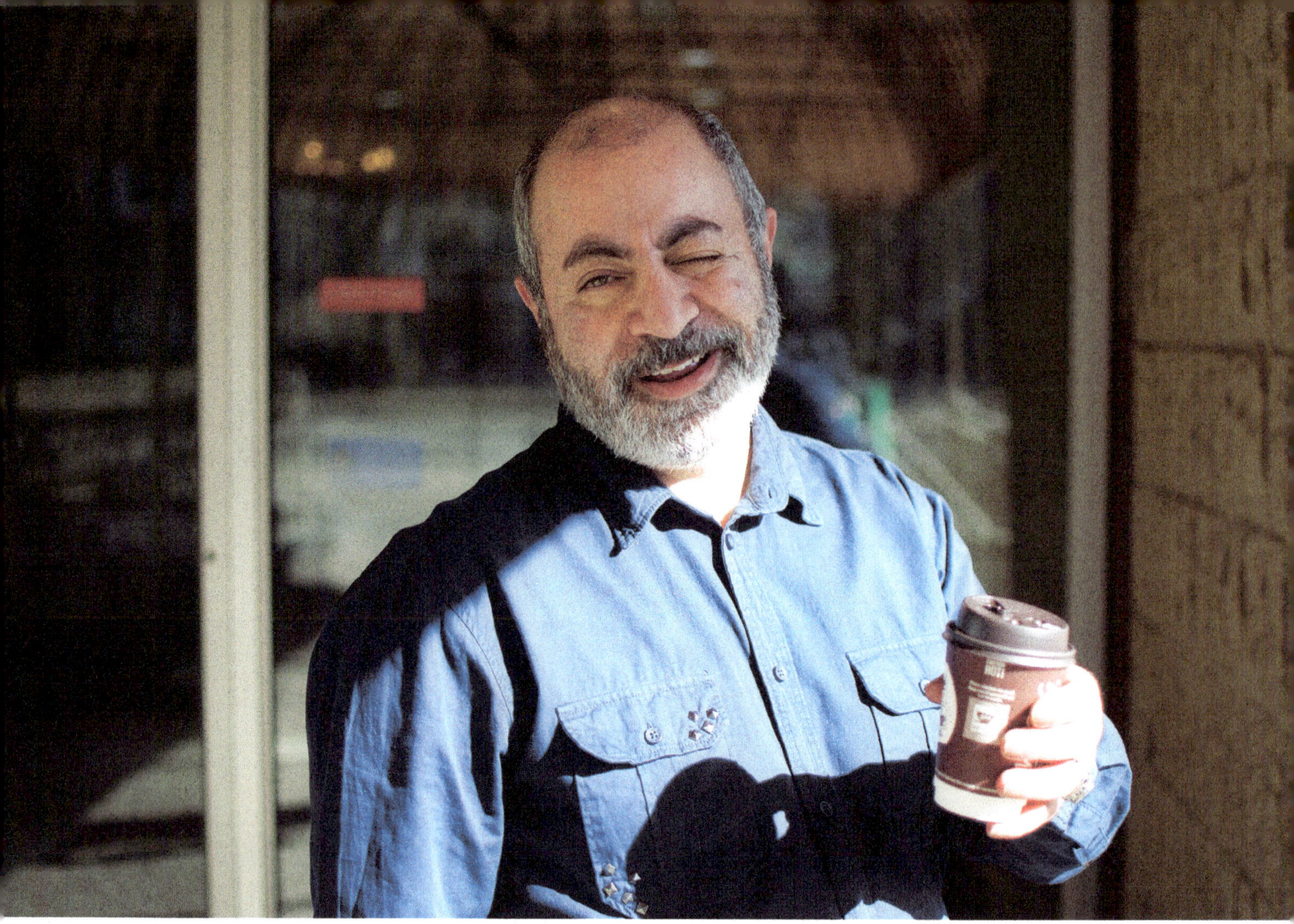

ARTINE

"You know what? I'm having some Moroccan green mint," he says, hold up his cup. "They say it's good for you." He takes a sip. "We'll see. I have a little salon here. I'm just hanging out, waiting for my next client."

"What's a decision you're happy you made?"

"Being a hairdresser. This year will be thirty years. It's funny. My clients ask me, 'How long are you going to do this for?' As long as I'm standing up and can use my hands. That's probably my biggest thing in life right now. People say they had a job, and I used to say I had a career. I no longer say I have a career. It's more like a lifestyle, you know."

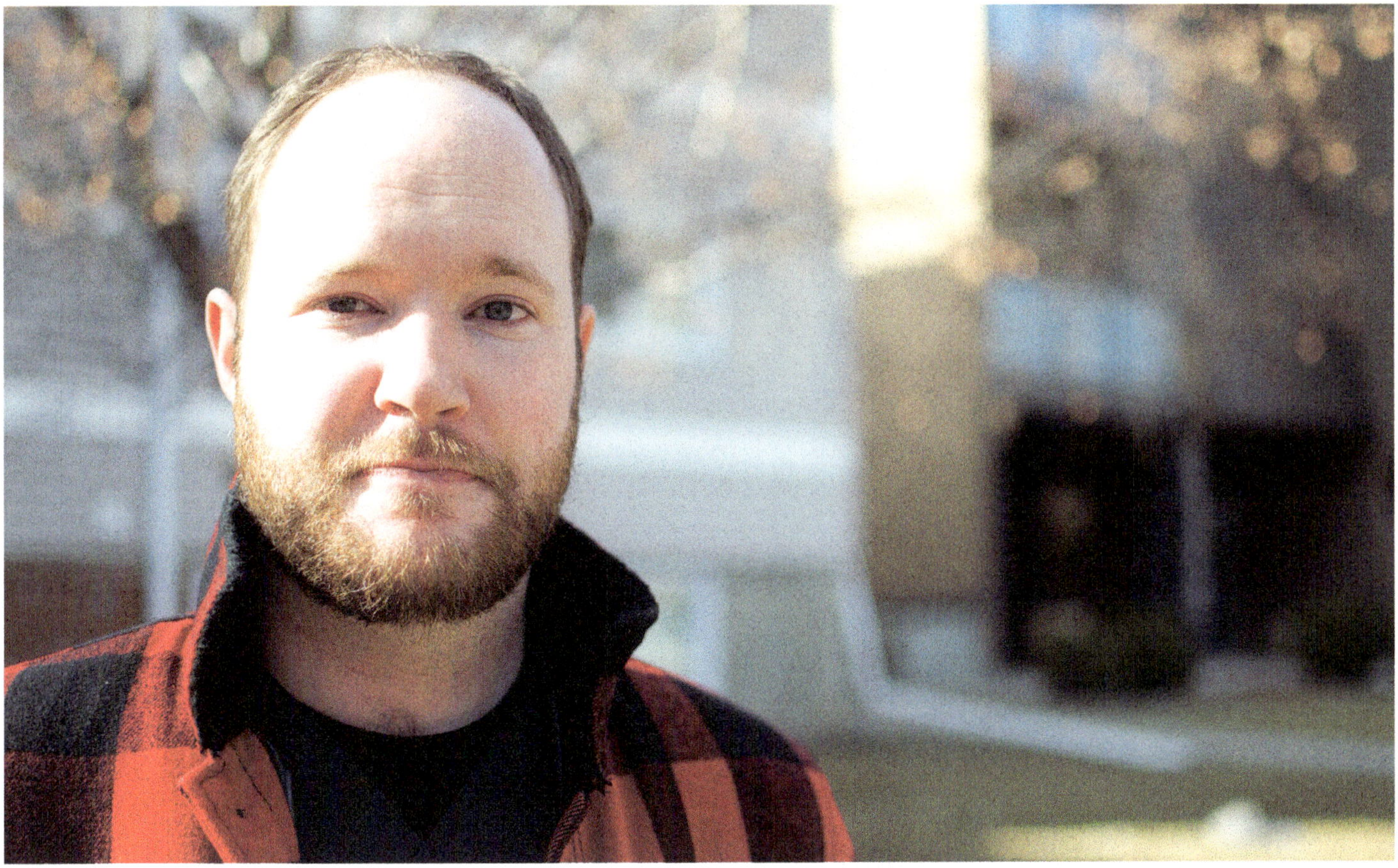

ANDREW

"What's one of the hardest decisions you've had to make?"

"What can I say publicly. Um, it's going to sound lame, but the decision to put my cat down. It was last year. He was an old cat. He was twenty-seven. And so he'd been with me for a long time. He had a urinary tract infection. He started to develop dementia, which was kind of cute in a strange way. But it was time to go I think. It got me thinking about assisted dying in my career, which is nursing."

"What was his name?"

"Gerflax. That was the name that he came with from the SPCA."

HOPEFULLY I CAN DO IT RIGHT THIS TIME

"I was an artist for many years and I gave it up. I couldn't stand it anymore. I was going to end up with one ear and dead. It's the purest thing that you can do with your life. There's no doubt about it. It's absolutely fabulous when it's good. You know, the higher the high, the lower you go on the other side. There seems to be a kind of balance, an organic balance of some kind so that when you're an artist, you have ecstasy. Literally, total and utter and absolute freedom of your inner self. Every artist ... it can't be communicated so artists talk about how they paint. They don't talk about the ecstasy and why they do it, why they're so obsessed and absorbed and ... anyway, I just got sick and tired of being a crazy ... artist, who can't function in the world because I'm so nuts about this thing I'm doin' that's not giving me any money. So, at any rate, I gave it up for several years and now I'm getting back into writing and painting and drawing. I even stopped reading. And I was also going blind from cataracts. So now I'm getting back into it and hopefully I can do it right this time."

"How's the art going now?"

"Well, I'm just at the beginning. I'm back on the bike and wobbly ... What appears to be happening, and I never thought it possible, I'm now going back, a return to art is a return back. Only this time, unlike that little kid, I know that that little kid had the goods. And the world doesn't want you to just do that because you love doing it. Oh, you gotta make money, da da da da da, and so you get stolen away from yourself and you don't even know it's happening. I used to love doing this. There was no struggle, no suffering, I picked up a pencil." He mimes drawing on the page in his lap. "And bang. I was there. Boom. So what appears to be happening is I'm going back to where I started. Only now I know that that's where I started. Now I know who I am. Now I know that what I had was better than anything in the world. Anything."

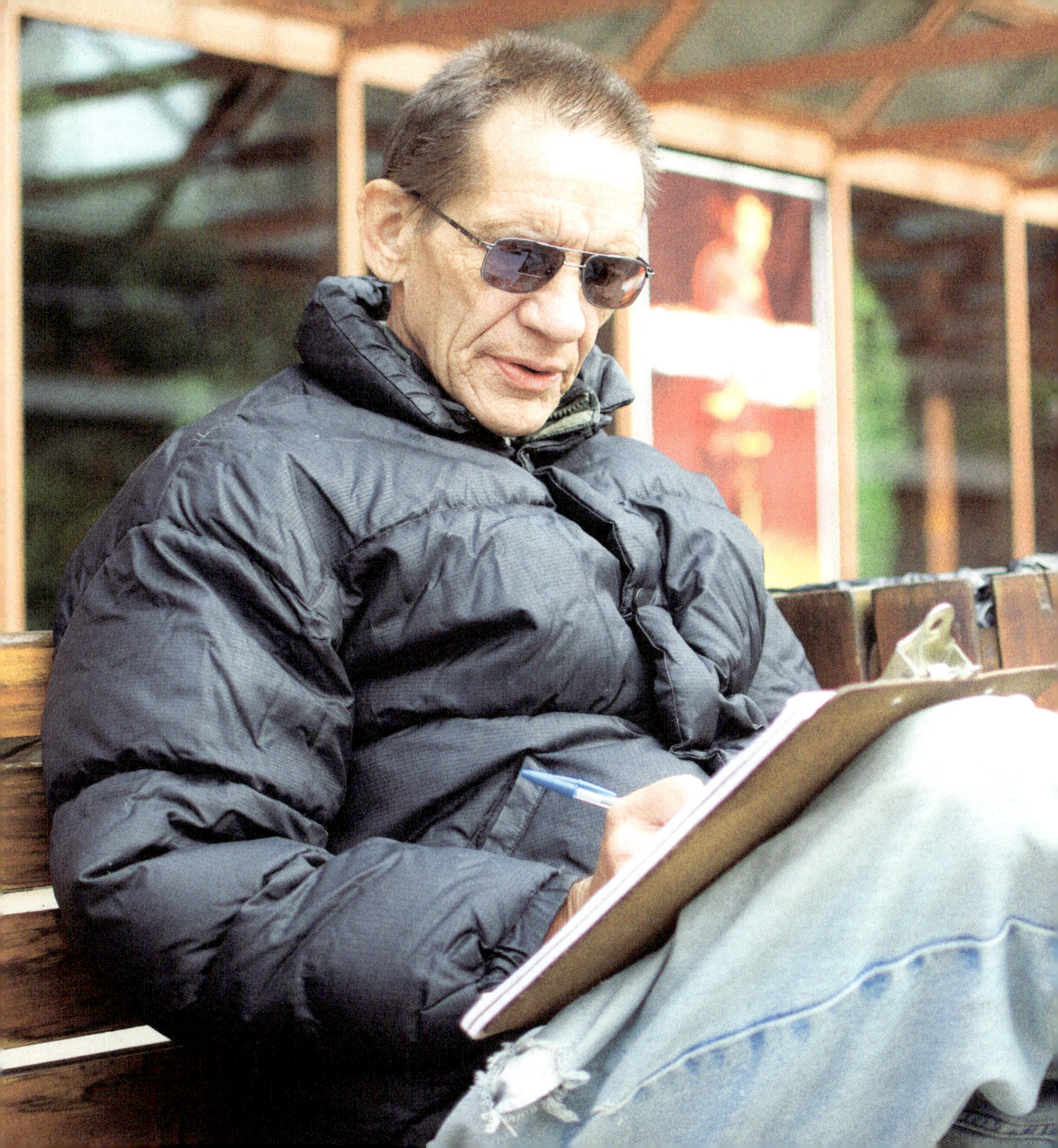

"How's your day?"

"Not too bad. It'd be nice if I had the old lady with me though."

"Where is she?"

"That's a good question. I don't know. She likes her drinkin'. Me, I don't like to drink that much. That's why I'm down here, keeping away from the downtown area. I had a home at one time but now I'm back here. The cops showed up. The nosy neighbours went down to the office and complained. They gave me a warning and then it happened again so ... that's it. It couldn't have happened at a better time. The winter was pretty cold this year. I had a home but now ... now the weather is warm, and I'm homeless, you know. I wouldn't want to be sleeping outside. Not yet. I'm staying at the Remand. They've got a gym in there with one hundred and five mats. You have to be sober to be in there. If you're drunk, they won't let you in. She goes overboard with her drinking and then she'll get barred out of the Hope Mission. She's not even supposed to be drinking; she's on probation right now. If she breeches, she goes back inside. She's been in there twice already. She's stubborn. She won't listen to me. She likes her beer. I have a part-time job right now but that's weekly, so I'm broke until Friday. I just don't like the Hope Mission anymore. I've been there only when I'm drinking. When you're drinking, you can go downstairs, but it's too noisy and the mats are too close. People tend to come and crawl on you, coughing or snoring. I just don't like it."

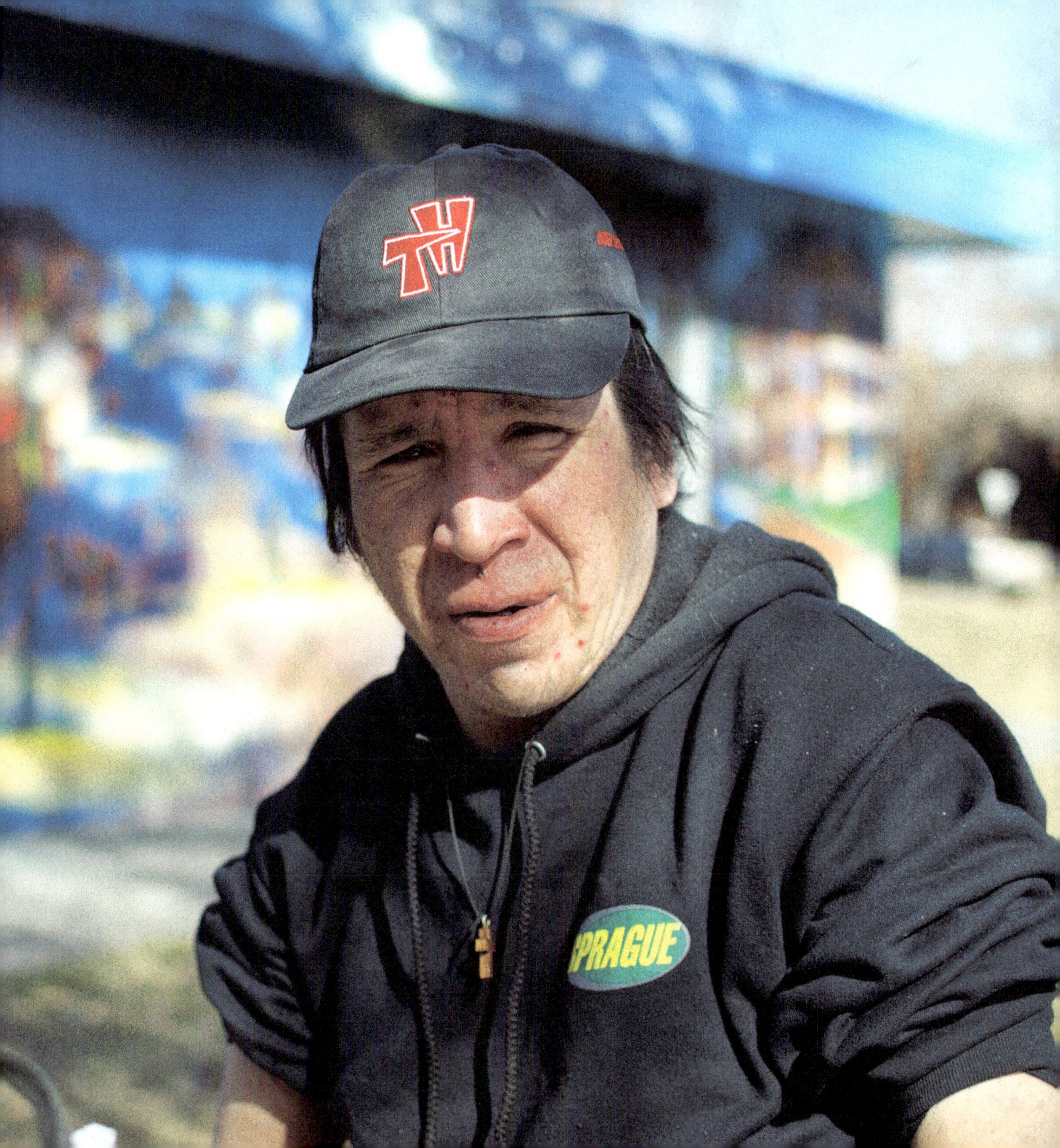
SPRAGUE

SOMETIMES, THE CART'S SO FULL, I NEED A HALF-TON TRUCK

"I can't smile today; I got no dentures. I lost them about fifteen years ago. I got all drunked up and left them somewhere and I was thinking, 'I can't figure out where the hell I left them'. They wanted six hundred for the top and six hundred for the bottom. Twelve hundred bucks. My name's Ron. I'm old. Sixty-nine years old. Old age pension, I could get that. I never collected welfare, AISH, or nothin'. Collect bottles seven days a week and live in the shelters."

"When did you start collecting bottles?"

"Nineteen seventy-nine. Collect bottles, stay in the shelters. I gotta go to the bottle depot. Cash 'em in."

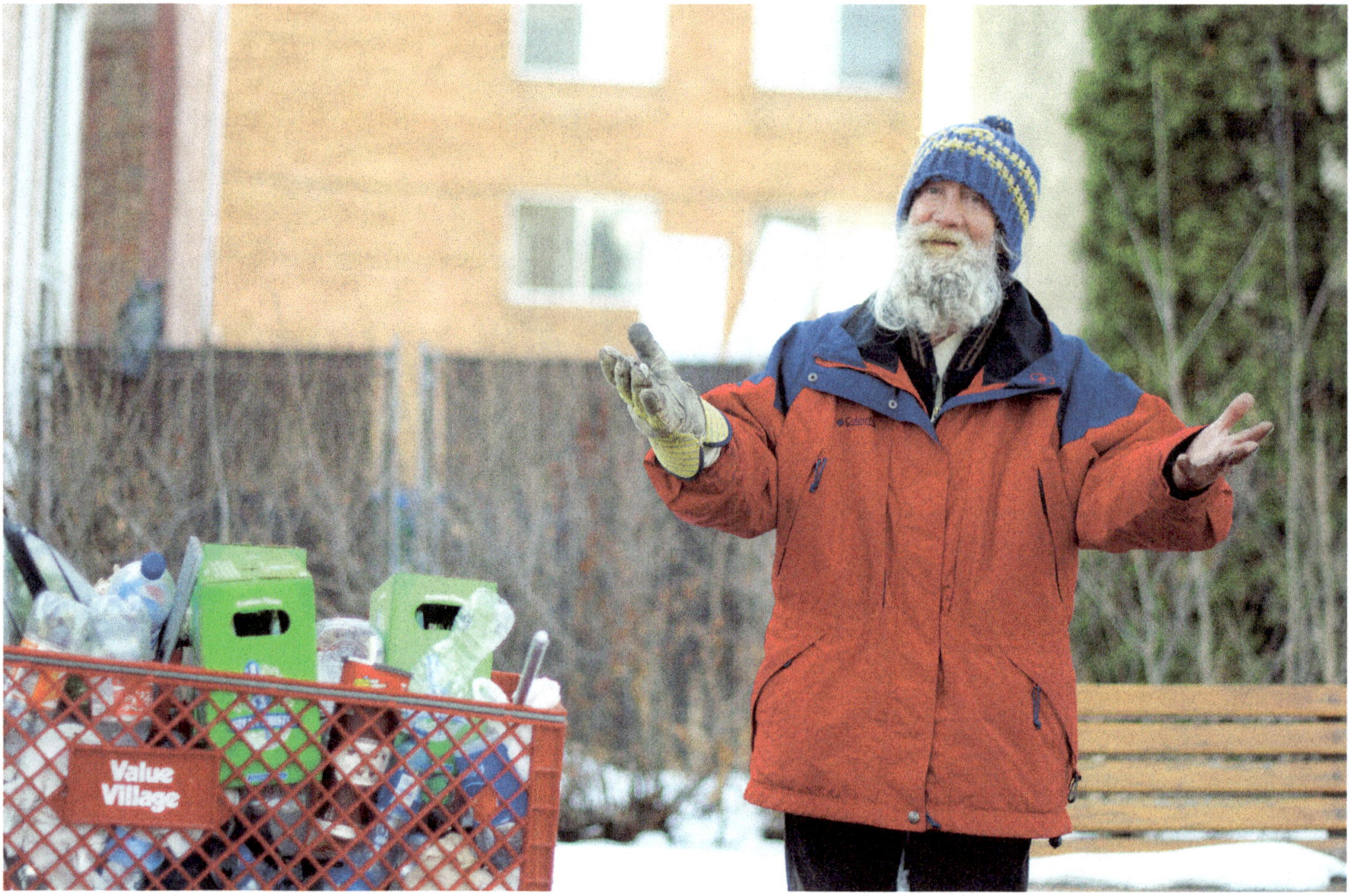

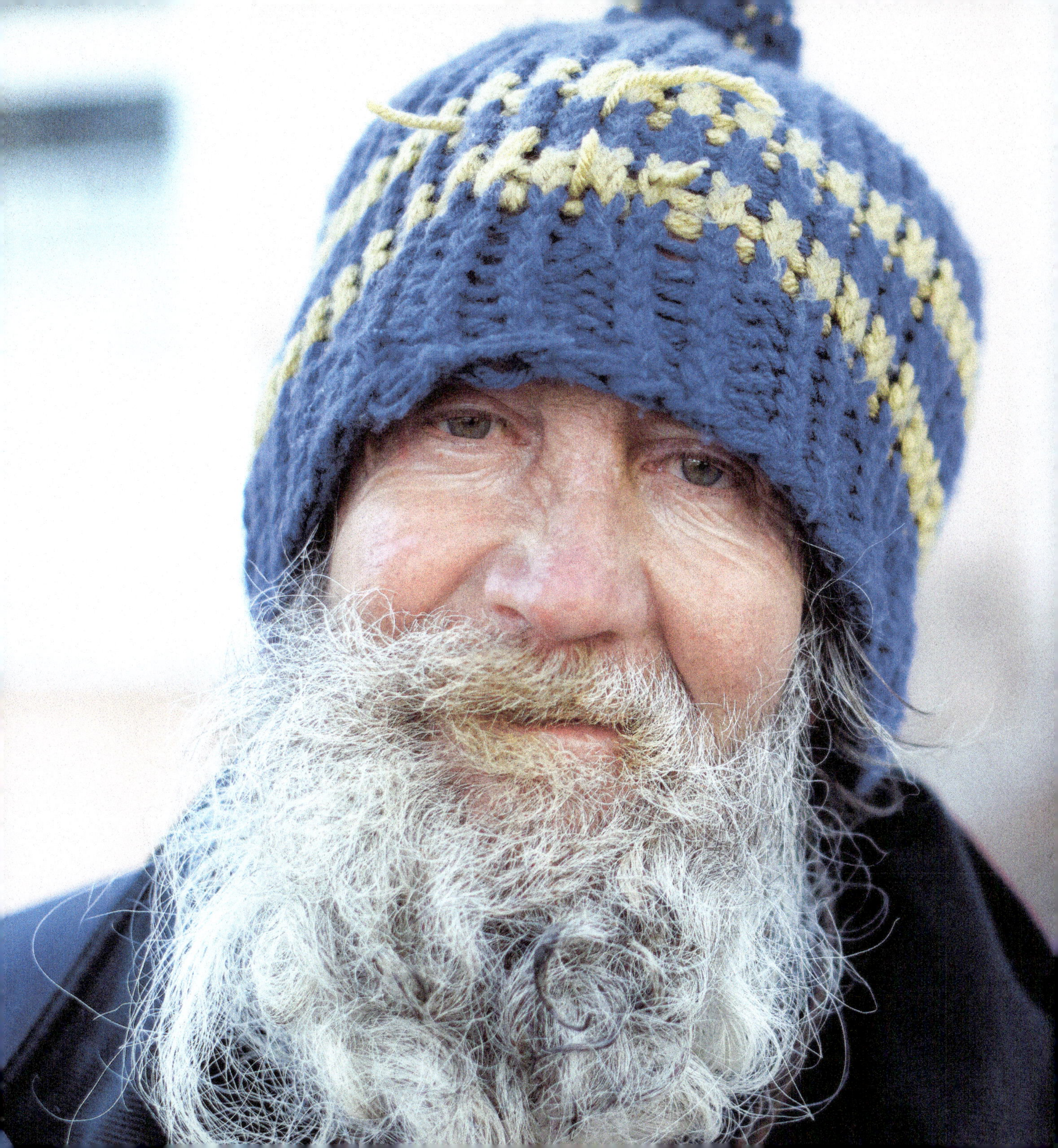

I'VE ALWAYS WANTED TO CATCH THE FIRST FLIGHT OUT AND JUST GO FROM THERE

"What's one of your hidden talents?"

"Piano. I've been playing piano since I was four. I don't really play for anyone else. I just play for myself. It's not something I share with people."

"What do you get from playing the piano?"

"It makes me happy and it makes me ... just feel. It's my heart and my soul."

"If you could do anything right now, what would you do?"

"I would pack my bags, buy a plane ticket, and get out of here. That's exactly what I'd do."

"Where would you go?"

"I've always wanted to catch the first flight out and just go from there. Be spontaneous."

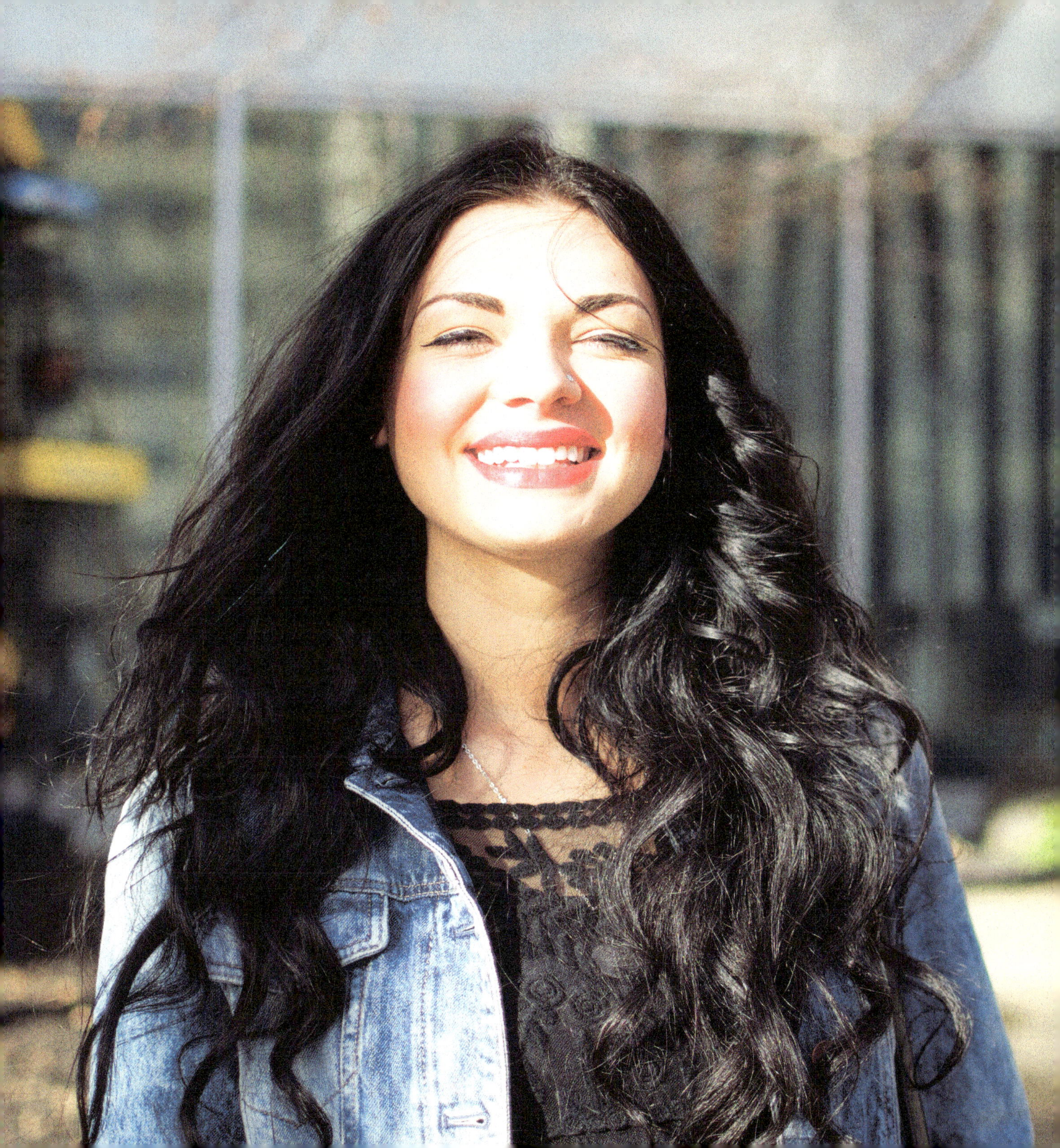

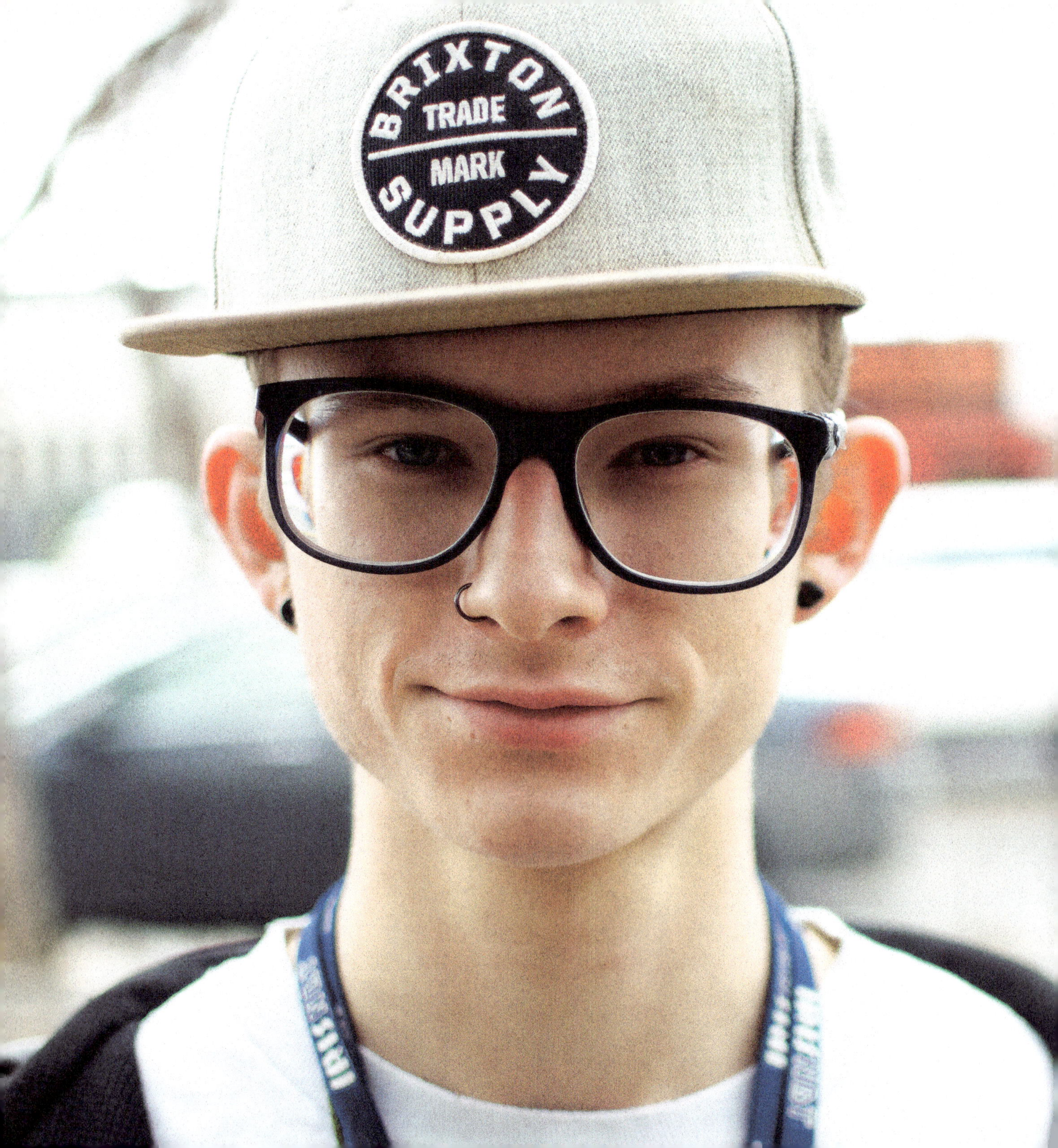
BRIXTON
TRADE
MARK
SUPPLY

WE ... DECIDED TO END THINGS ON VALENTINE'S DAY

"What are you struggling with these days?"

"Relationship issues."

"How was your Valentine's Day?"

"The worst Valentine's Day I've ever had actually. We had a lot of issues leading up to that point and decided to end things on Valentine's Day. It was a three-year relationship."

"Are you okay?"

"Yeah. It's fine."

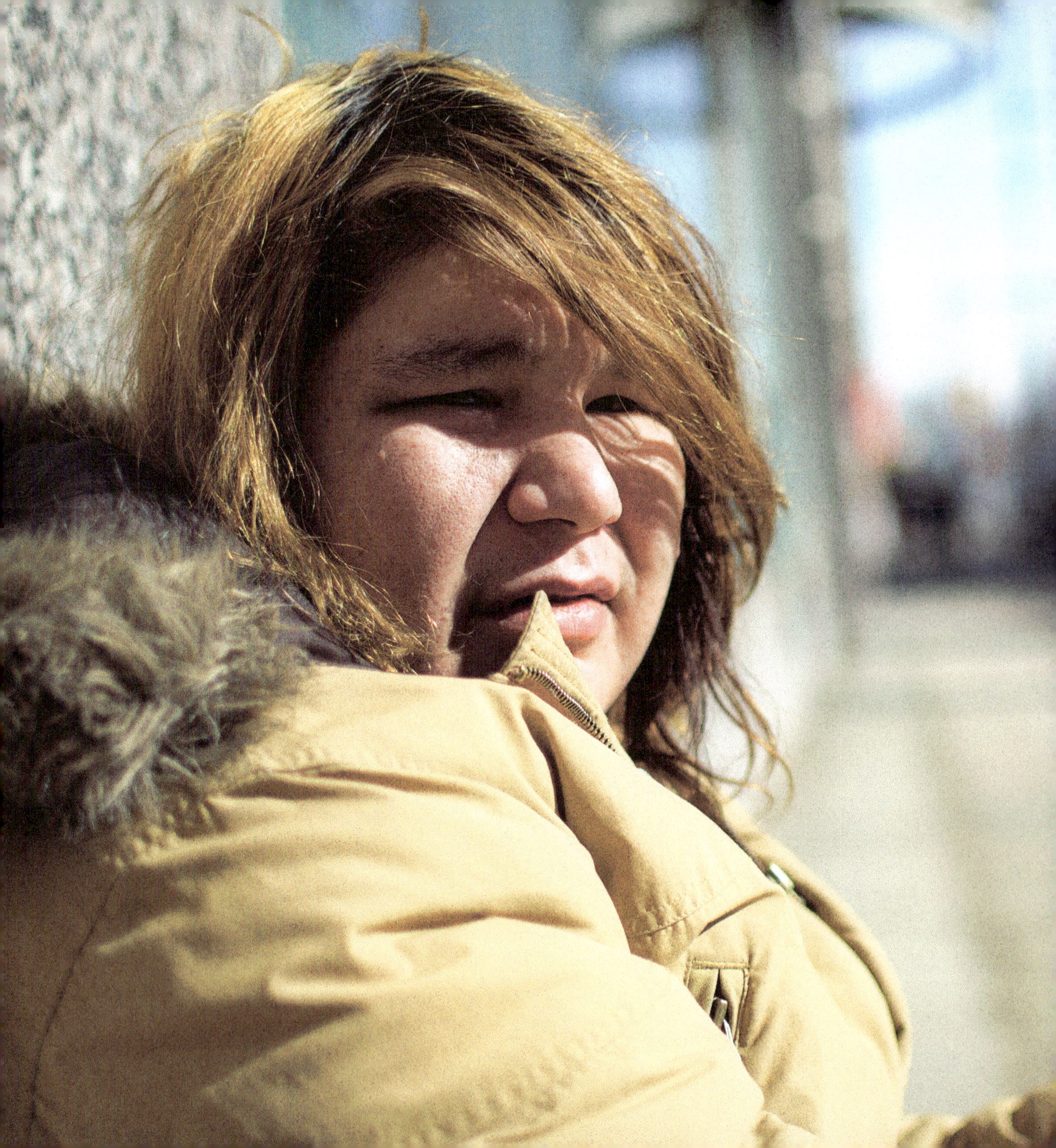

"Where I live I pretty much live on the streets. It's been a rough life. It's a struggle. I'm trying to get ID so I can get a hotel room or something."

"Why can't you get ID?"

"Mainly because I need all this other information and I don't have it. They tell me to go to the cop station. I go to the cop station, and they tell me that there's no such thing as the forms they're trying to get me to sign. So they're running me around. Back and forth to different places."

"Did you have an ID before?"

"Yeah."

"What happened to it?"

"It got jacked. It's kind of hard to find a place without an ID. I can't find a job or anything. It sucks. I'm going to try again this week and bring in my brother-in-law. Maybe that'll help. Because I don't want to be on the street forever."

"How old are you?"

"Twenty-four."

"How long have you been on the streets?"

"Since I was twenty." He pauses, rubs his eyes, and says, "I quit drinkin'. I quit drinkin' now for about a year. It's difficult because everywhere I go people are trying to offer me a drink. So I just say no." He lowers his head for a moment. "I feel sad now." Then he looks up again, sighs, and says, "Well, I'm going to stay here and try to make enough for something to eat. Thank you for your time and consideration."

He flattens cans and bottles under his foot before putting them in the garbage bag he holds.

“How was your winter?”

“Pretty rough. Cold. Weird weather. I’ve got my little spots here and there. I’m always alone. I keep it like that. Stay out of trouble.”

“Do you collect bottles all day?”

“Not all day. In the morning. Then find a place somewhere to squish ‘em. Then take ‘em to the bottle depot.”

“Is not having a home the hardest thing about your life?”

“I quit drinking, smoking marijuana, smoking crack, sniffing coke, you know, doing lines, which is a good thing. When I was on that stuff I was always in jail, always getting into trouble. If I was doing this and I was drinking, some guys would laugh at me, and I’d get into trouble, right. But now, today, if they’re laughing at me because I do this, so what. It doesn’t bother me. At least I’m making money. I’m out here every day. I’m used to it.”

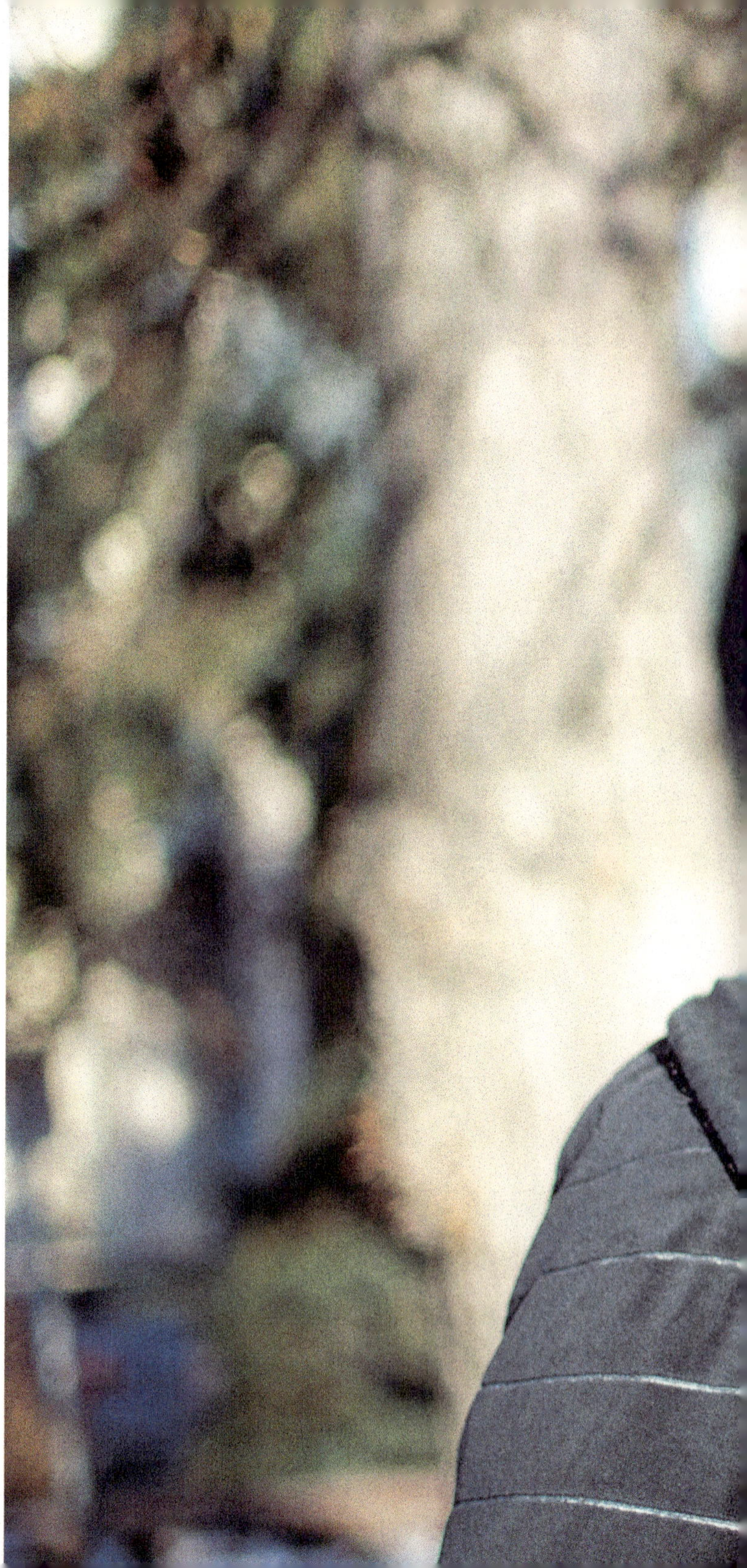

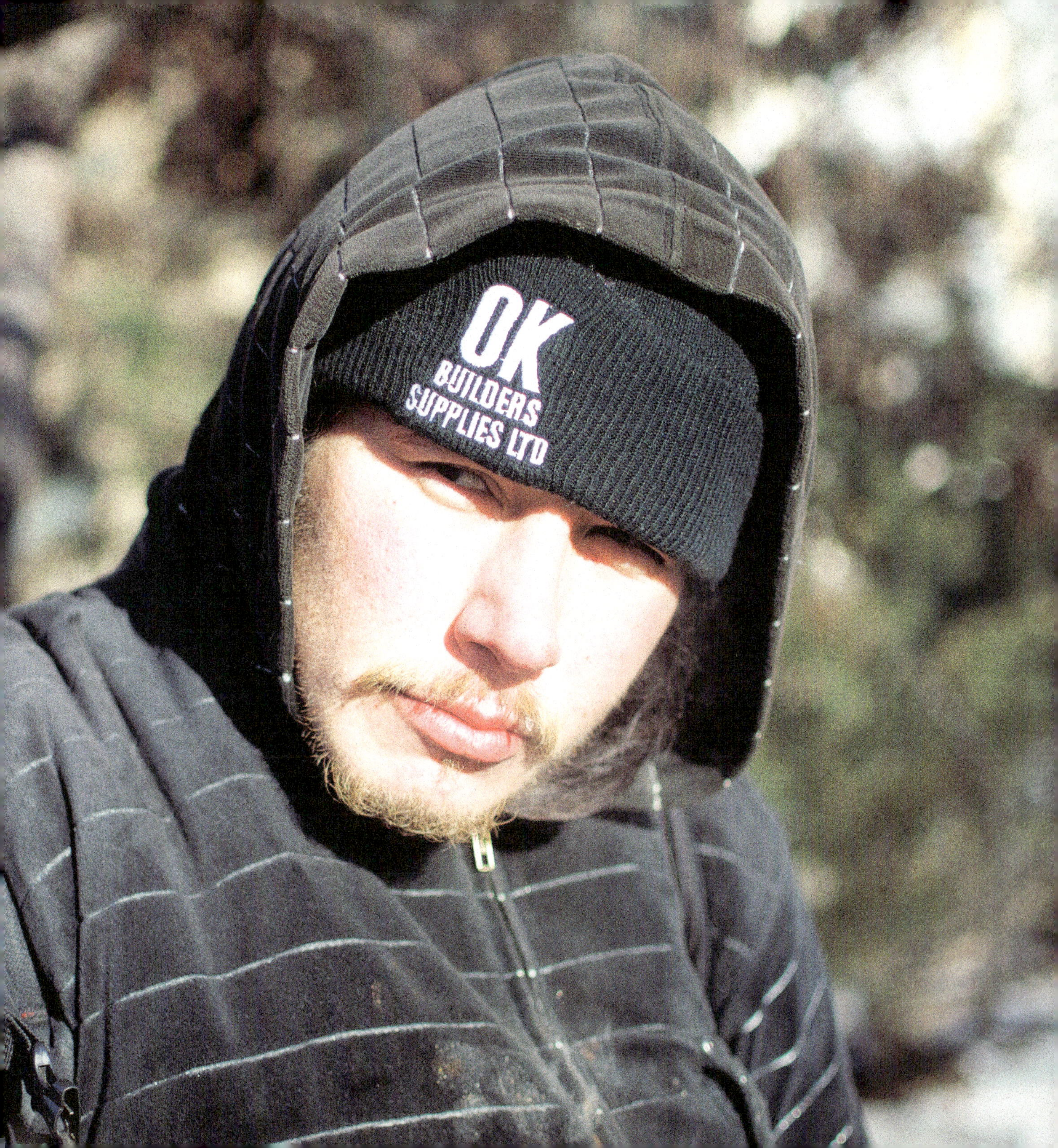
OK
BUILDERS
SUPPLIES LTD

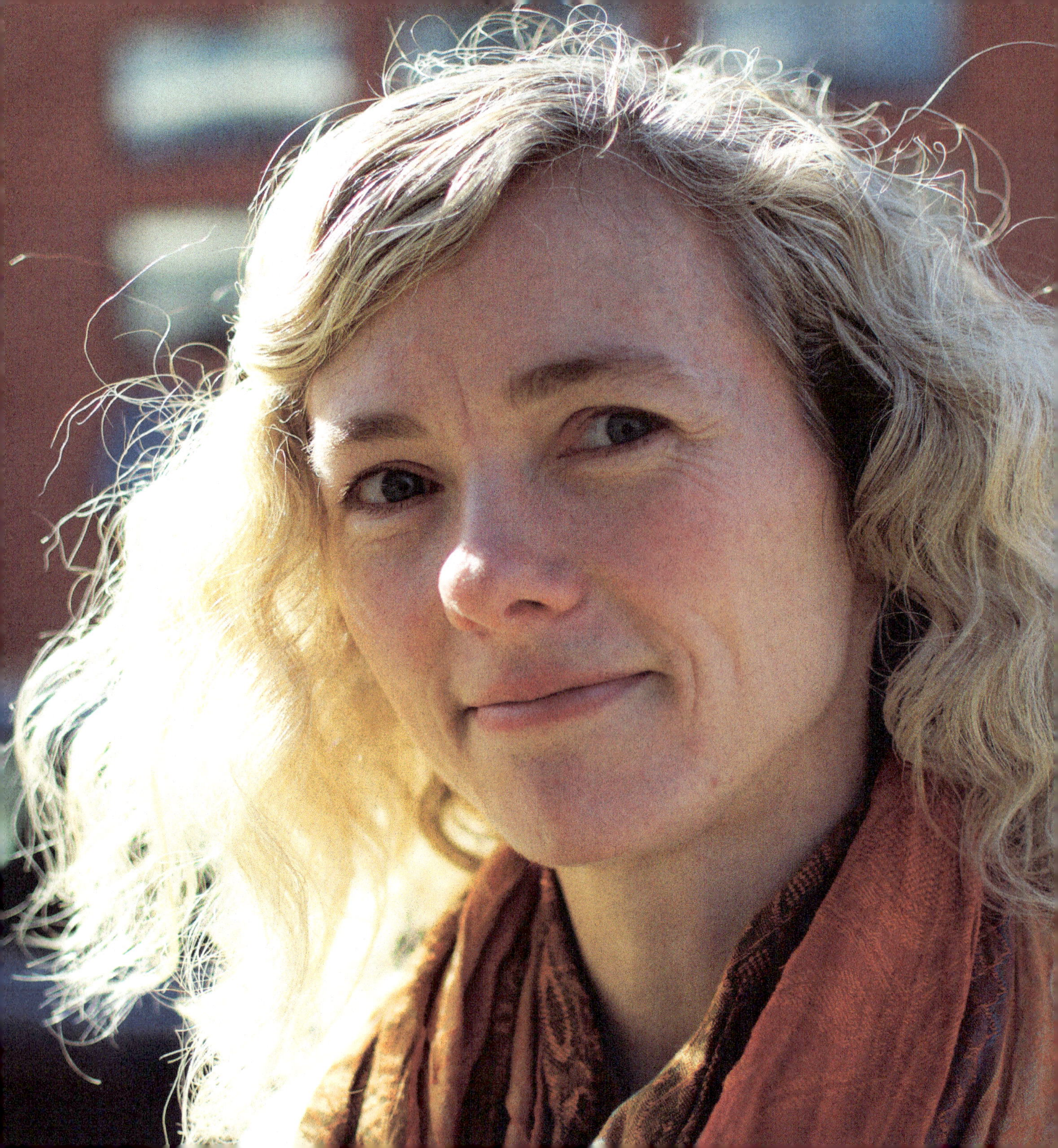

WHAT'S ONE OF THE HARDEST DECISIONS YOU'VE HAD TO MAKE?

"I think it's often when you have to surmount your fears, so they can be emotional or psychological. Once I was living with some other people and came back from work and they had my suitcase at the bottom of the stairs. We were all housesitting, and the owners came back. Some of us weren't supposed to be there, and they were like, 'Sorry, Claire. You have to leave the house'. It was seven p.m. and you come back from work, and you have to work the next day but you don't know where you're going to be that night or the next day, you have no housing. The hardest decision was to decide I was going to sleep in a church that night and figure out what the next day was going to be. You know, you see a lot of people on the street and think. 'How did they get there?' It's very easy to have a job and be homeless, and to build yourself back is very hard. Life throws things at you all the time and you rebuild and fight back. I think that's the hardest thing, rebuilding when your life falls apart. You can never tell. You look at a person and think that they have it together or look at a person and think that they are totally broken, and sometimes it's the opposite. The faces don't always say everything. The stories can be surprising."

WAS THERE A PARTICULAR MOMENT IN YOUR LIFE THAT MADE YOU BECOME MORE ENVIRONMENTALLY CONSCIOUS?

"There were a few moments, but I do remember one in particular. My son was four at the time, and I was helping him dress, pulling this T-shirt over his head, a T-shirt a grandparent had given him, and I noticed that it was a big-box store brand. You know how Superstore has Joe, and Walmart has George? And I had just read about how those were some of the worst, ethically speaking. So the irony struck me as I was pulling this T-shirt down over his head that here I am pulling a T-shirt over a little boy's head that could have maybe been made by another little boy on the other side of the planet who doesn't ... so that was a real moment where I went, 'I can't shop there anymore. I can't do that.'"

Tears gather in her eyes as she recounts the story.

"It brings a tear to my eye thinking about it. I stopped and looked, his head got stuck in there, and I stopped pulling for a minute. A little slapstick there too. But, yeah, it was really eye-opening to think about that kind of thing."

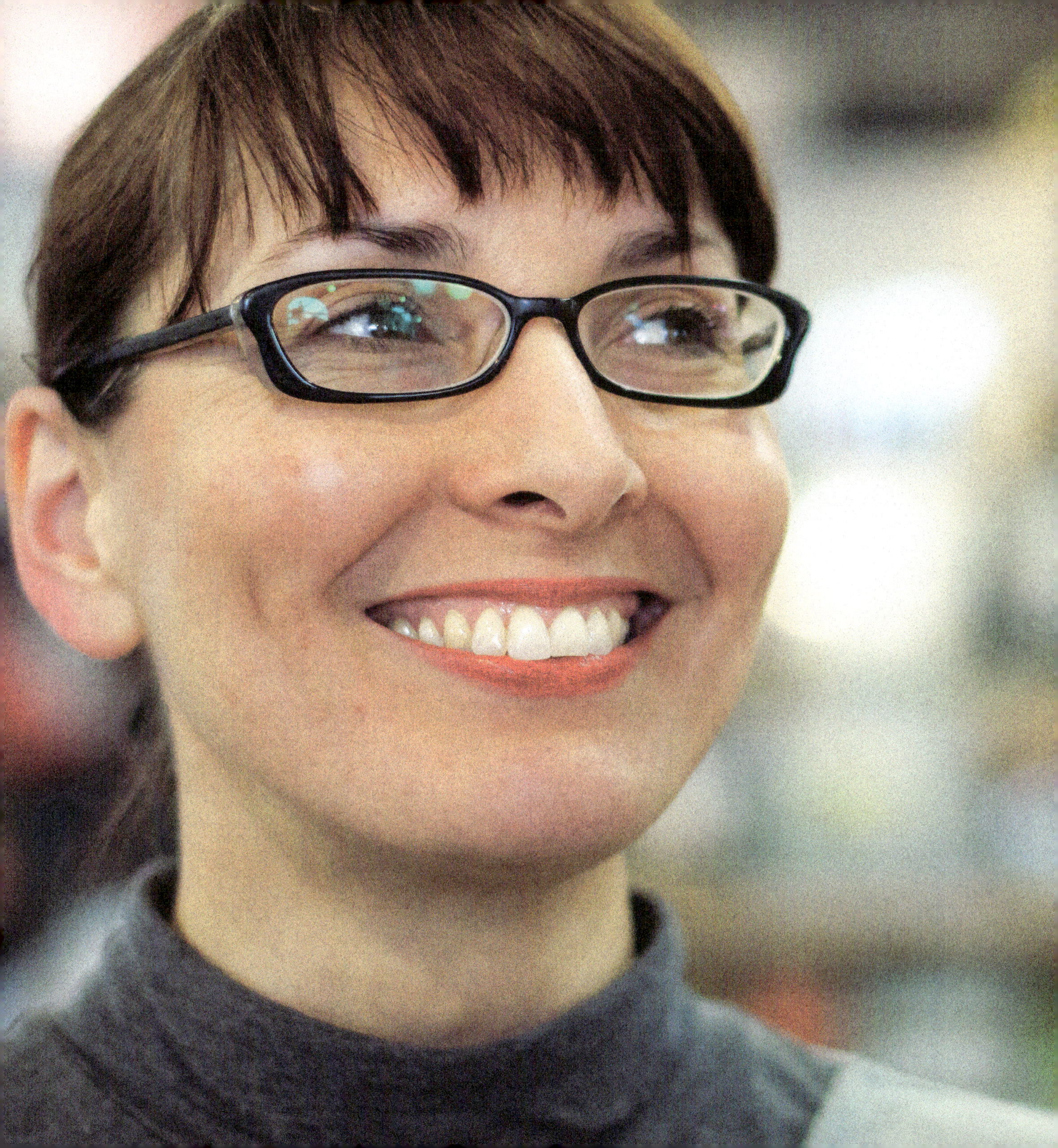

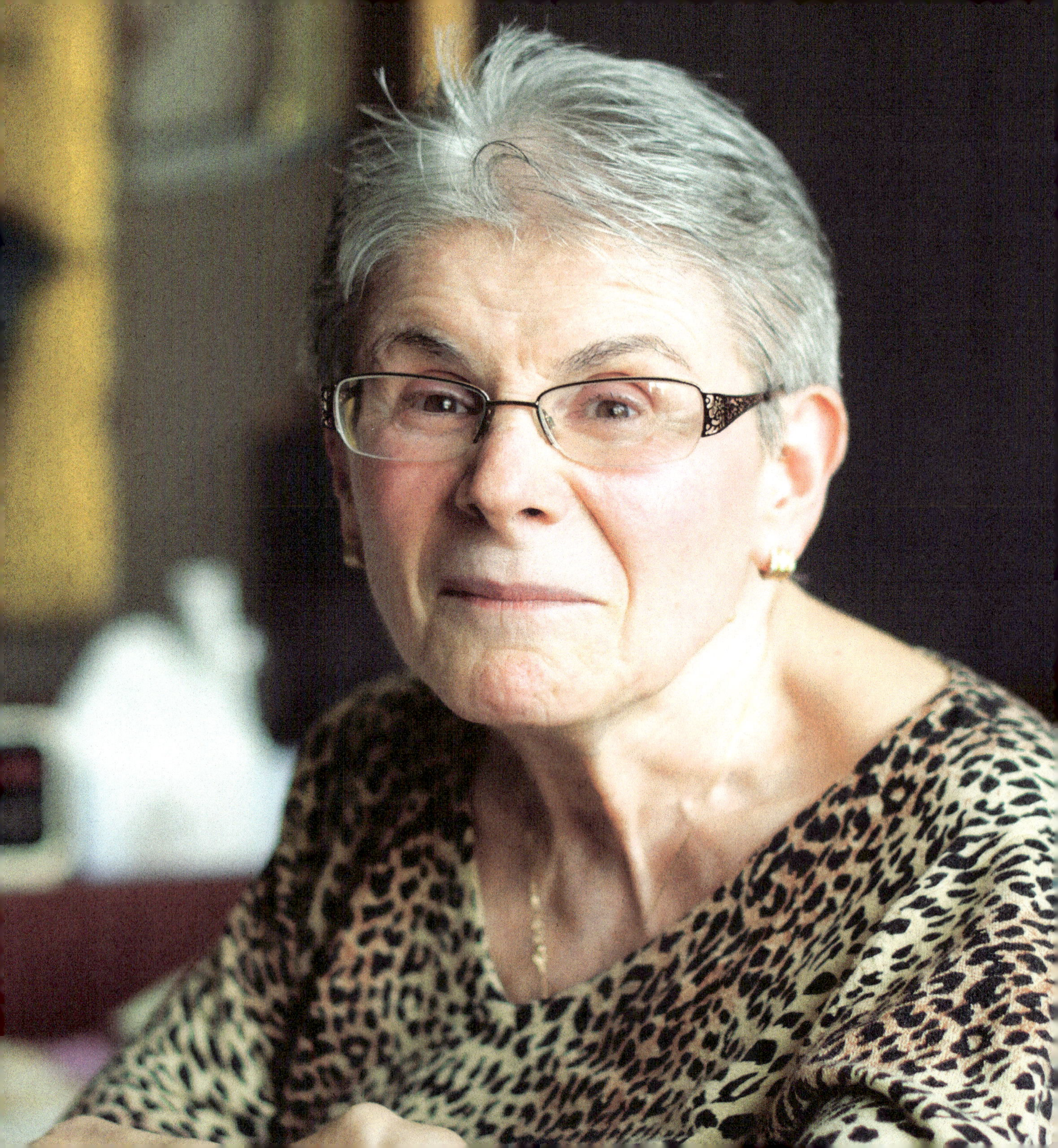

WHEN WERE YOU DIAGNOSED WITH MS?

“Twenty-eight years ago. Diagnosed when I was thirty-five when I was still working full-time at the University Hospital, but my legs and arms were becoming weaker with some numbness. So after about two years, it was necessary for me to quit work and go on disability. I was still able to walk, drive, go to church, and do the things that I normally did. I walked with a quad cane. As I got weaker, I had to graduate to a wheelchair. When you’re used to helping people and now you have to get somebody to do everything for you—because at this point I’m unable to even feed myself, so I have to get someone to feed me. Now that’s okay because then I get to interact with them.”

“Was it hard to accept help from other people?”

“It was very very hard at first because I’m not a dependent person so I wasn’t used to reaching out to others. Always having to say, ‘Please do this,’ was very difficult. But as time went on, I realized that as I had helped people for ...” Clare’s voice fails her for a moment as tears rush to her eyes. “For eighteen years, it was my turn to get helped. Then it became easier. It was a big learning curve. I learned all my life lessons in the chair. I still have things I’d like to do with my life. I have two daughters and three grandchildren and I would like to be able to enjoy more time with them, with, hopefully, my great grandchildren as time goes on.”

“What’s something you really want to do?”

“I think reaching out more to people, being able to share what I’ve learned with others. It’s being a teacher. Still being a nurse but doing it on a different level than I used to do it. Not with my hands but with my heart.”

"Why do you write?"

"Probably like many people of our generation, I have an existential crisis that I'm working out," she says, chuckling. "It hasn't been happening lately, and I think it's probably because I feel like I'm living my life's purpose now. There was a time, most of the past three years, where I would go to bed at night and as I was falling asleep, I'd go, ' Okay, so this is what death is like. You're just going to fade into the darkness and you're not going to know when it happens or how it happens but this is to kind of psychologically prepare you for when death happens.' And it was a very anxious feeling. I didn't write for awhile. I think there was a period of almost ten year when I didn't write. And then just this past term I wrote out a lot of that anxiety. A lot of it came out but it seems like everything I write has an element of death to it."

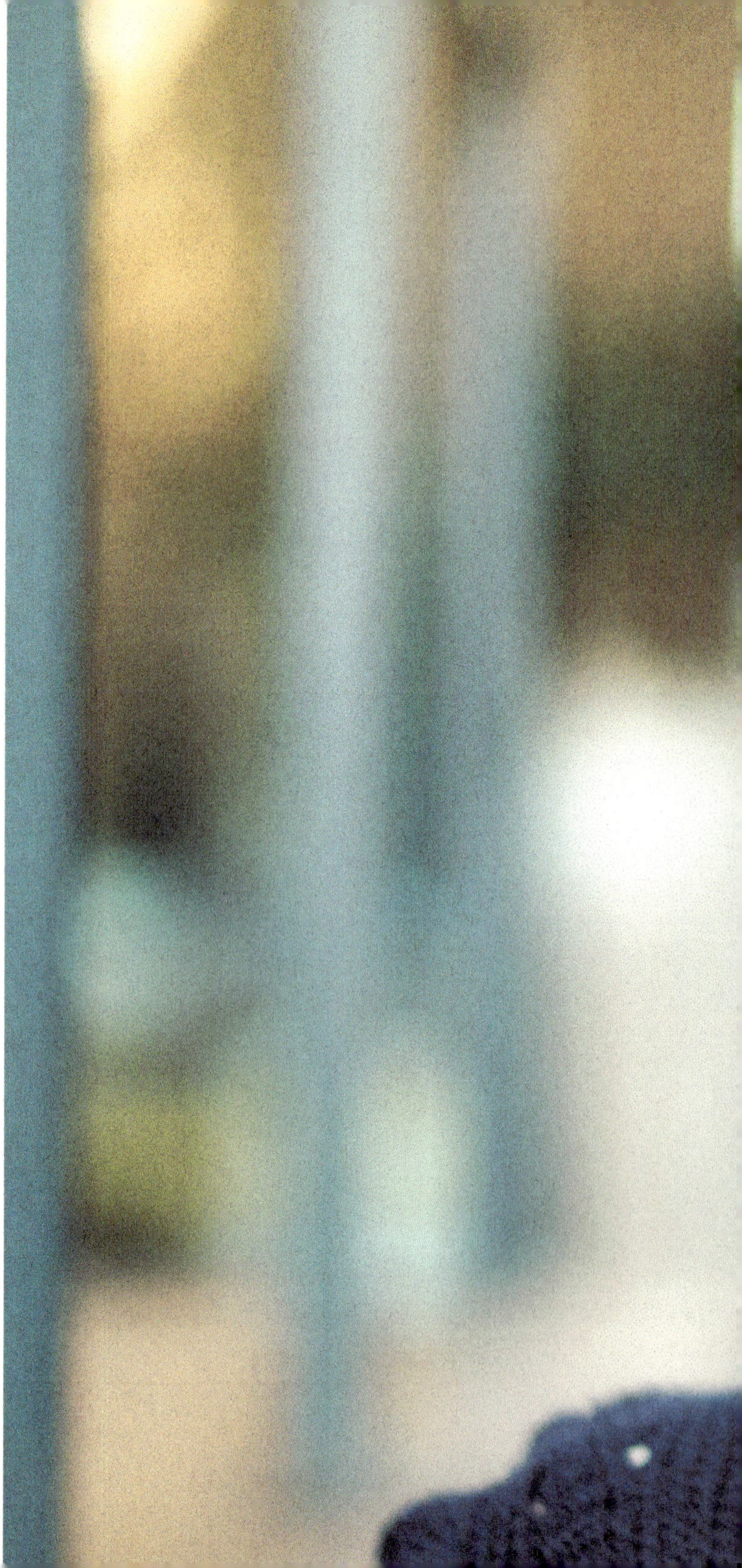

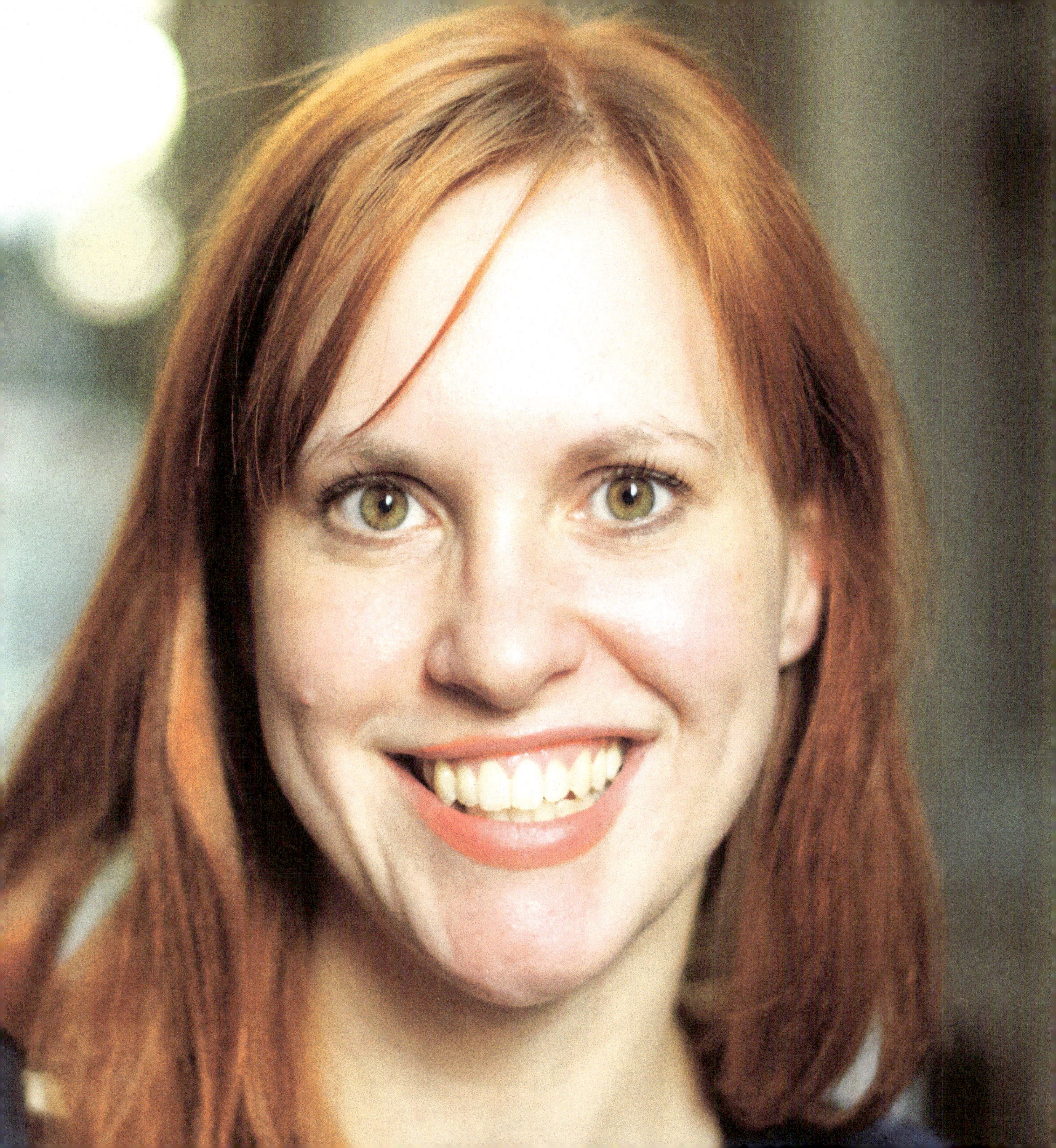

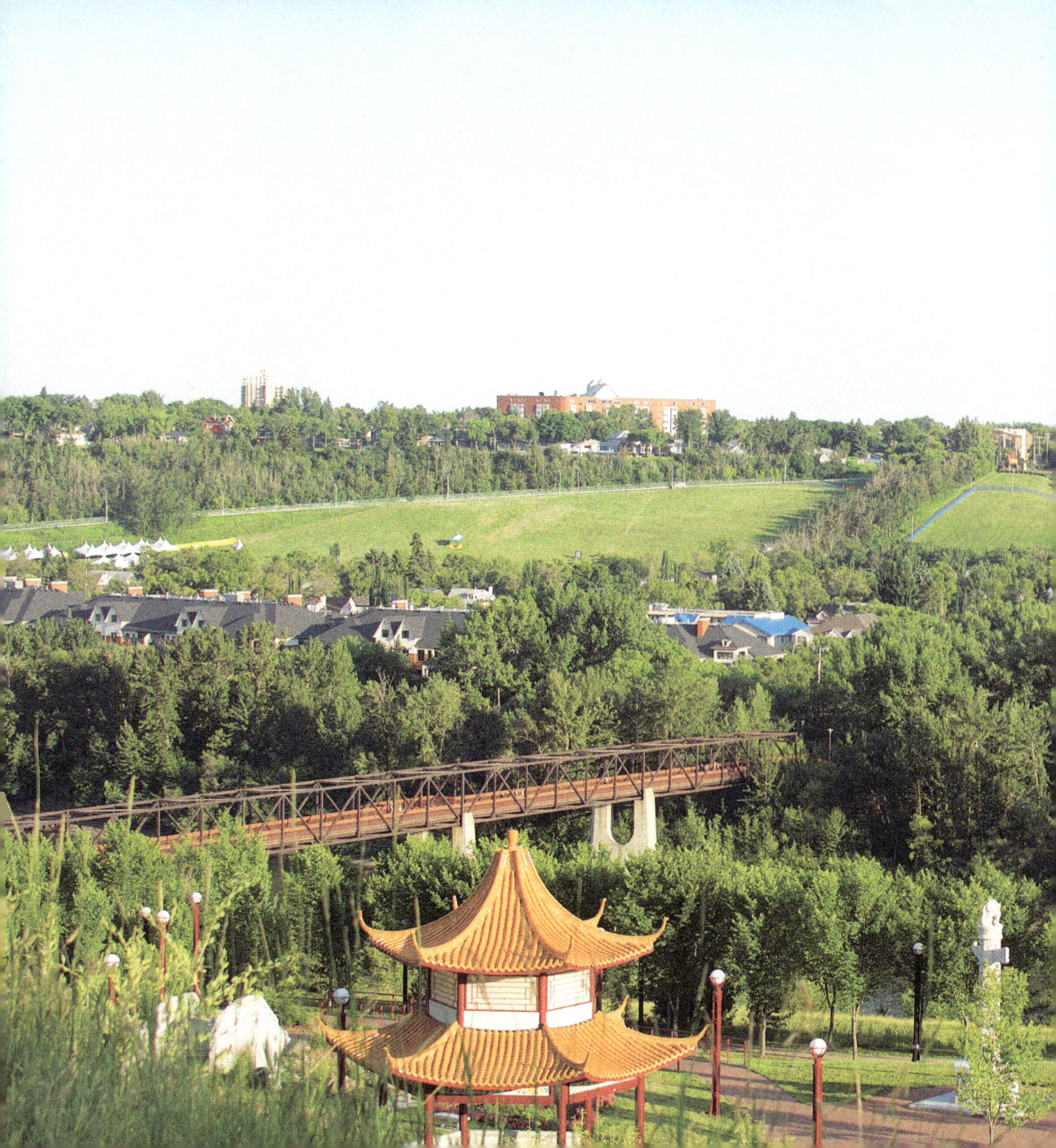

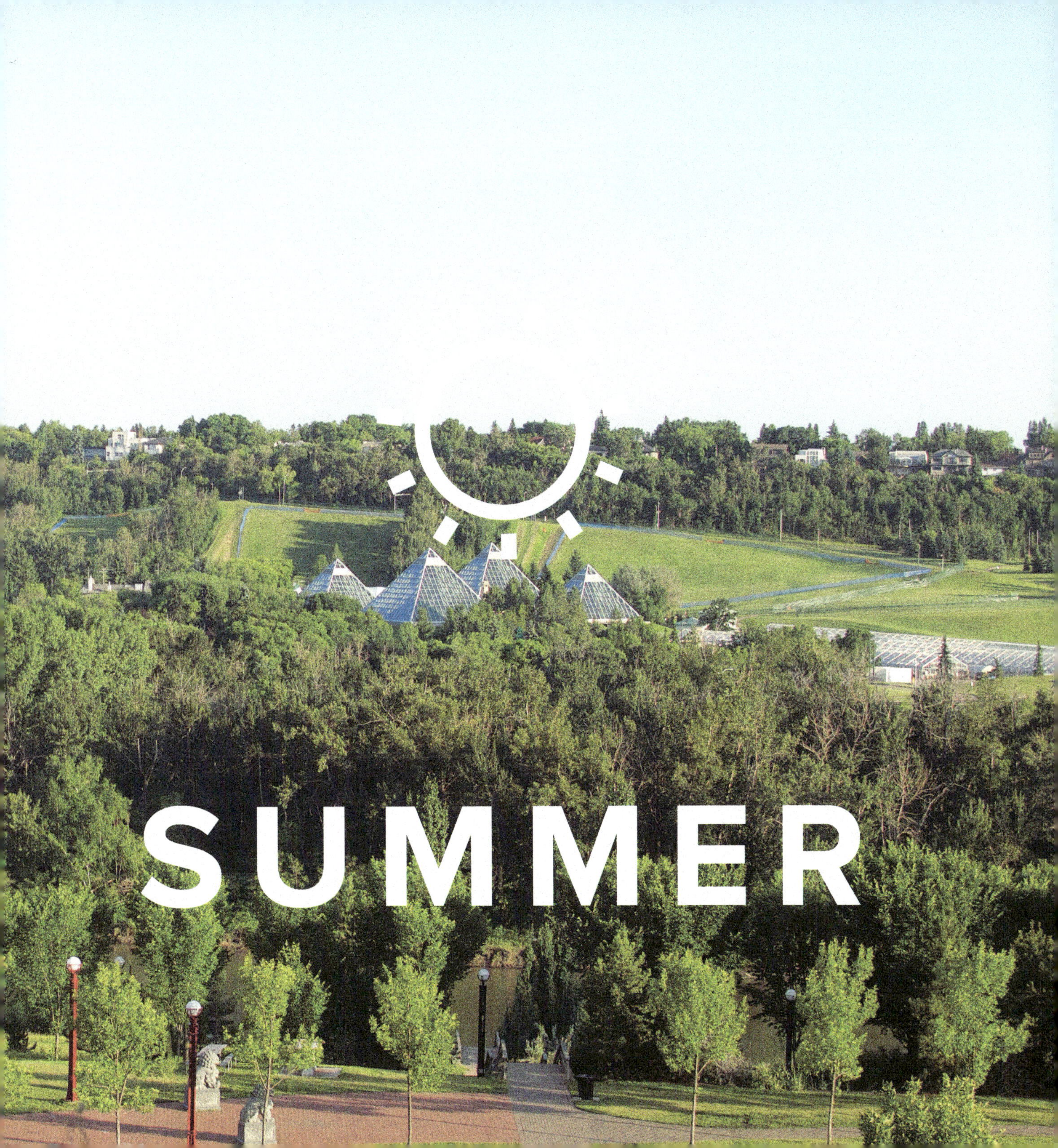
SUMMER

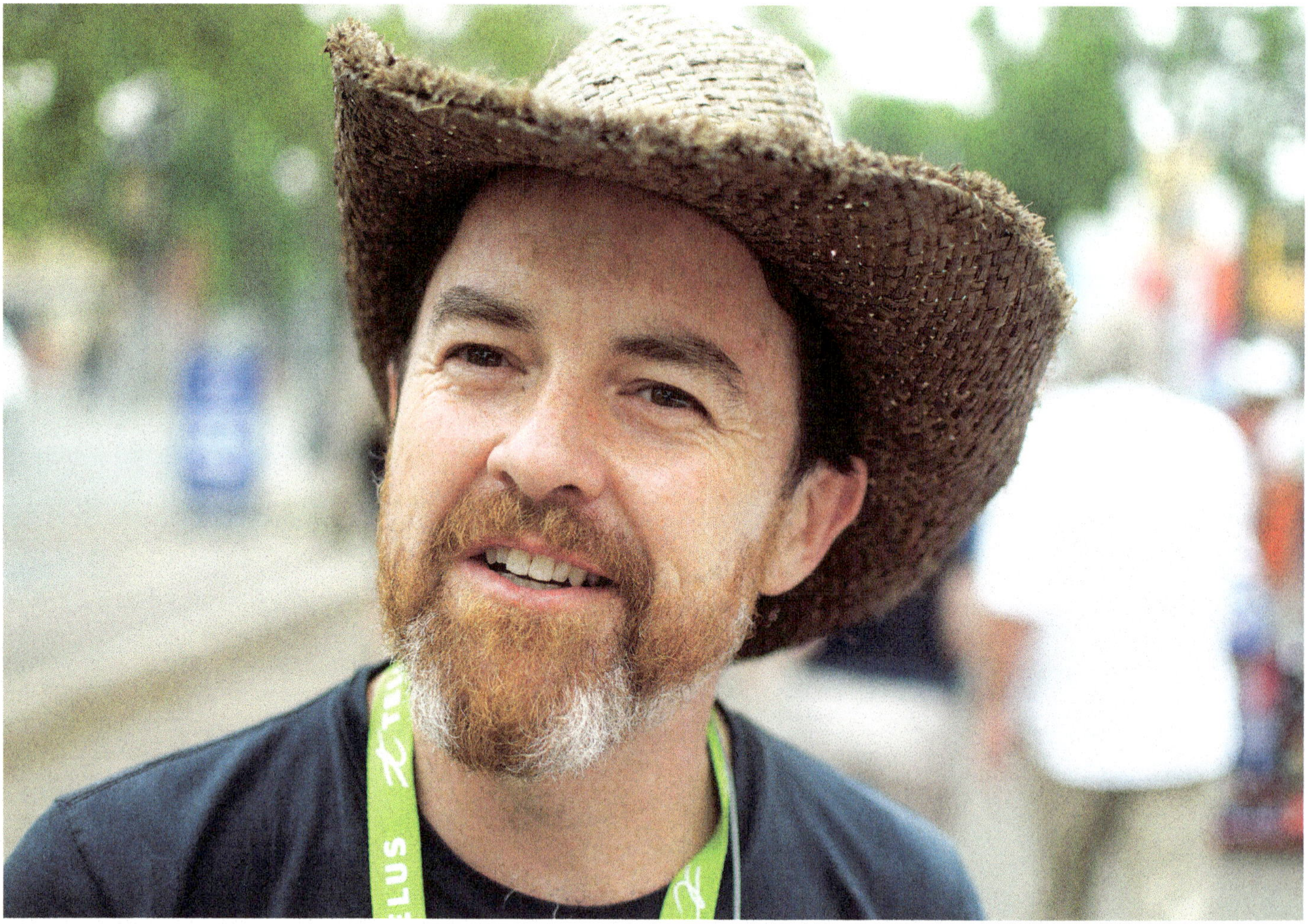

"What's the most rewarding thing about putting on a fringe play?"

"The most rewarding thing is when people come along and they get it, and they respond to it, and it moves them. It's what being an artist is all about."

"What's the most difficult thing?"

"In Edmonton, it's that there is so much stuff on at this festival. And a lot of it's great. The trouble is you get so many one-man, storytelling shows just because of the economics and logistics of it all, and the larger shows are generally local because it's so difficult to get enough people out to cover costs."

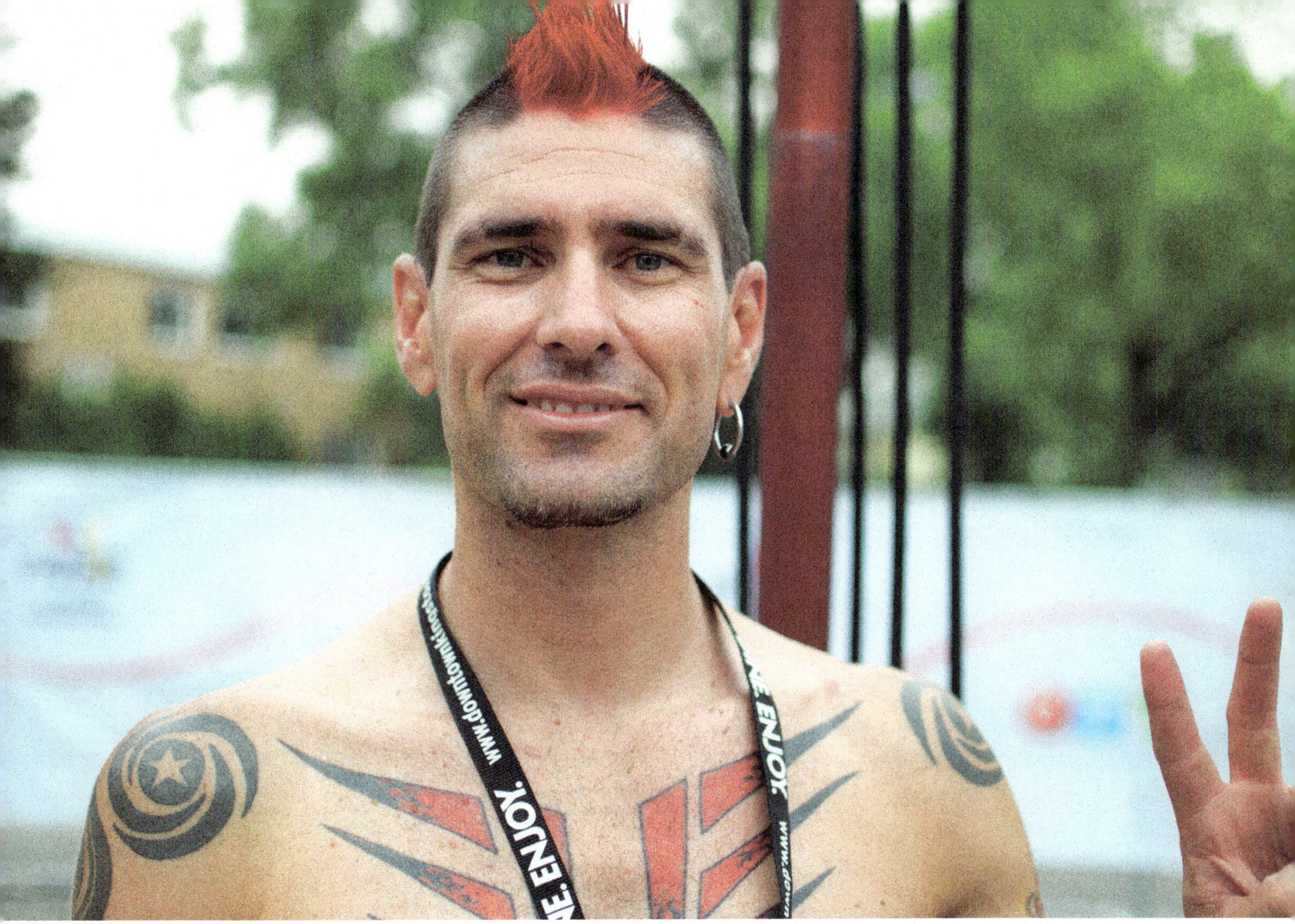

“Don’t be nervous,” he says, holding a started chainsaw that was verified to be real by someone from the audience. “I’m a professional,” he says, pausing, glancing around, smirking. “That’s why I’m performing on a street corner.”

After the show:

“Don’t push and shove,” he says into his mic, holding out a bag to collect tips from the crowd of people huddling around him, his voice amplified through the speakers around his stage.

“Unless you have a hundred. Then push the kids out of the way.”

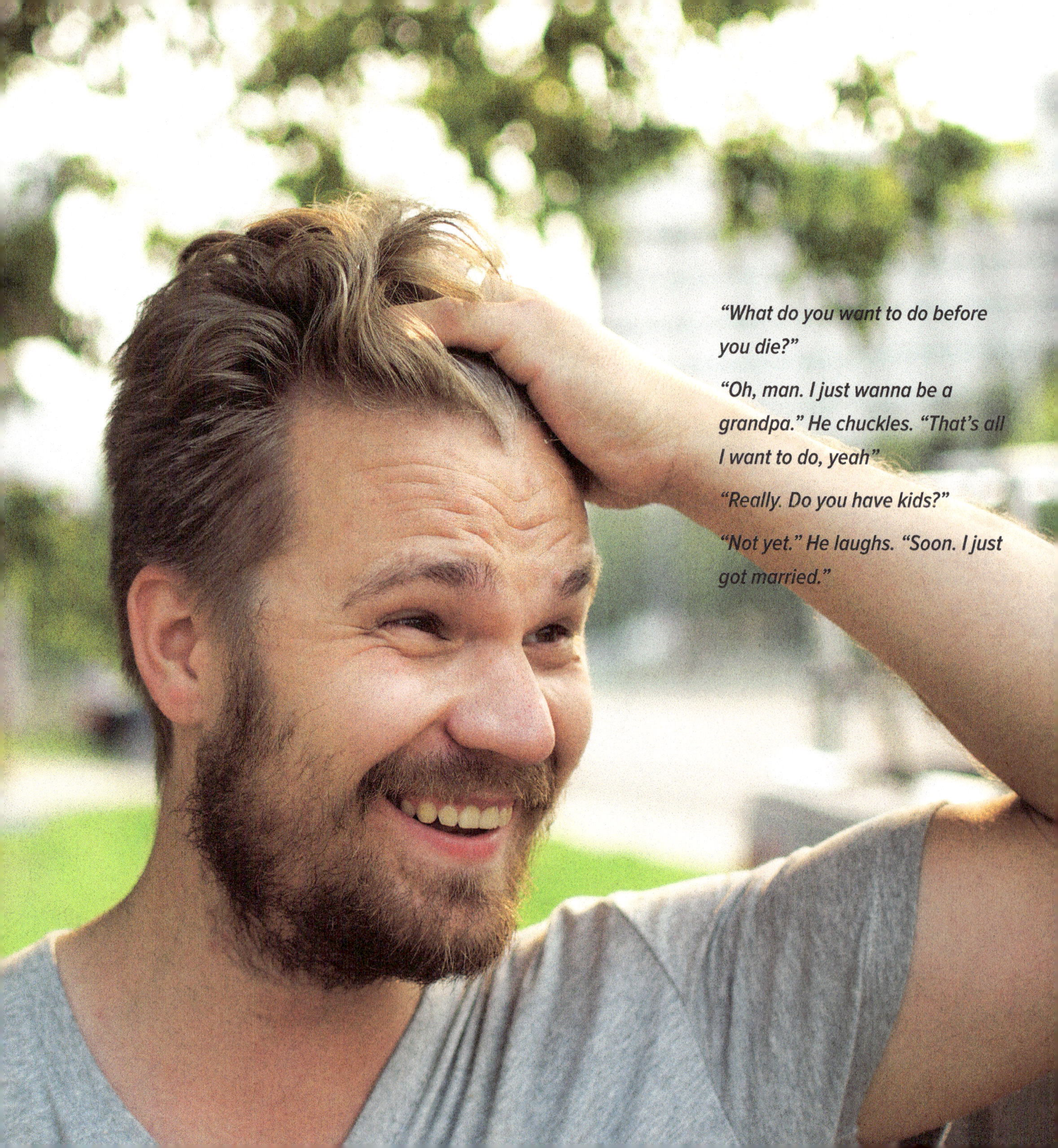

"What do you want to do before you die?"

"Oh, man. I just wanna be a grandpa." He chuckles. "That's all I want to do, yeah"

"Really. Do you have kids?"

"Not yet." He laughs. "Soon. I just got married."

“Ballet is like a relationship because it makes you so nervous and so scared all the time, so it’s like an emotional ... like terror. I don’t know. Like when you’re on stage it’s a moment of terror and elation all wrapped into one.”

“Can you remember a moment when ballet made you really happy?”

“I think my first contract was my happiest moment. I cried, ‘I did it guys. Life goal done. I can die now.’”

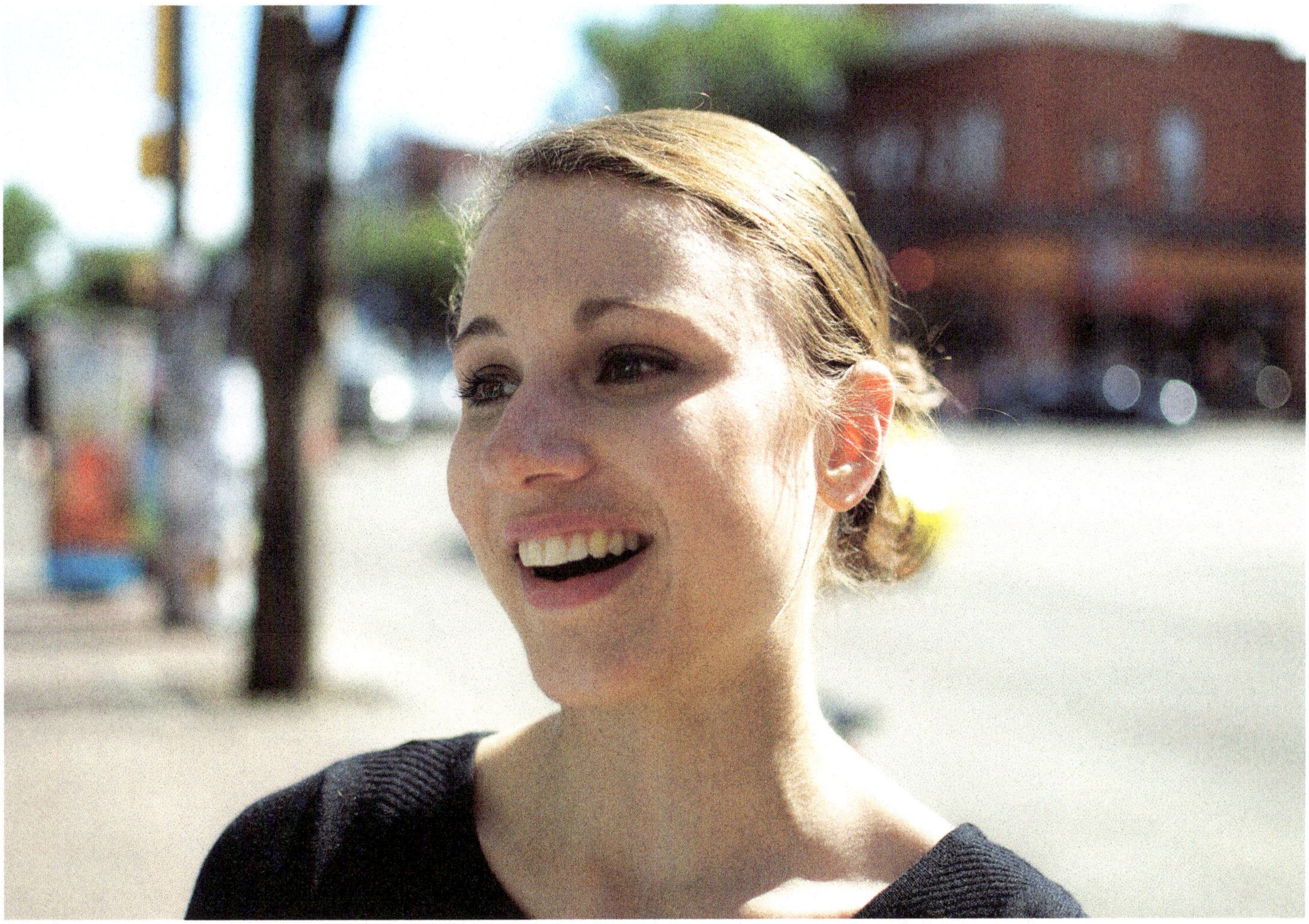

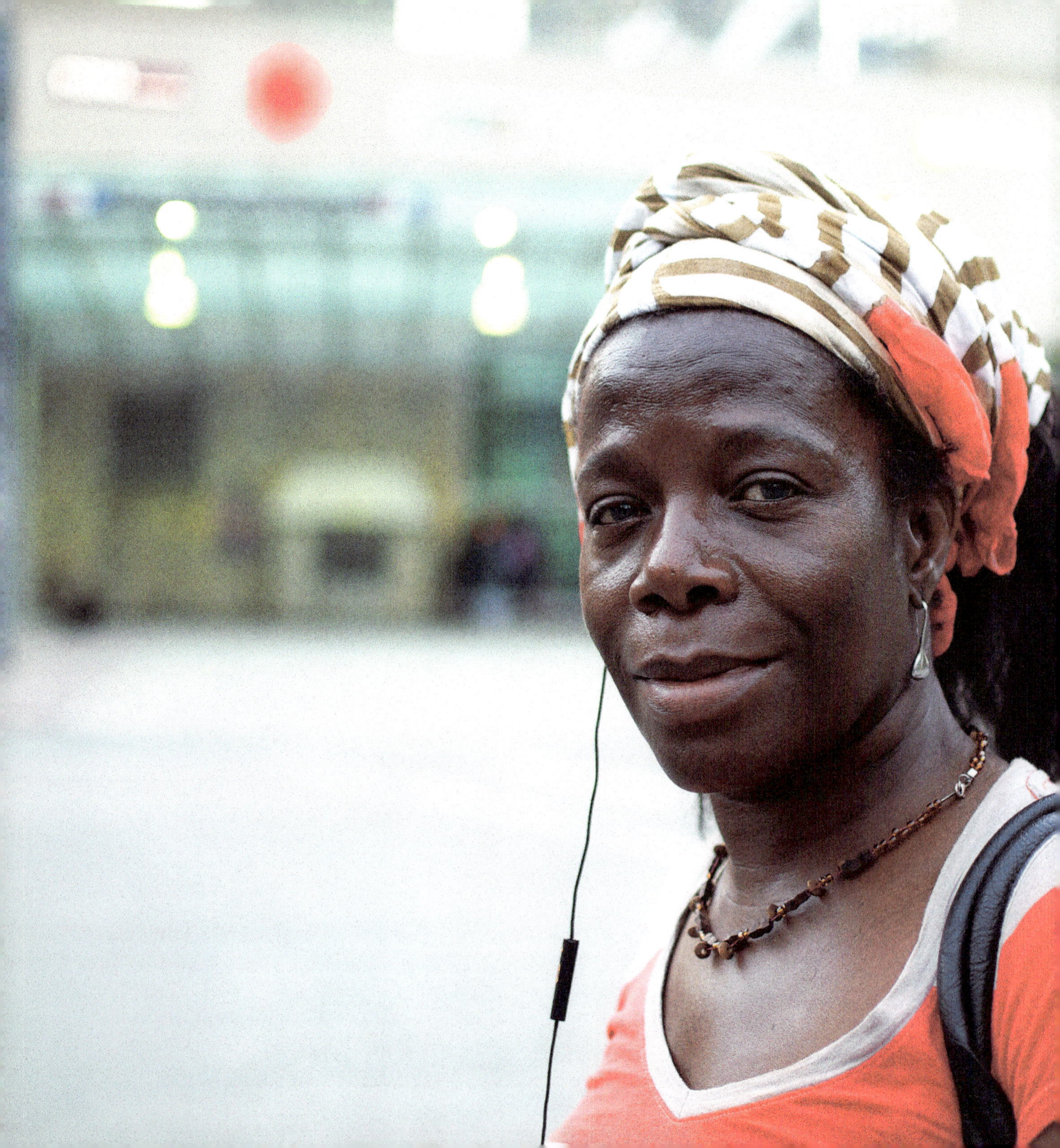

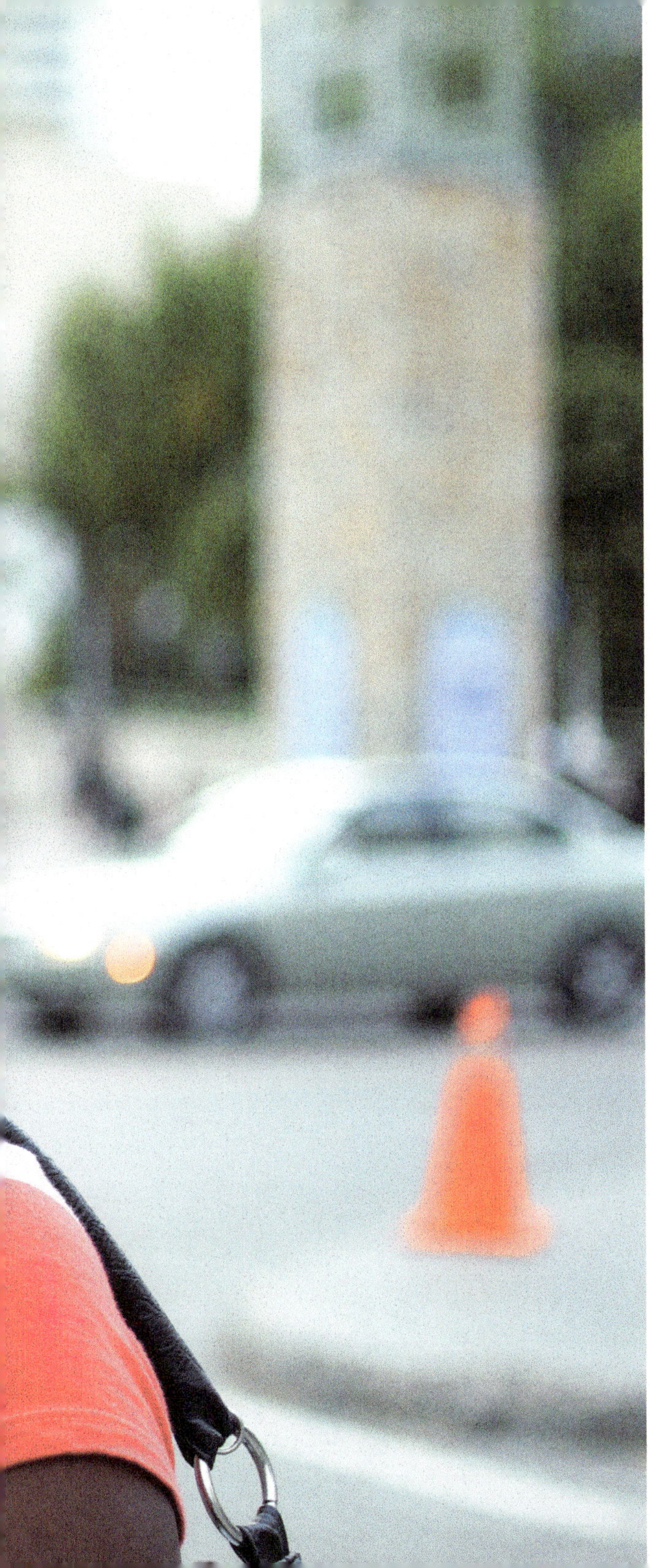

We stand at a street corner together, waiting for the light to change. When it does, we cross.

"I like helping other people," she says. "I used to coordinate a program called Housing First to help homeless people. So that's what I like to do."

"What is it about helping people?"

"It's just the satisfaction that you get after you help somebody, knowing that you've made a difference. Just two days ago I was walking over there," she says, pointing. "At the corner there, and I saw a lady who was going to fall and I knew something was wrong. So I just observed her, and she just went down. Then I asked someone to hold onto her; I called 911 and stayed on the phone until the ambulance came and took her to the hospital."

“I plant this garden every year. I’m seventy-seven and have nothing else to do. I have arthritis and had an operation. What else am I going to do?”

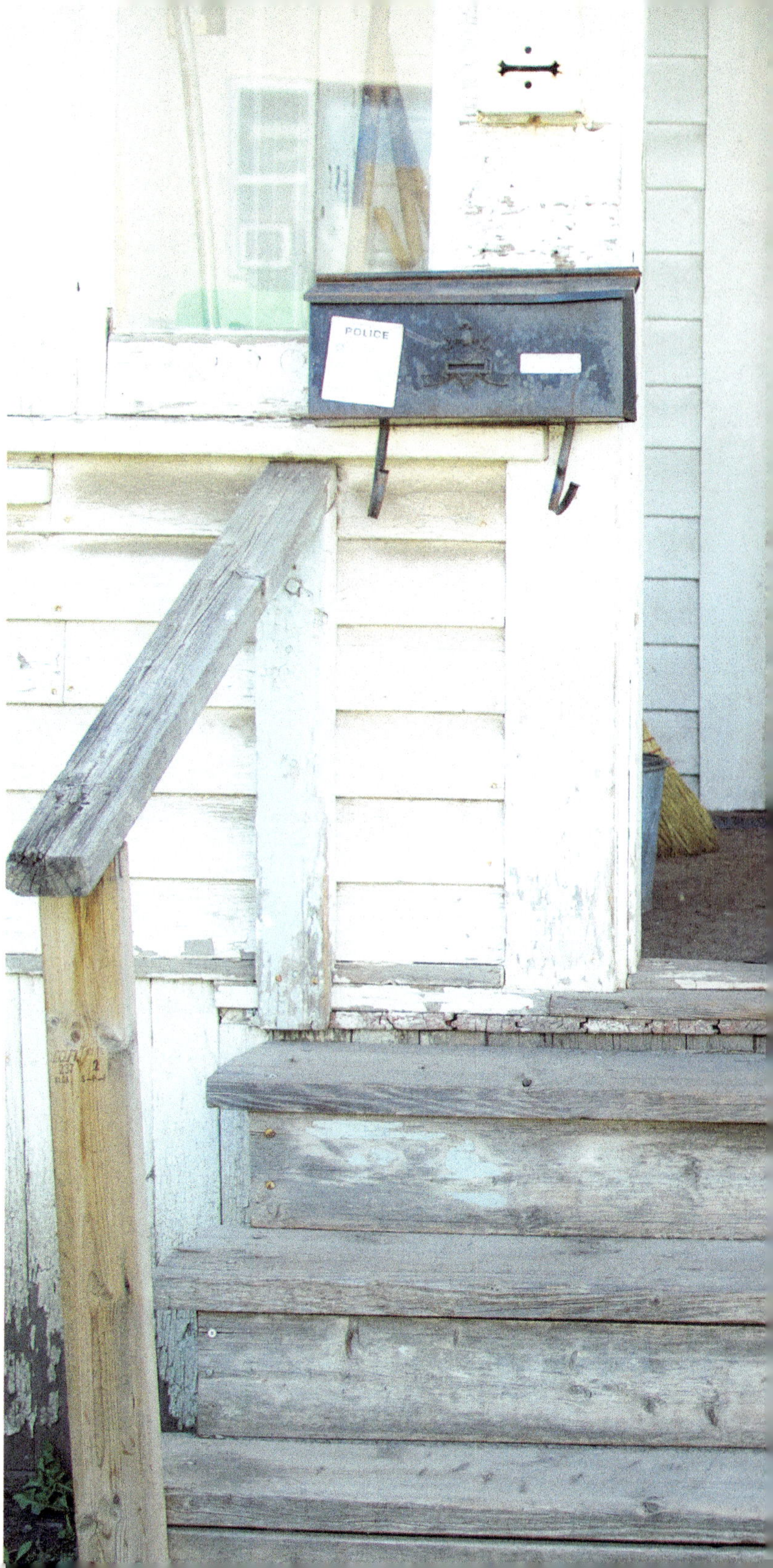

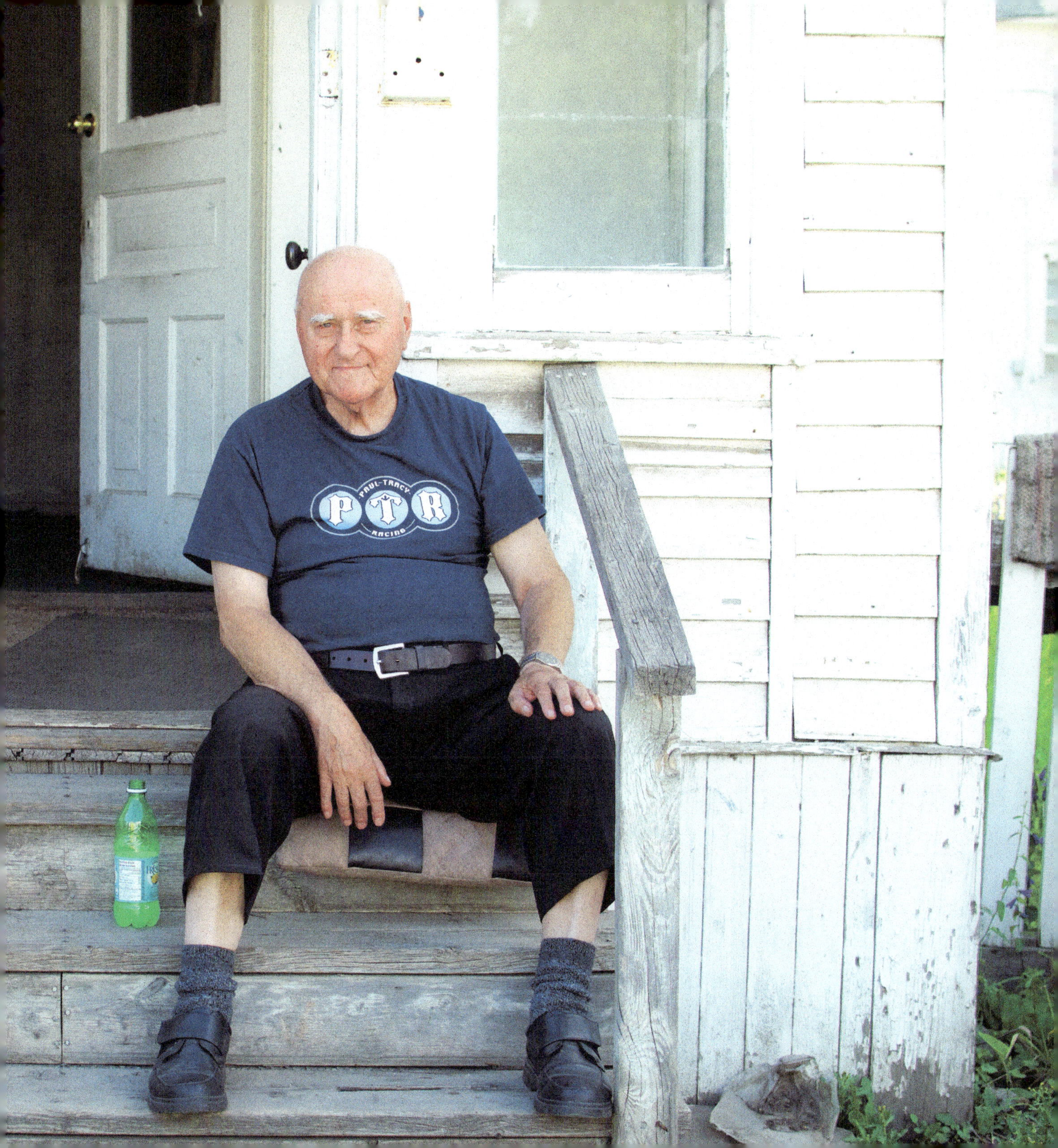
PAUL-TRACY
PTR
RACING

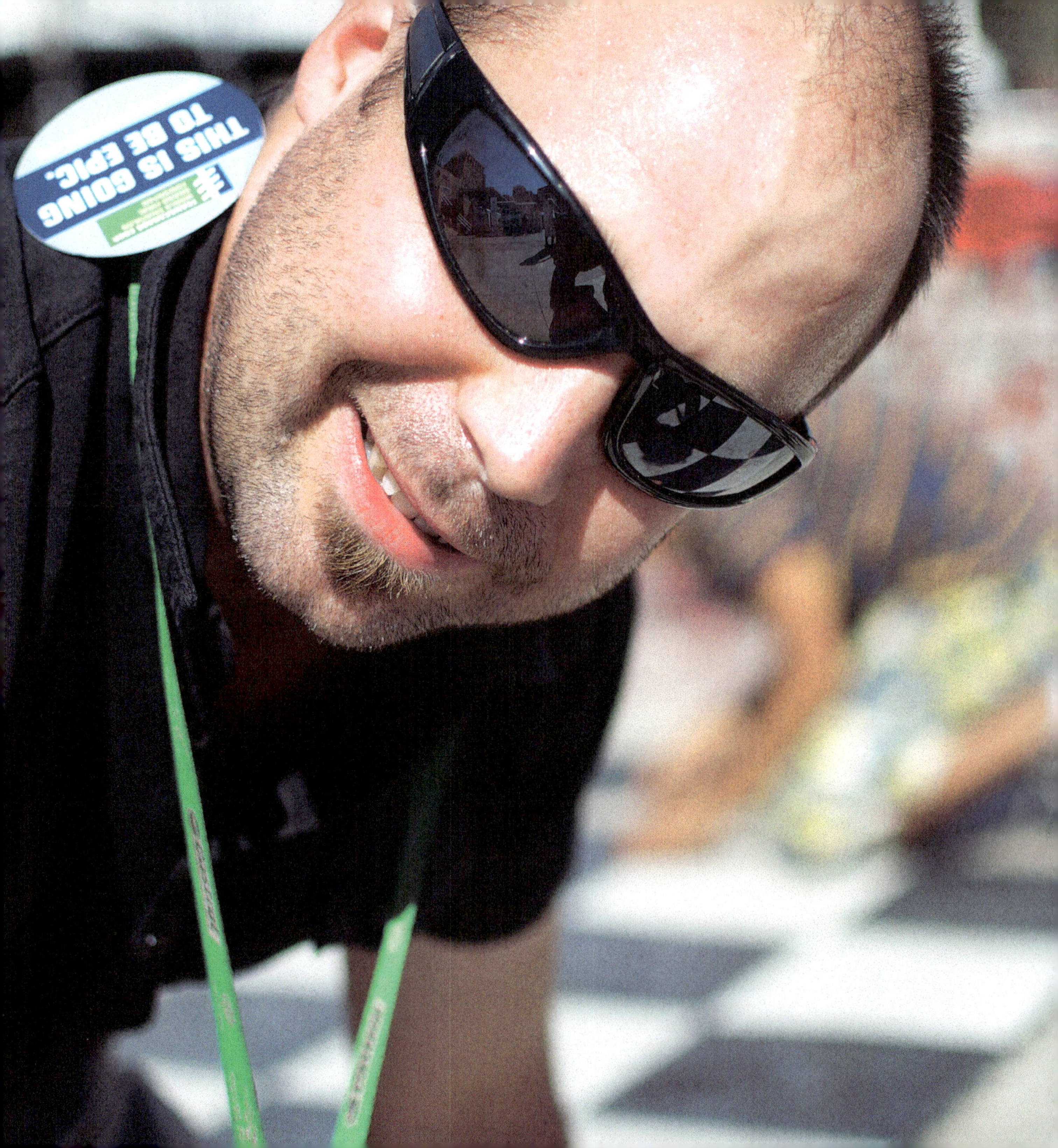
THIS IS GOING TO BE EPIC.

I LIKE WATCHING PEOPLE PLAY

At Churchill Square, the Zumba class is in full hip thrust, Ricky Martin's Livin' la Vida Loca blaring through unseen speakers and filling the square. None of the games are set up yet—the ping-pong tables, gigantic chess and checkers boards are nowhere in sight. And then I see him, pushing a blue cart, a THIS IS GOING TO BE EPIC button pinned to his collar.

"ZUMBA. ZUMBA," booms through the speakers.

He stops to unload chess pieces the size of a small child.

"You'll catch me as I ponder how to do this. It's like a fresh puzzle everyday," he says, standing with his hands on his hips, looking down at the pieces of black and white squares.

"They don't have numbers on the bottom or something?"

"No. They ah, usually it's pretty easy. Um ... as long as all my hoops are facing the same way, there's only one direction and then, ah, as long as they're all in the same direction—"

"ZUMBA. ZUMBA."

"And I get white black, white black then hey," he says chuckling, squatting now and putting the puzzle together. "Then you've done your job."

"So, do you like doing this? Setting these up?"

"It's a little tedious, but I like watching people play."

"When you see people playing these games, how does it make you feel?"

"It's great. One of my favourite things is watching people who don't speak the same language trying to negotiate a game. That's always wild. So you'll see someone who's hanging out here waiting and waiting for someone to come by, and it's the best when they clearly don't speak the same language, but you can see the negotiation, you know. And then it happens, and it's great. I mean, it's a language unto itself, so you know, it's great to see that happen. You see some pretty interesting games. Some pretty interesting rules that come up."

I'M OLD AND TIRED. BUT I'M OKAY.

"How old are you? If you don't mind me asking."

"Oh, I don't mind." He has a thick accent. "Guess how old I am," he says.

"I don't know. Seventy-one?"

"Oh no," he says, laughing through his nose and shaking his head. He waves his hand up and down in the air and says, "Much more."

I shrug.

"I'm eighty-three. I was born in 1931 in Portugal. In 1952, I joined the army, and then I ran like a rabbit to Canada. This has been my home for fifty-five years."

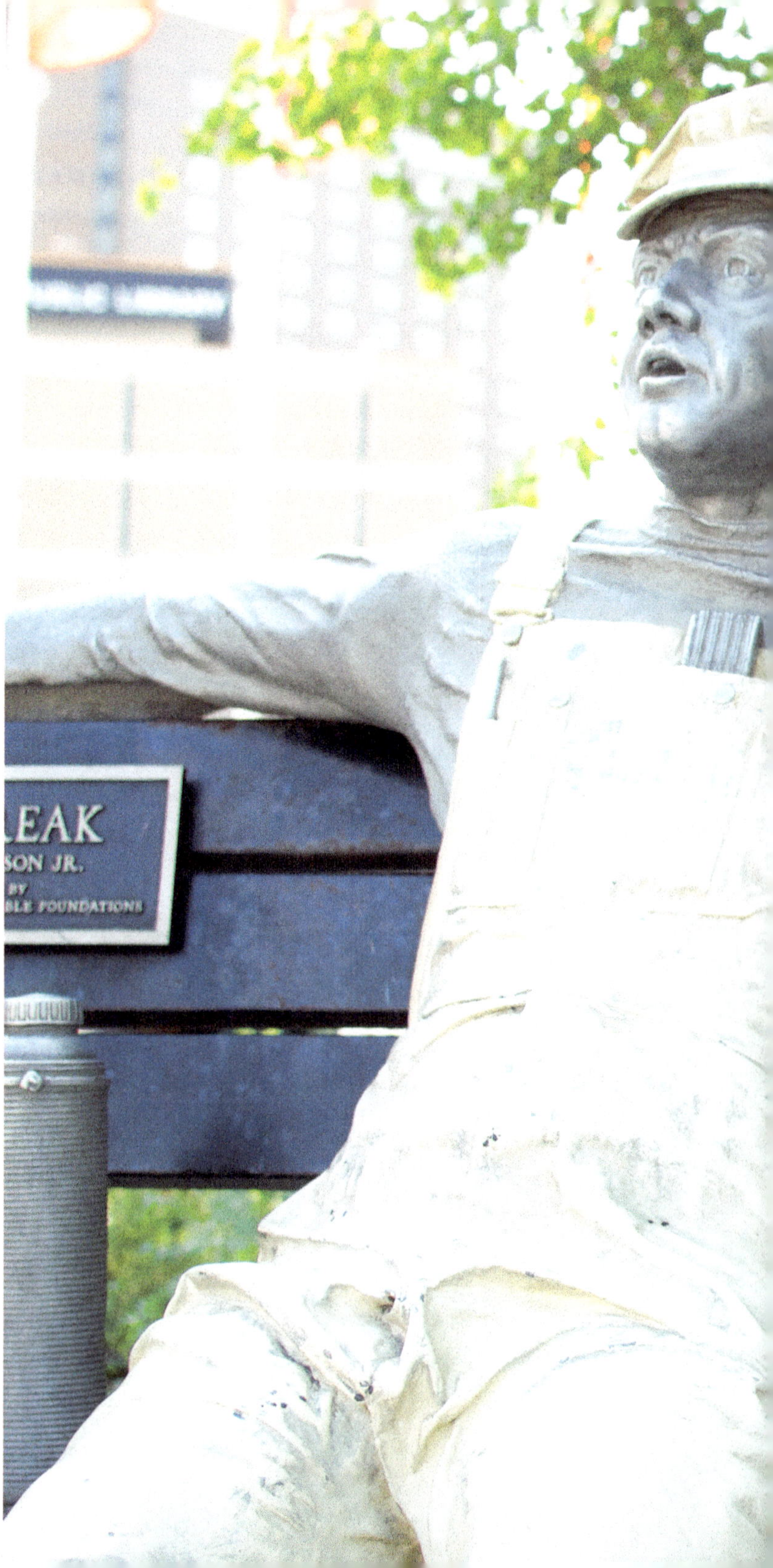

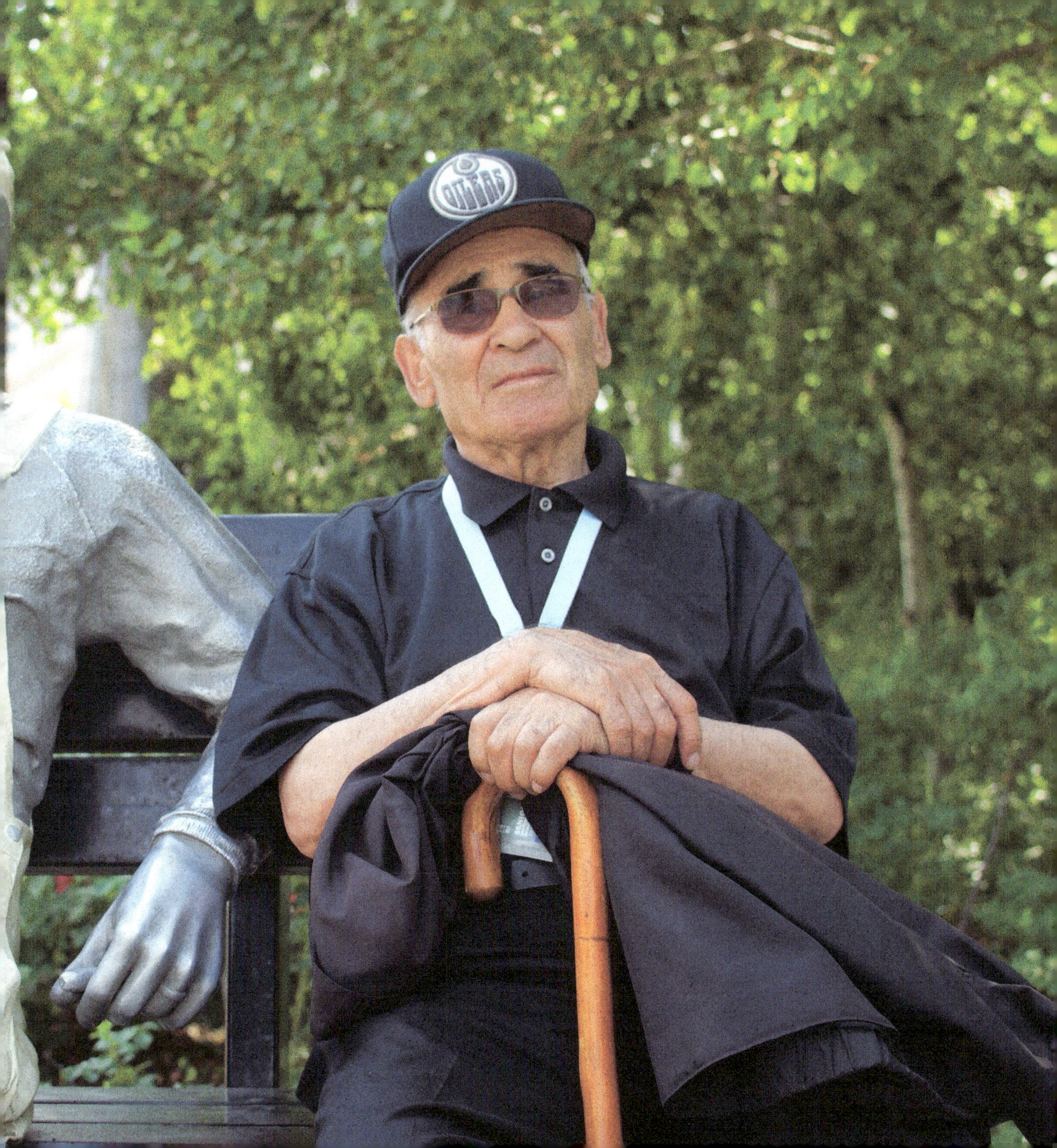
OILERS

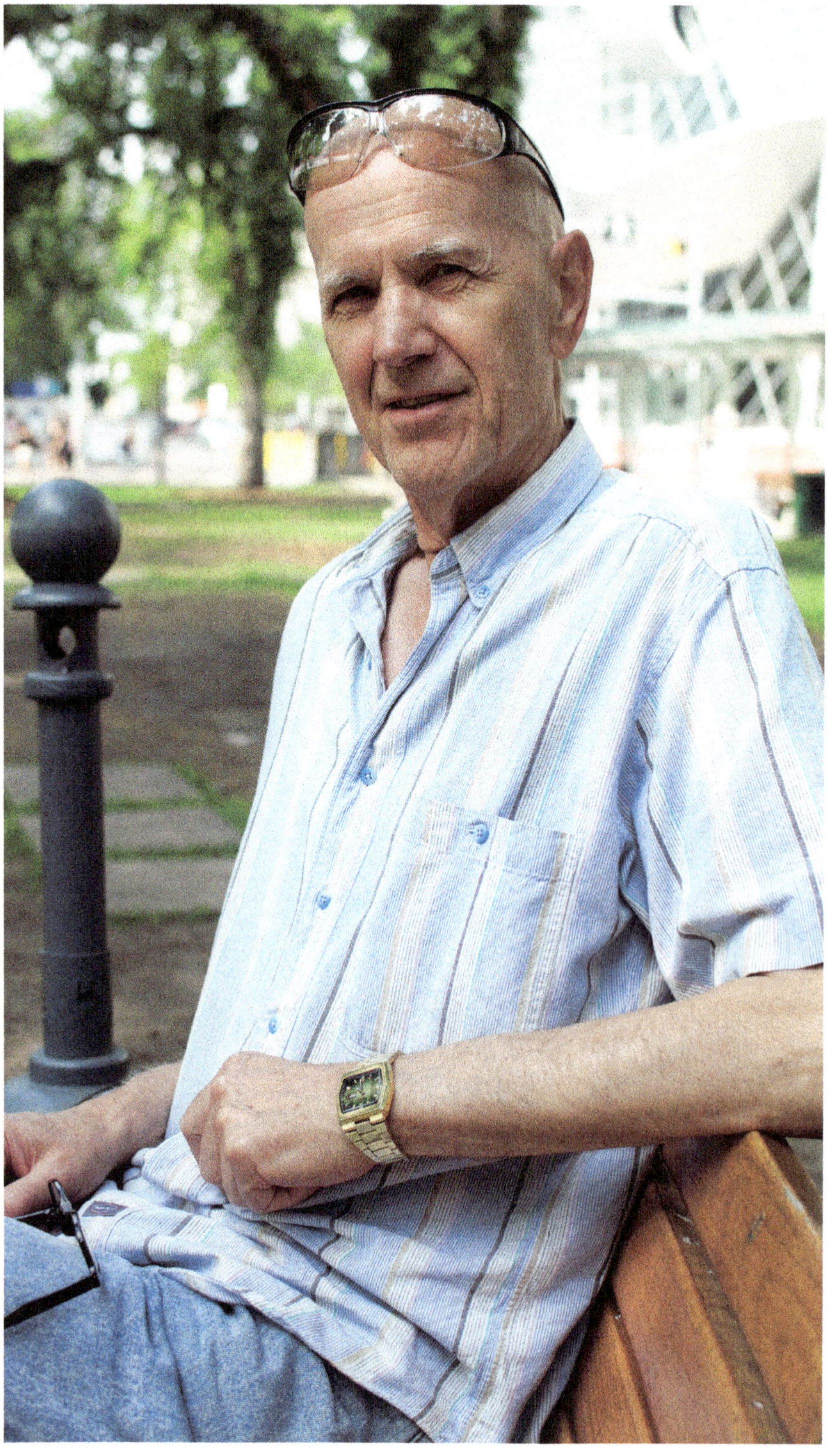

He sits on a bench overlooking Churchill Square. He wears two pairs of glasses, sunglasses resting on his head and reading glasses perched on his nose.

"May I join you?" I ask.

"Absolutely," he says. He's reading the Metro edition that has an article about Faces of Edmonton in it. I smile, don't say anything about the article, and we start talking. "I sing karaoke once a week. Hank Williams, Johnny Cash's Folsom Prison. Songs like that.

"Every week?"

"Every week. One time I got in and there was standing room only. There must have been a hundred people in there. I was so nervous I almost didn't go up. But then I did and people loved it, and it was great. Singing's good for the soul."

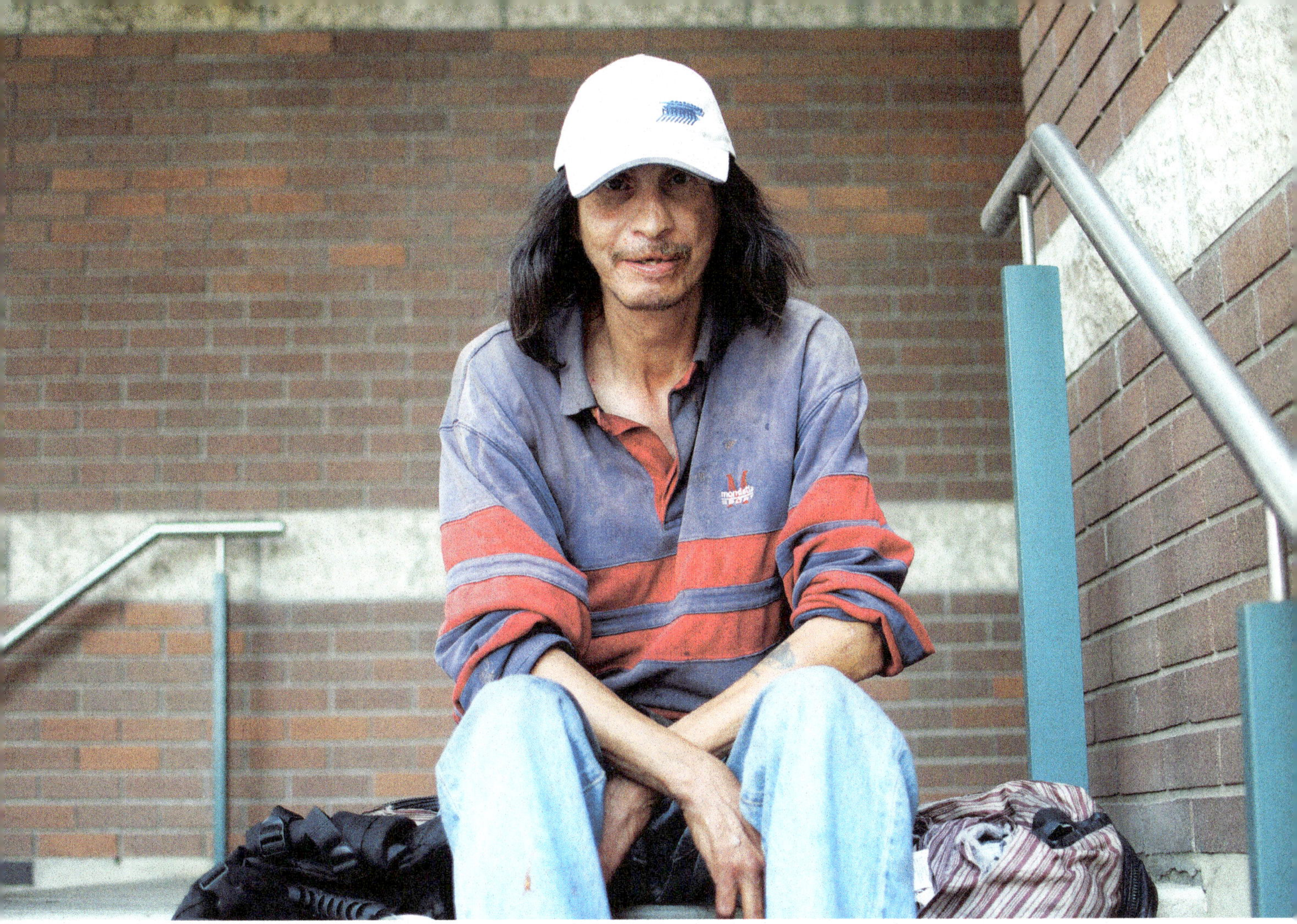

RENÉ

“If you could change one thing about your life, what would it be?”

“Stop drinking. I don’t need drugs no more. I quit that years ago. Thank god. It’s so expensive. I can’t afford it. I’m homeless. So … What’s your name?”

“I’m Shayne.”

“René.”

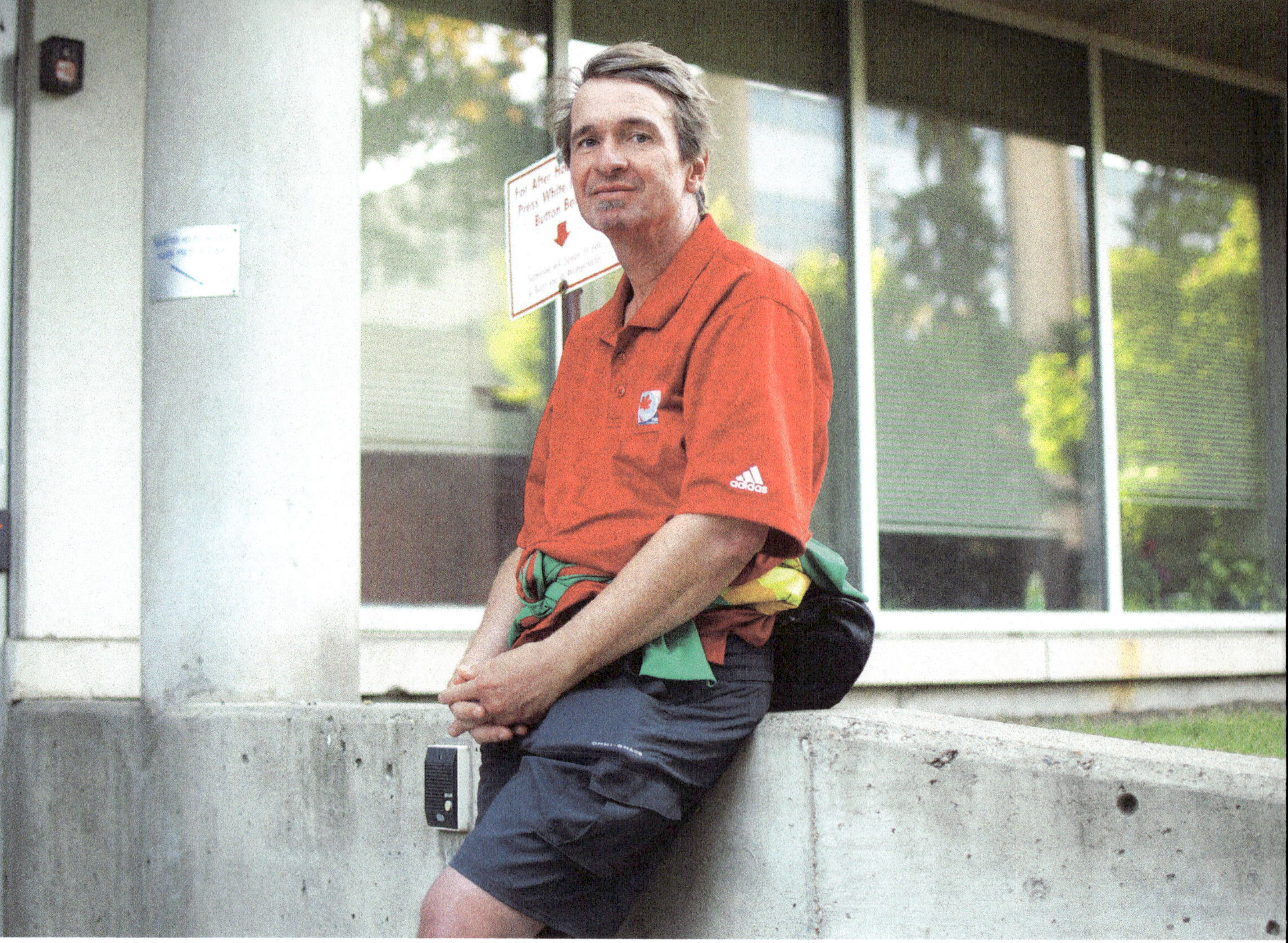

WALTER

"I volunteer. I volunteer for the Red Cross, many of Edmonton's festivals and special events. I like being able to help with so many different causes. It's everyone's right to volunteer."

"I just finished an interview," she says, laughing.

"How did it go?"

"Pretty good. They really wanted me but ah … I'm not going to do door-to-door sales again. I did it for a year and a half. I was good at it but too much frostbite. Maybe in California I'll do it but not in Edmonton."

"Do you have any crazy stories from your door to door sales days?"

"Plenty. Lots of naked people. Lots and lots of naked people. There was one time when these two people were actually having sex, and I interrupted them. They covered themselves with a blanket, and then I got them to sign a contract. Yeah," she says, pausing and grinning. "It was pretty interesting."

We both laugh.

"Lots of crazy stories like that."

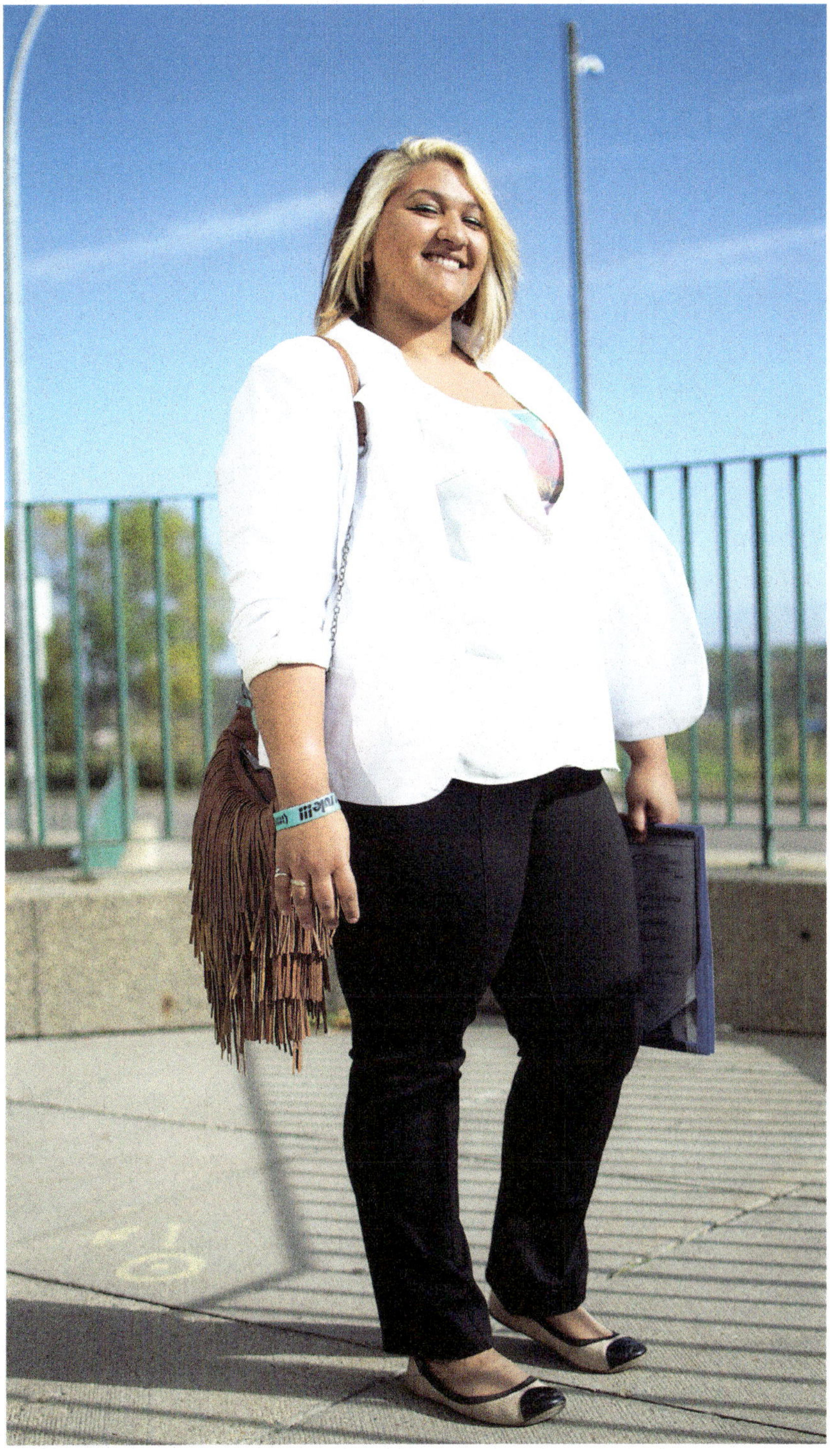

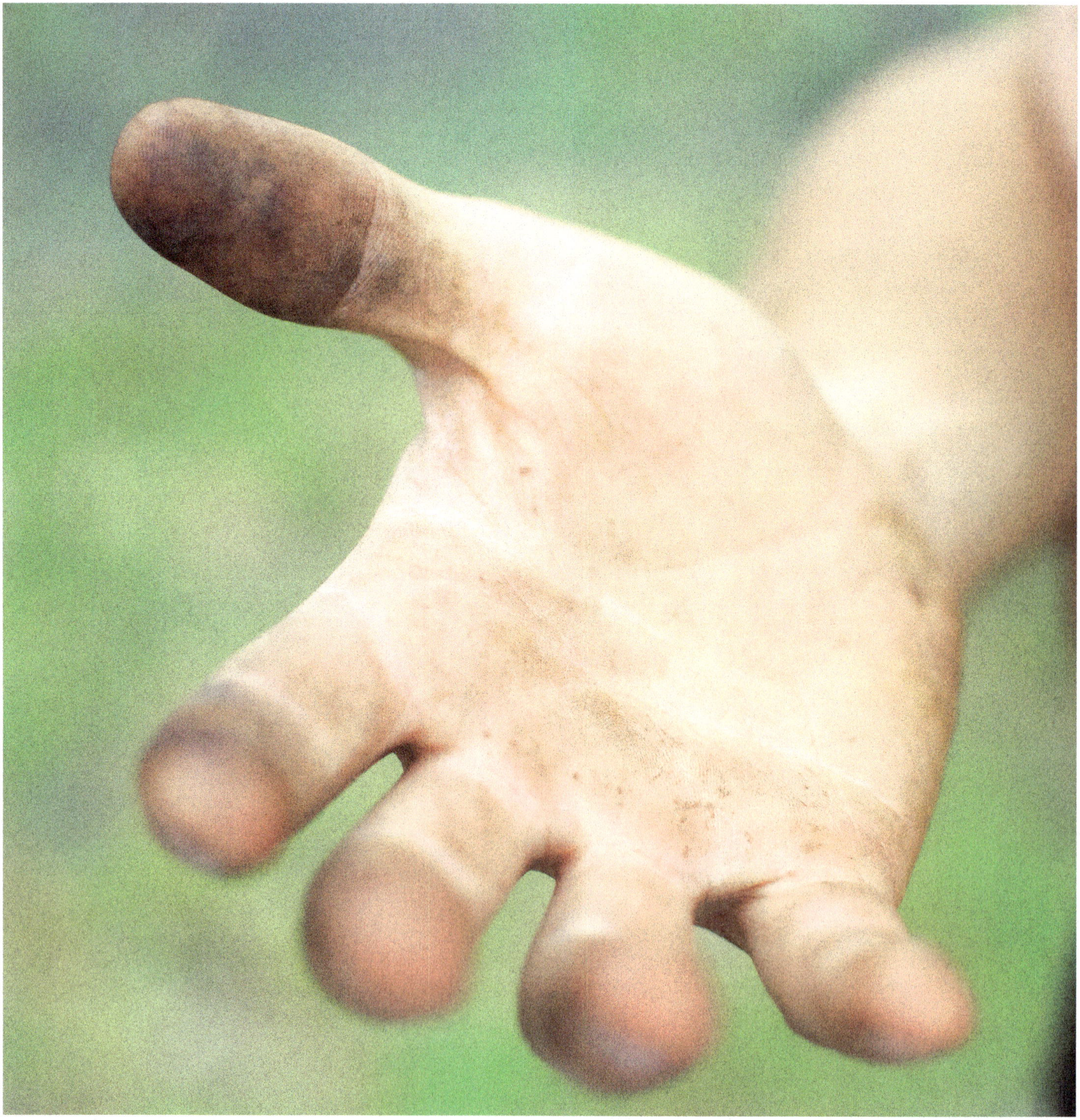

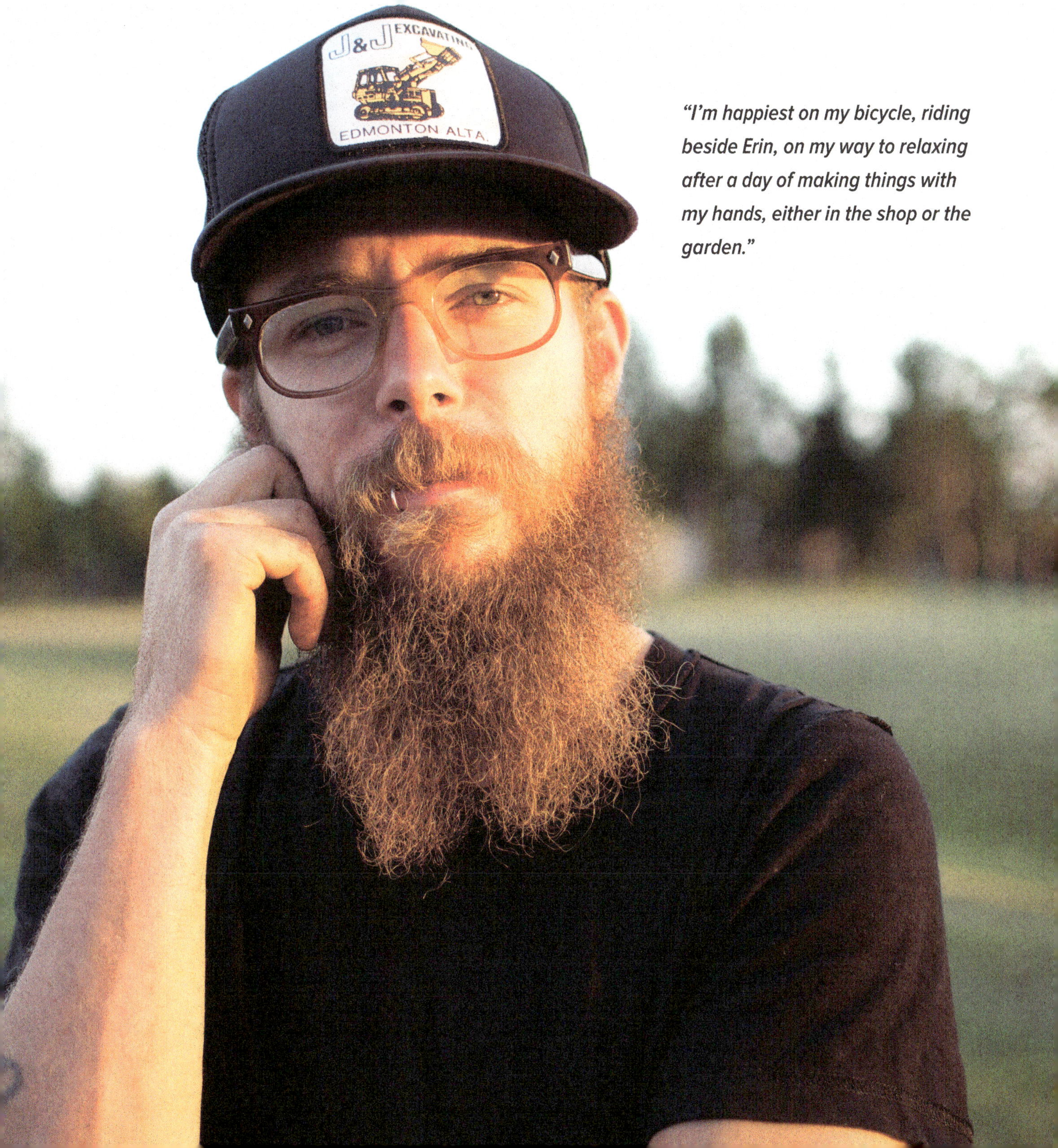

"I'm happiest on my bicycle, riding beside Erin, on my way to relaxing after a day of making things with my hands, either in the shop or the garden."

“One of the best things in my life is my wife,” he says, smiling and pointing to a van that just pulled up. “That’s my wife there.”

“How long have you been together?”

“There’s kind of a complex answer. We’ve been married for five years but we actually dated back when we were in high school about thirty years ago. We kind of had separate lives as we moved from where we’re from. We’re originally from El Salvador. And then she had her life in the States, and I had mine in Canada, and then we met each other again about ten years ago.”

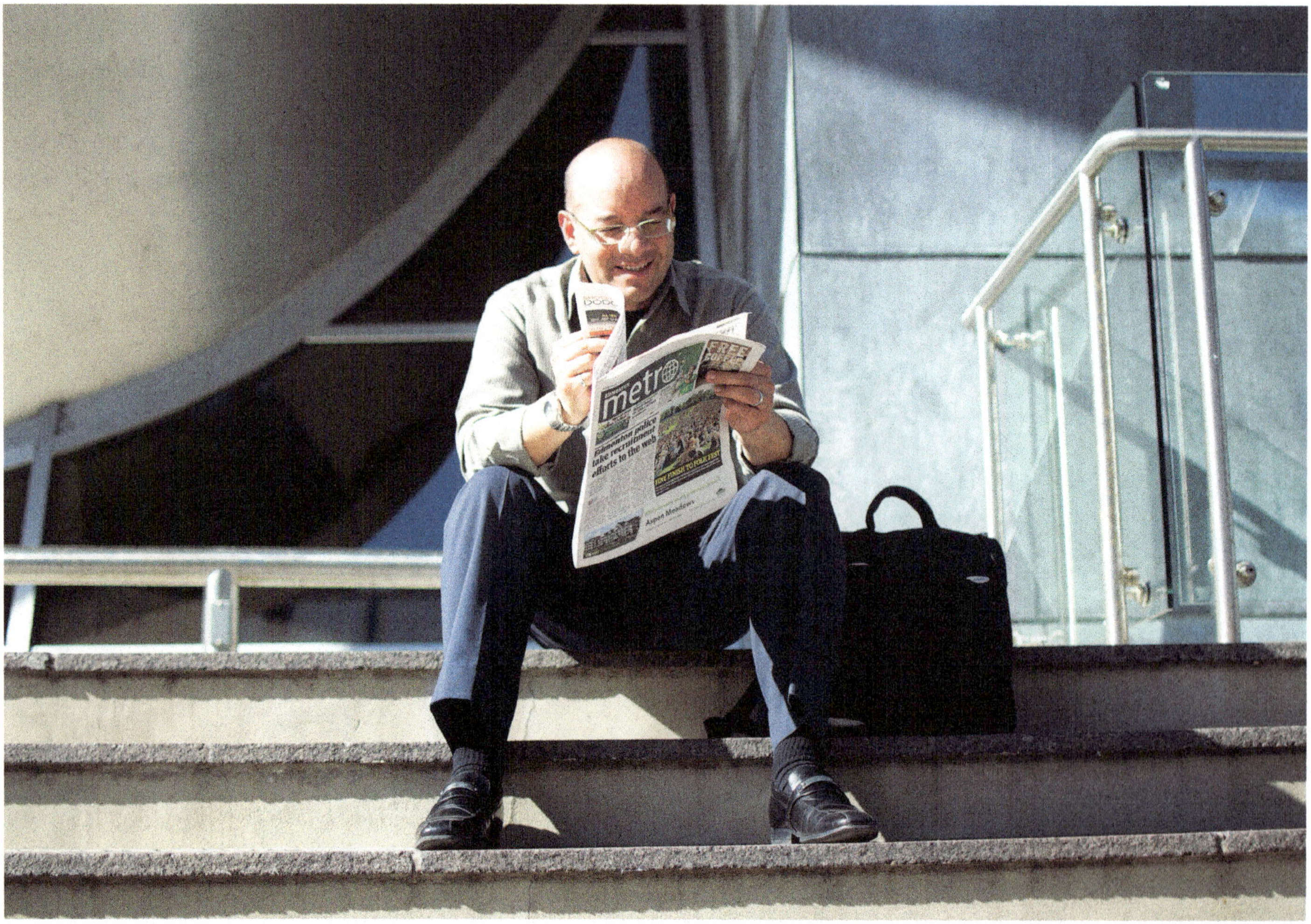

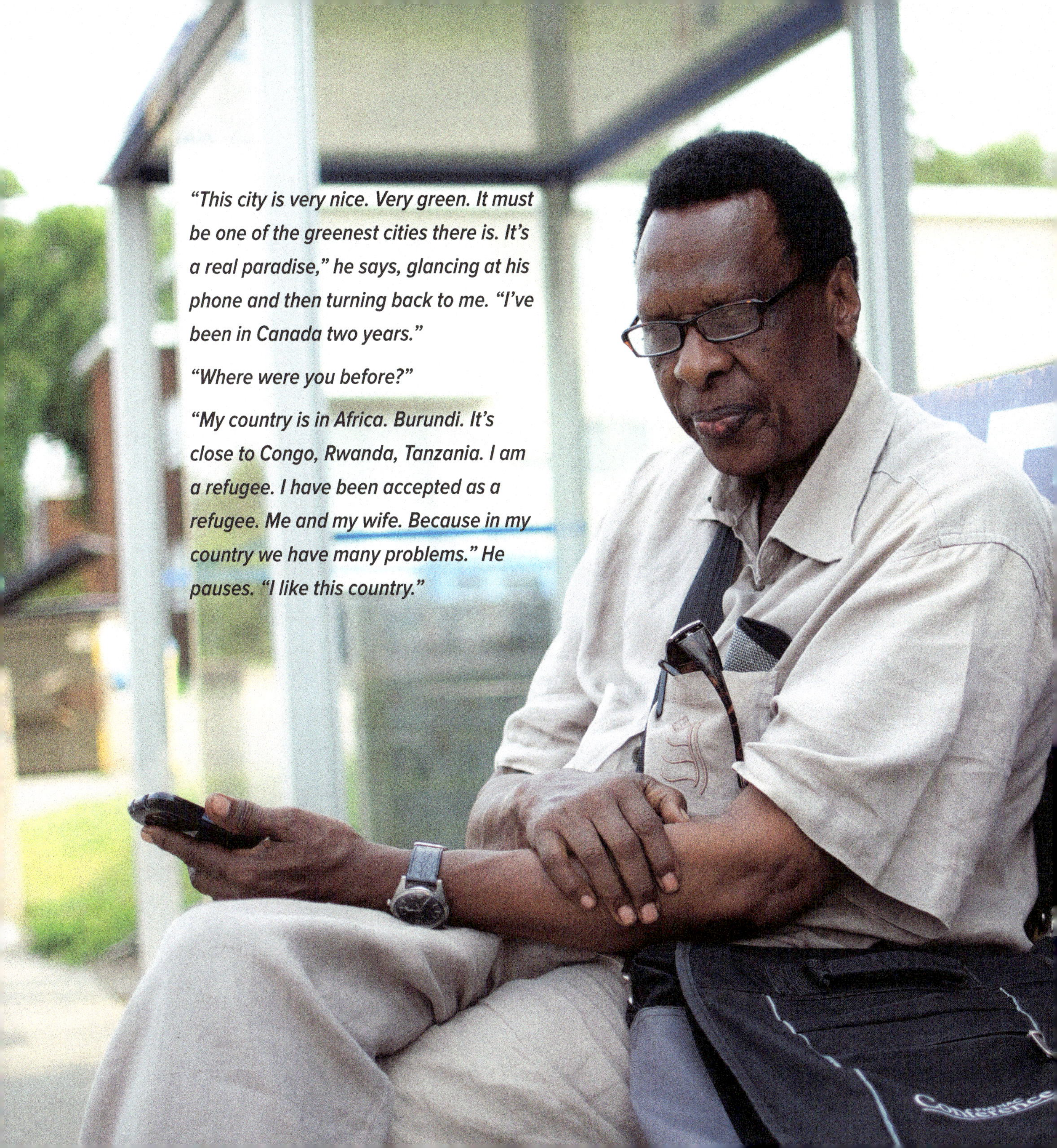

"This city is very nice. Very green. It must be one of the greenest cities there is. It's a real paradise," he says, glancing at his phone and then turning back to me. "I've been in Canada two years."

"Where were you before?"

"My country is in Africa. Burundi. It's close to Congo, Rwanda, Tanzania. I am a refugee. I have been accepted as a refugee. Me and my wife. Because in my country we have many problems." He pauses. "I like this country."

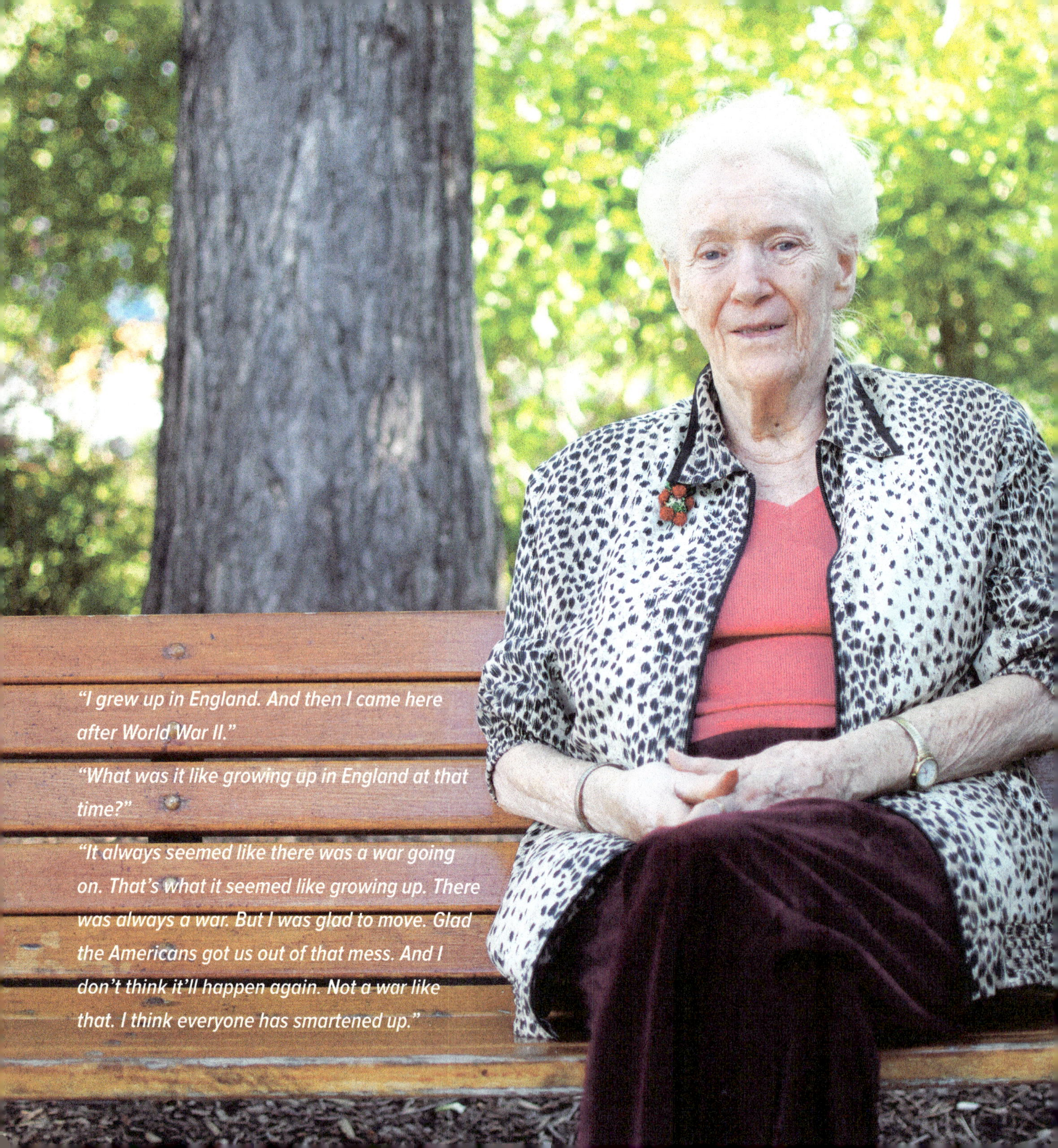

"I grew up in England. And then I came here after World War II."

"What was it like growing up in England at that time?"

"It always seemed like there was a war going on. That's what it seemed like growing up. There was always a war. But I was glad to move. Glad the Americans got us out of that mess. And I don't think it'll happen again. Not a war like that. I think everyone has smartened up."

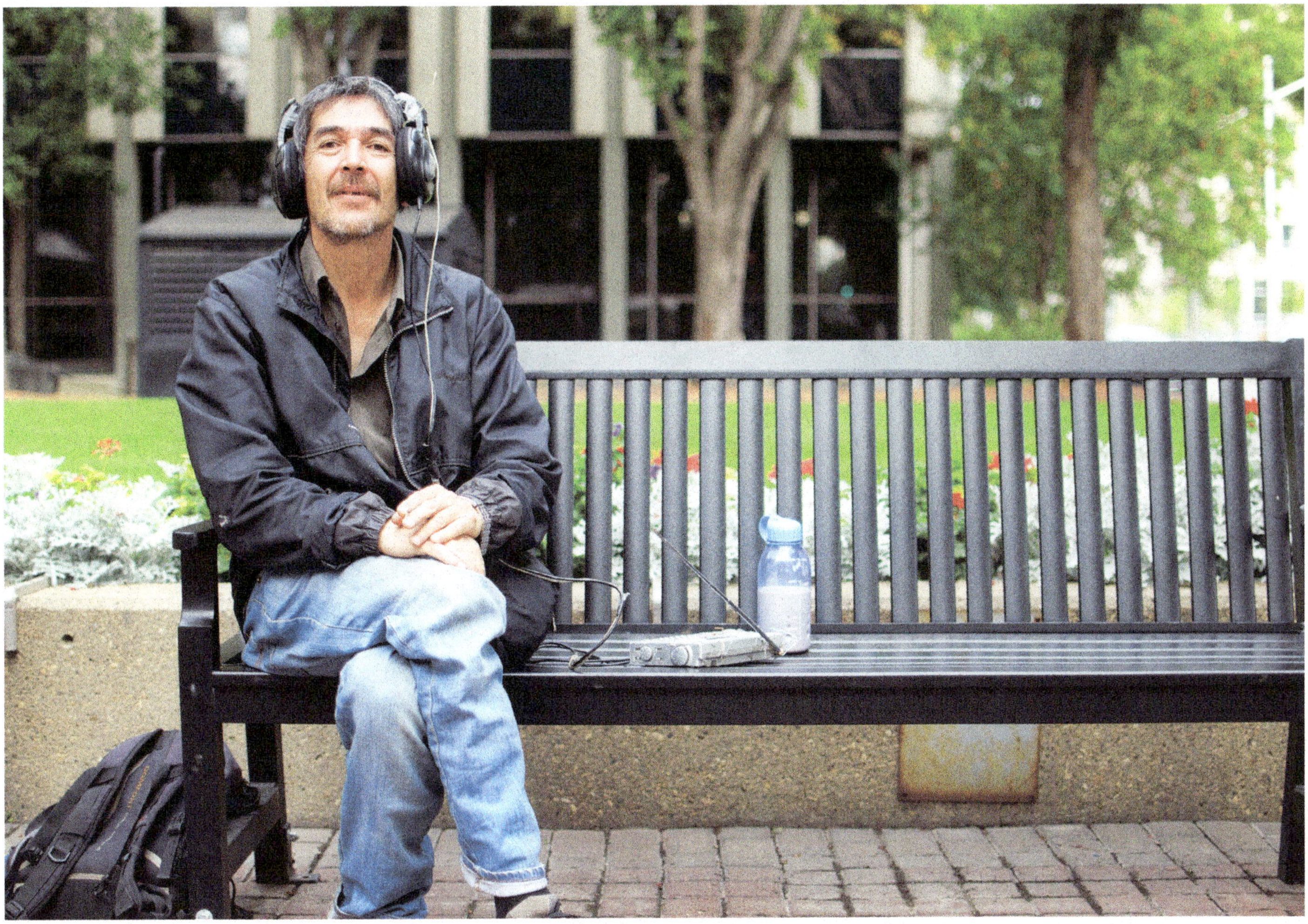

He sits alone, on a bench, singing, his head bobbing to the music coming through the vintage-looking headphones over his ears. I walk past and then turn toward him. His singing makes me smile.

"I basically just sing to the radio because I haven't bought any actual equipment to record. Well, I did have a tape recorder previously. But I'll have to get a better microphone and amplifier from the music shop at some point, and I'll start recording. I just keep on singing different songs. I've been working on it for seven years. I sing at home. I sing along with YouTube and Rock Band."

She sits on the curb, waiting, her blue dress practically glowing in the sunlight, her hat slightly askew. I step across the street and squat in front of her.

"What's one of your happiest memories?"

"When I was in grade eleven, I spent the day at—the person who I was most in love with—I spent the day at their house. We woke up, and it was raining and snowing at the same time, so we just spent the whole day in bed. And then we got up, and they said to me, 'I'm going to play the piano. Would you just dance for me?' And I danced for them while they played the piano. It was really beautiful."

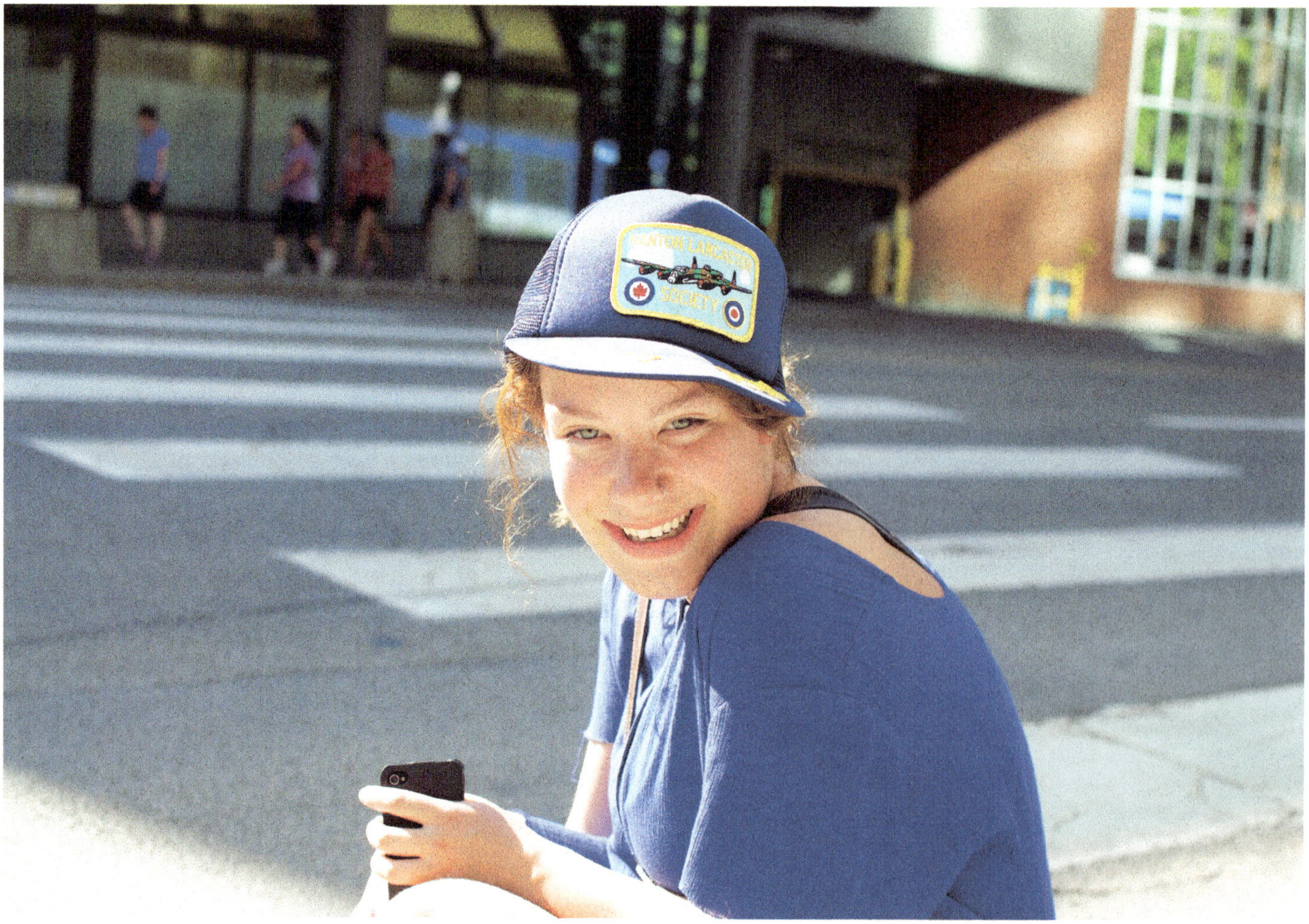

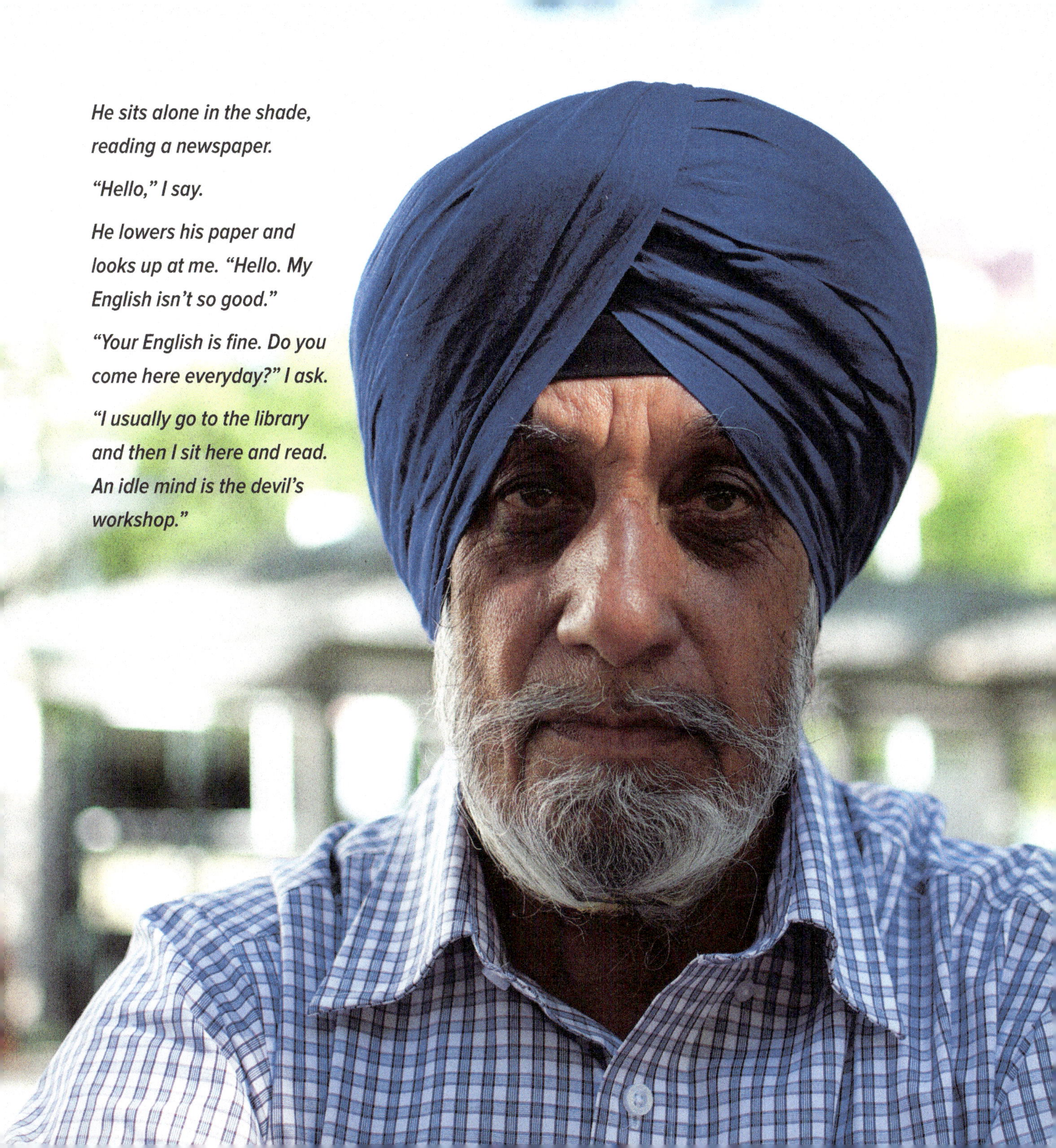

He sits alone in the shade, reading a newspaper.

"Hello," I say.

He lowers his paper and looks up at me. "Hello. My English isn't so good."

"Your English is fine. Do you come here everyday?" I ask.

"I usually go to the library and then I sit here and read. An idle mind is the devil's workshop."

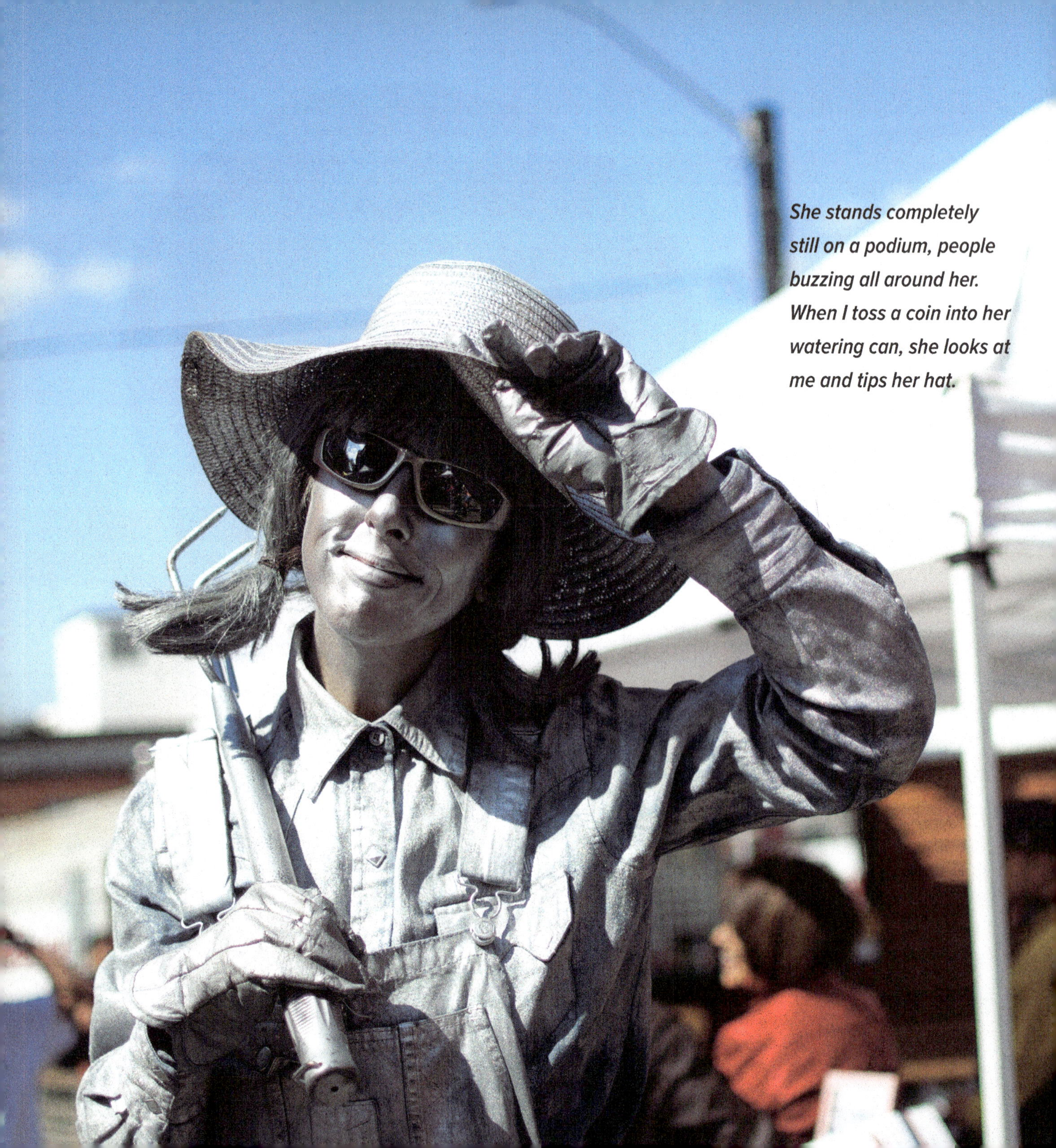

She stands completely still on a podium, people buzzing all around her. When I toss a coin into her watering can, she looks at me and tips her hat.

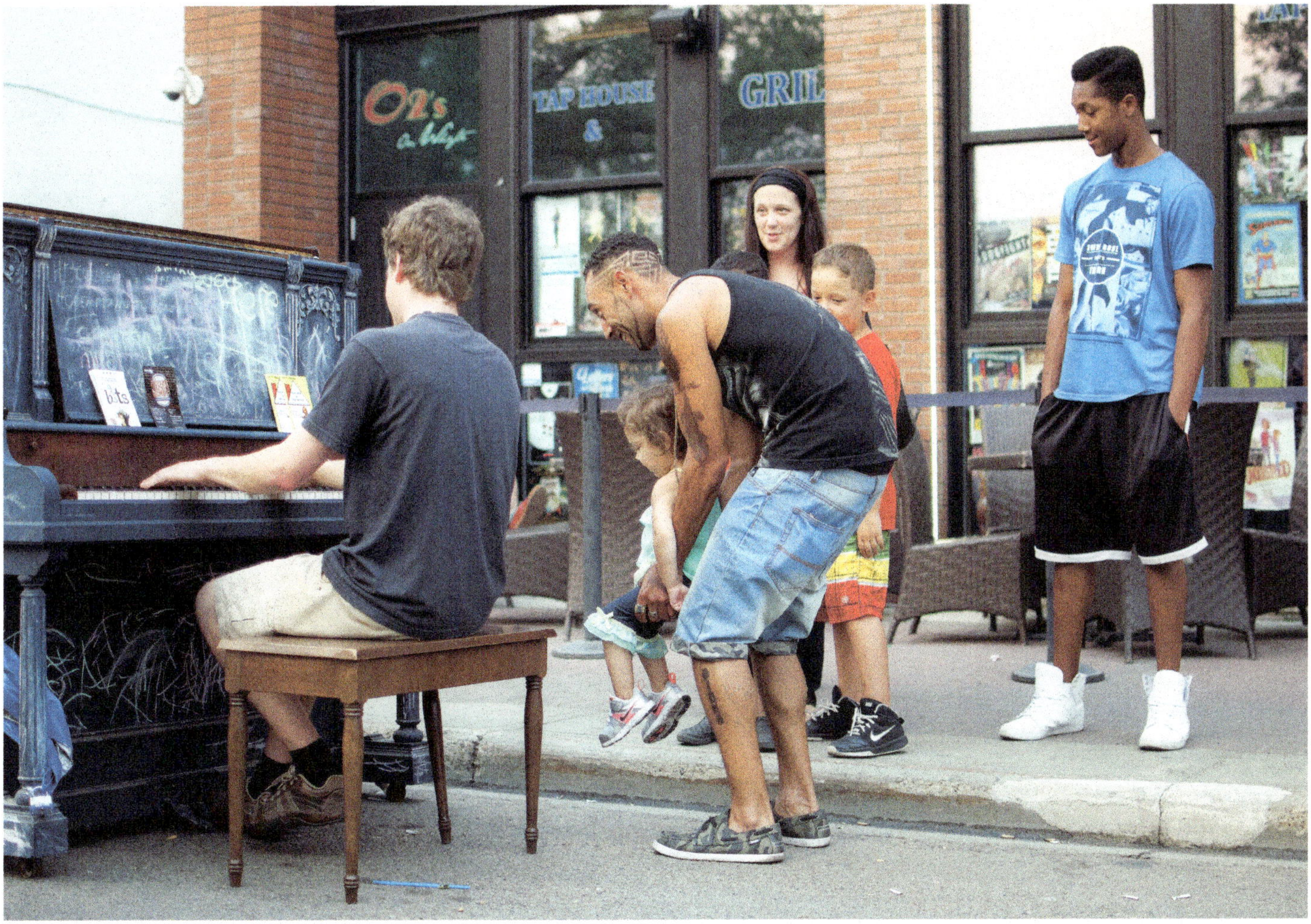

He plays a piano, covered in chalk and on the street, like a jazz club pianist. People walk by, stop, and can't help tapping a foot in time with the music. A man holding a child dances beside the piano, the little girl grooving in his arms. They dance as if they are alone, as if the pianist is playing just for them.

THIS DOESN'T SHOW YOU WHO I AM

"You can take a picture but you have to sneak it. They take pictures of me all day," he says, thumbing to the surveillance camera attached to the 7-Eleven beside him, his row of missing teeth visible when he speaks. "I'm not one for pictures and this picture doesn't tell the whole story, you know." He motions to his cart stuffed with clothes, plastic, and other stuff. "This doesn't show you who I am."

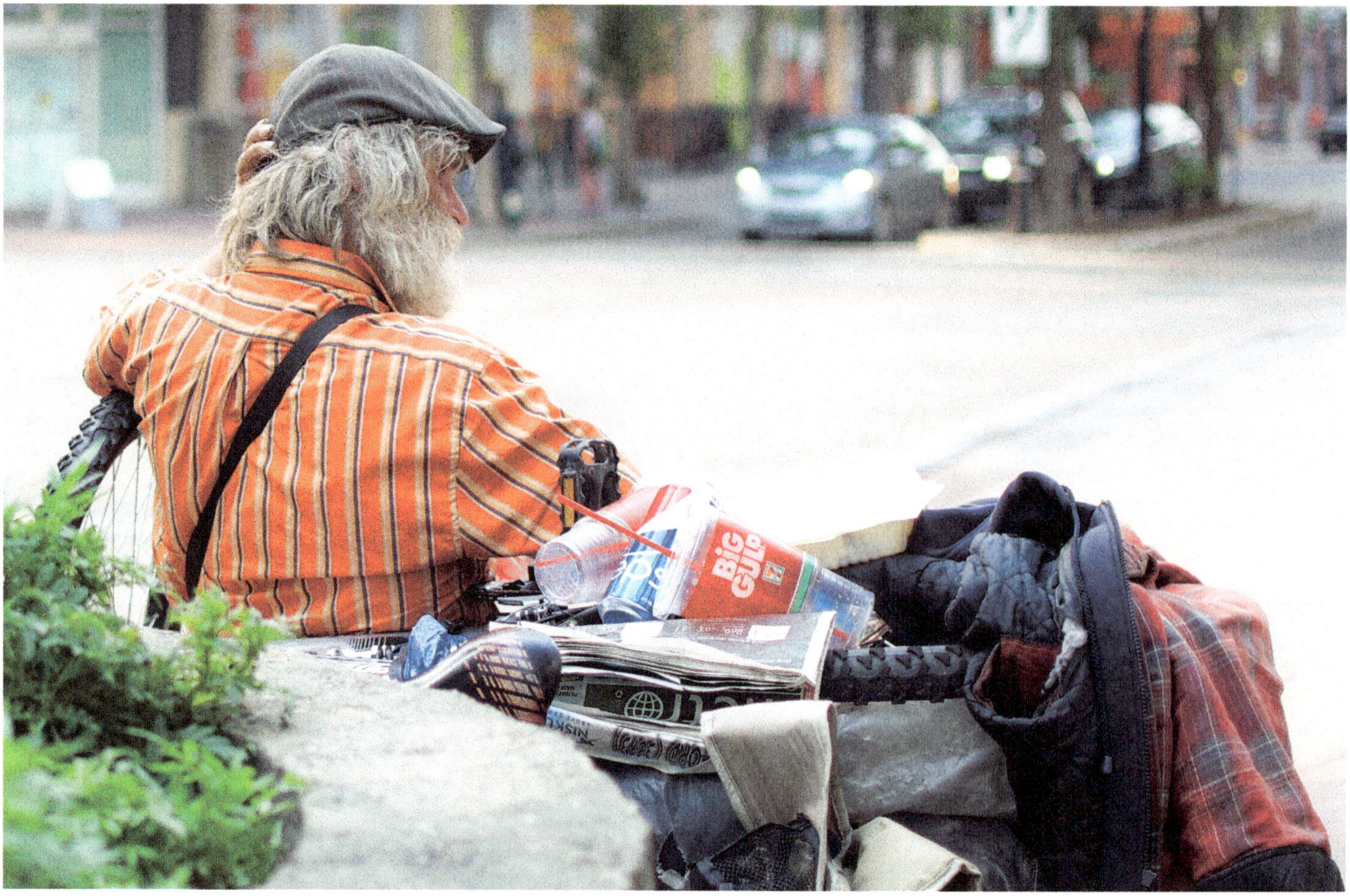

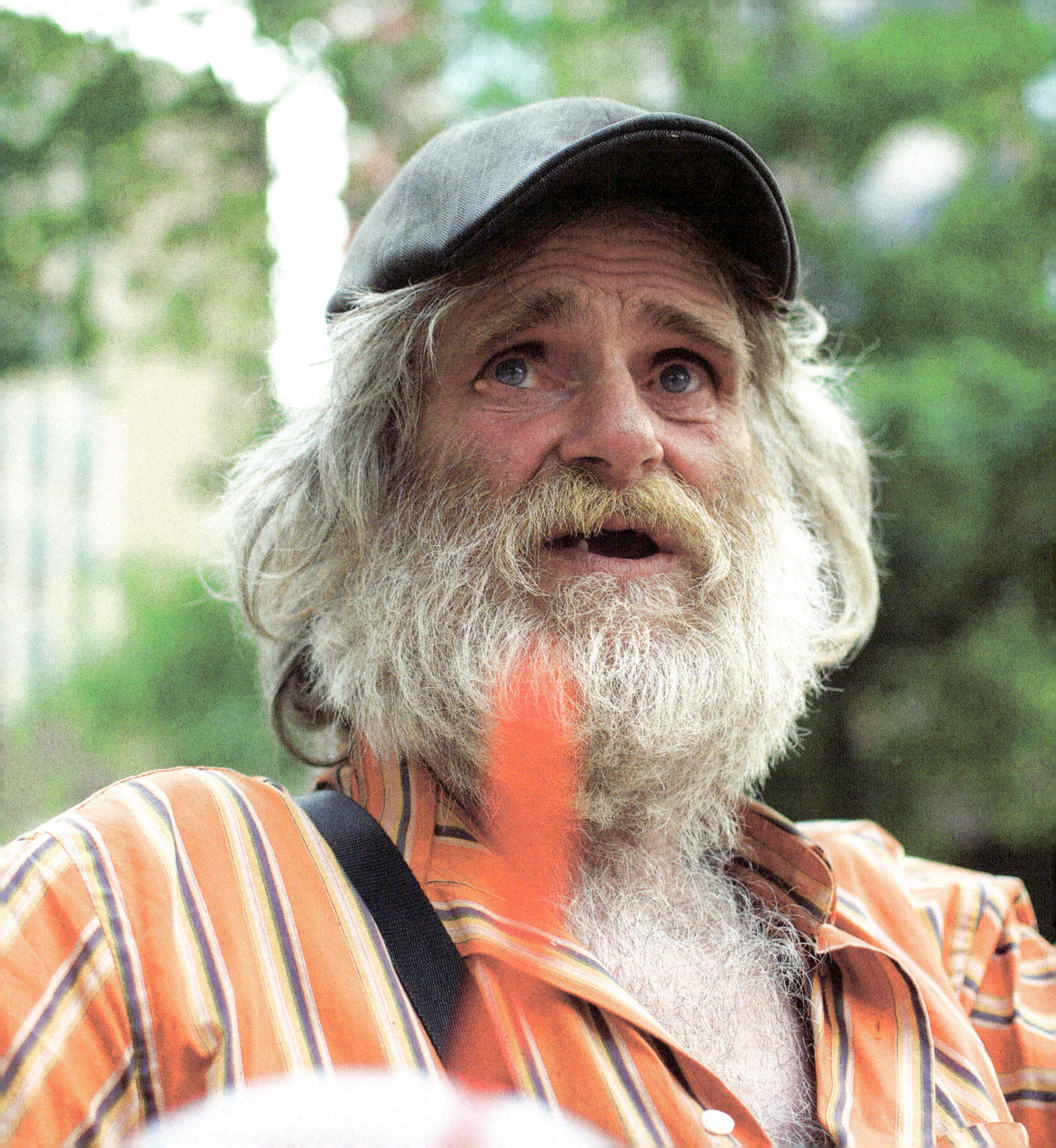

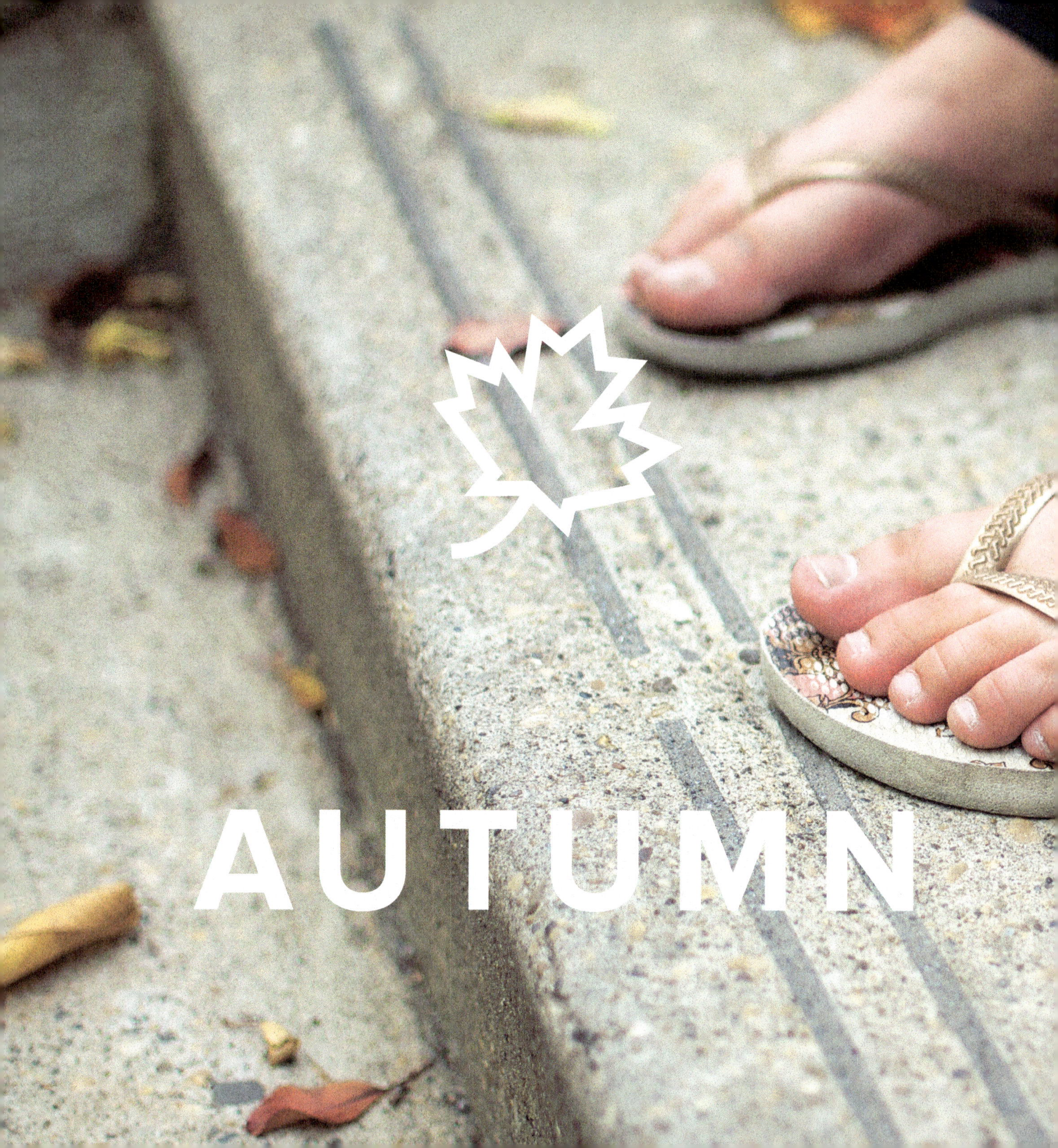
AUTUMN

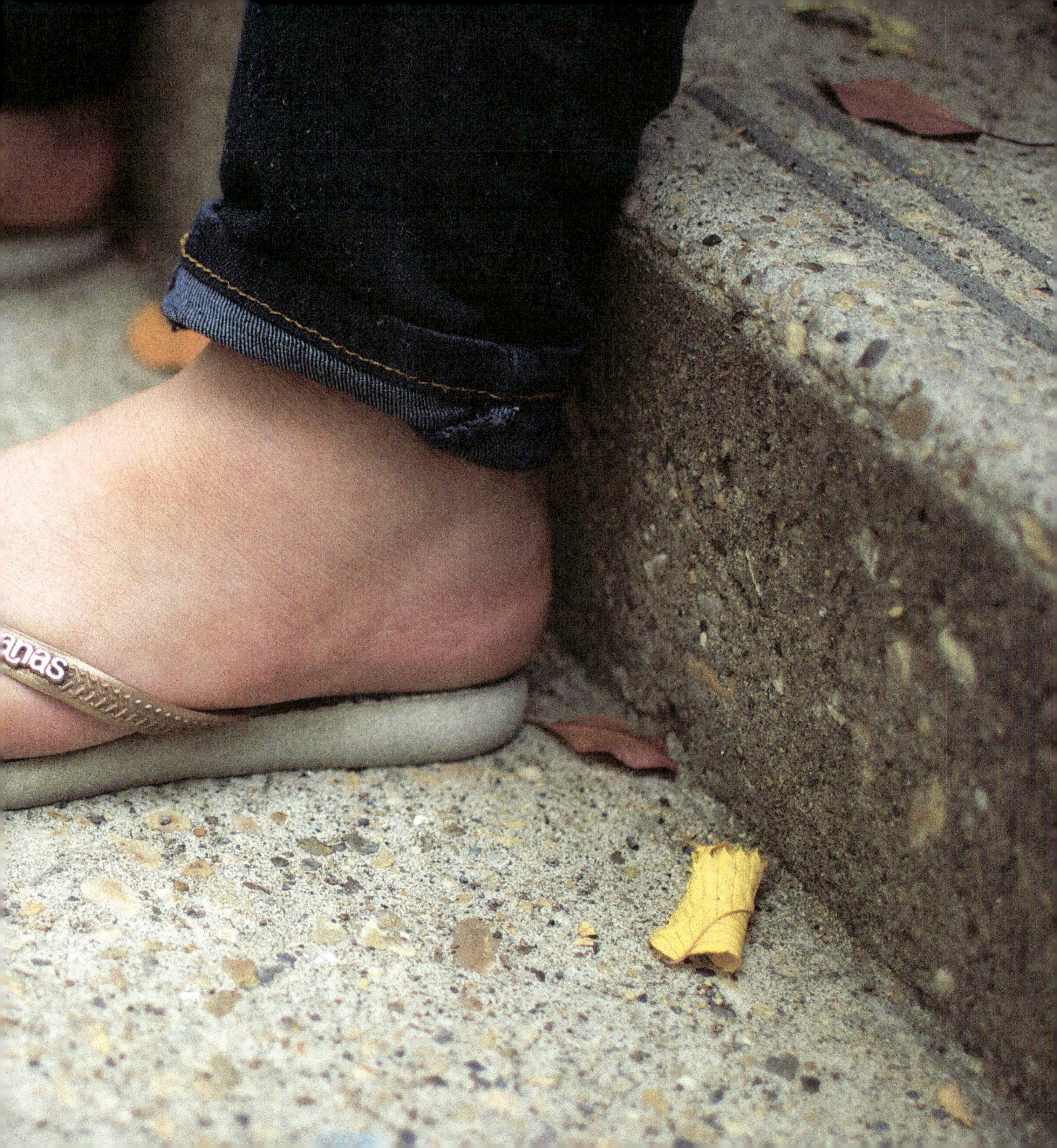

I CALL IT THE DISABILITY DIVIDEND

His guide dog helps him move past the fire hydrants, lampposts, garbage cans, and sandwich boards.

"What's the biggest challenge for you?"

"I think the biggest one is people's attitudes. If you can deal with attitudes and misperceptions around blindness and disability, you can overcome it. People are very compassionate, very kind, very sympathetic. They try to understand but that's half the challenge. It becomes something that pulls at the heart strings. I need to make a living. I need to provide for myself and my family. When I'm out knocking on doors, looking for a job, people don't focus on the ability. They focus on the disability. But the reality is that I can do anything that you can do except I just do it differently. I can't drive a car and I probably wouldn't be much of a photographer but there are lots of other things you can do without having to drive a car, take pictures, or be a brain surgeon. So focus on the ability. And getting around a city like Edmonton is tough. Construction. You've got sandwich board signs everywhere. I just walked here from the hotel I'm staying in and there has been major construction there for the last five or six months. It wouldn't take much to make it easier for people with sight loss to find their way around. And you know the side effect of that—I call it the disability dividend—is that if you make it easy for me or my friend in a wheelchair to get around, you're going to make it a whole lot easier for a lot of people to get around."

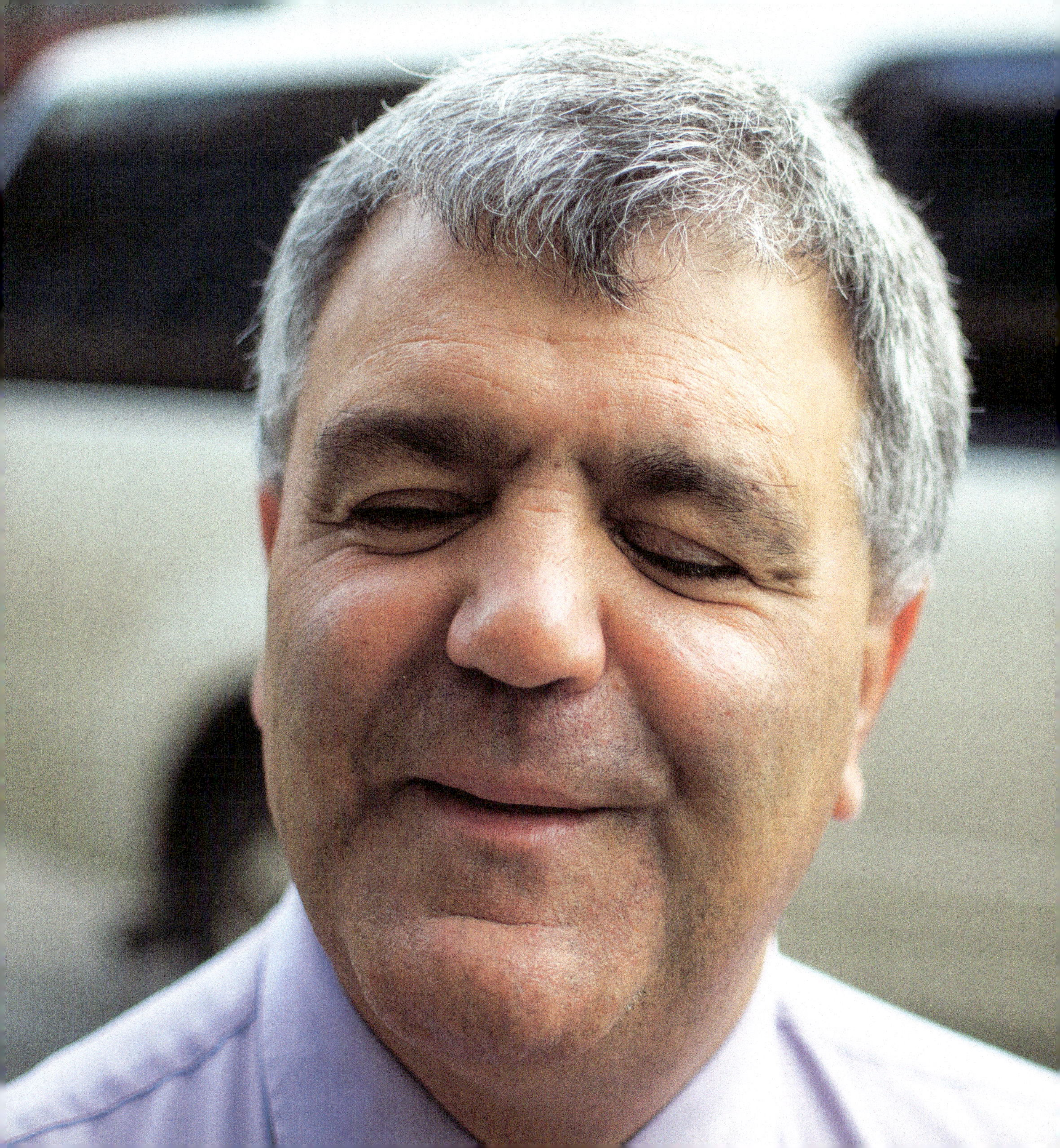

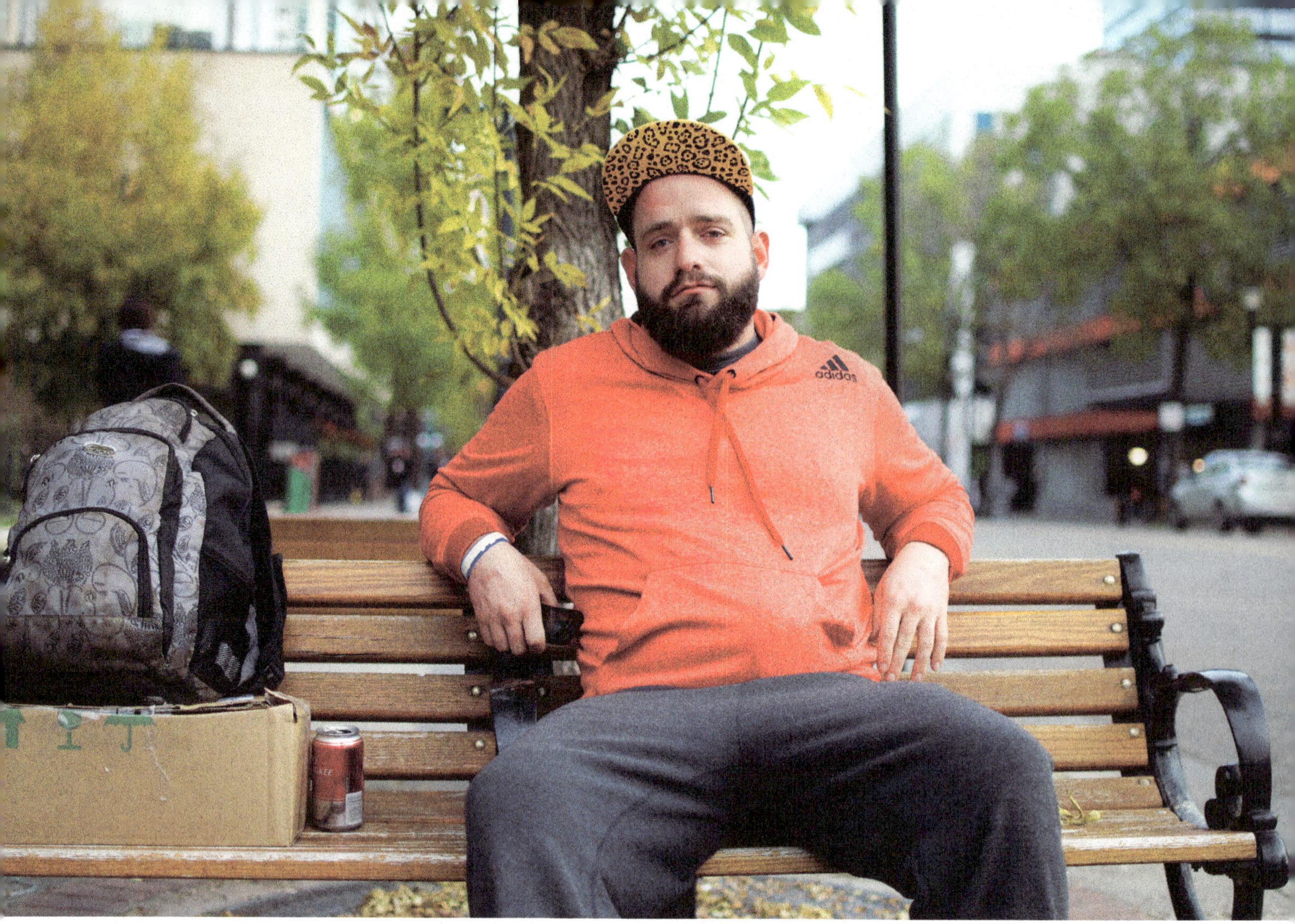

"If you could change anything about your life right now, what would it be?"

His eyes narrow, he looks past me for a moment before making eye contact again. "My girlfriend just moved to England, for two years. Like right now, just left. We just said goodbye so ... if I could change that, I'd keep her here," he says, wiping a tear away with the back of his hand.

"I'm sorry to hear that."

"It's life. She'll be back in a few years. She's coming back in May for a wedding. We'll see what happens."

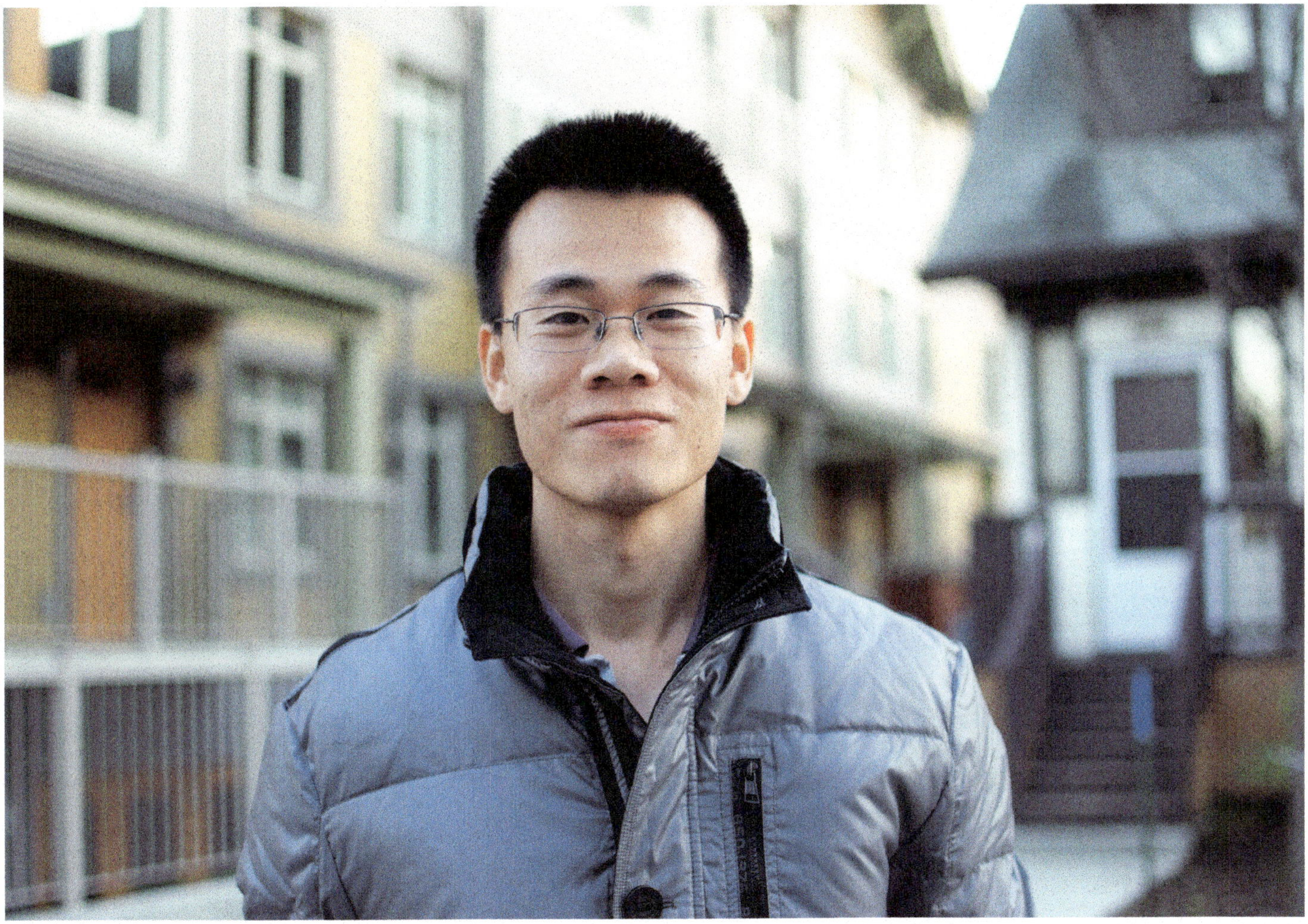

“When are you happiest?”

“With my family. They are in China so every time I go back to China or when they come here I am very happy. I will visit them, probably, two years from now.”

“What brought you to Edmonton?”

“Forestry. I'm a graduate student in forestry here. You know, in BC and Alberta forestry is very important and the career will be very good. I'm going to do some forestry survey work when I graduate in May and then I plan to go back to China some years later.”

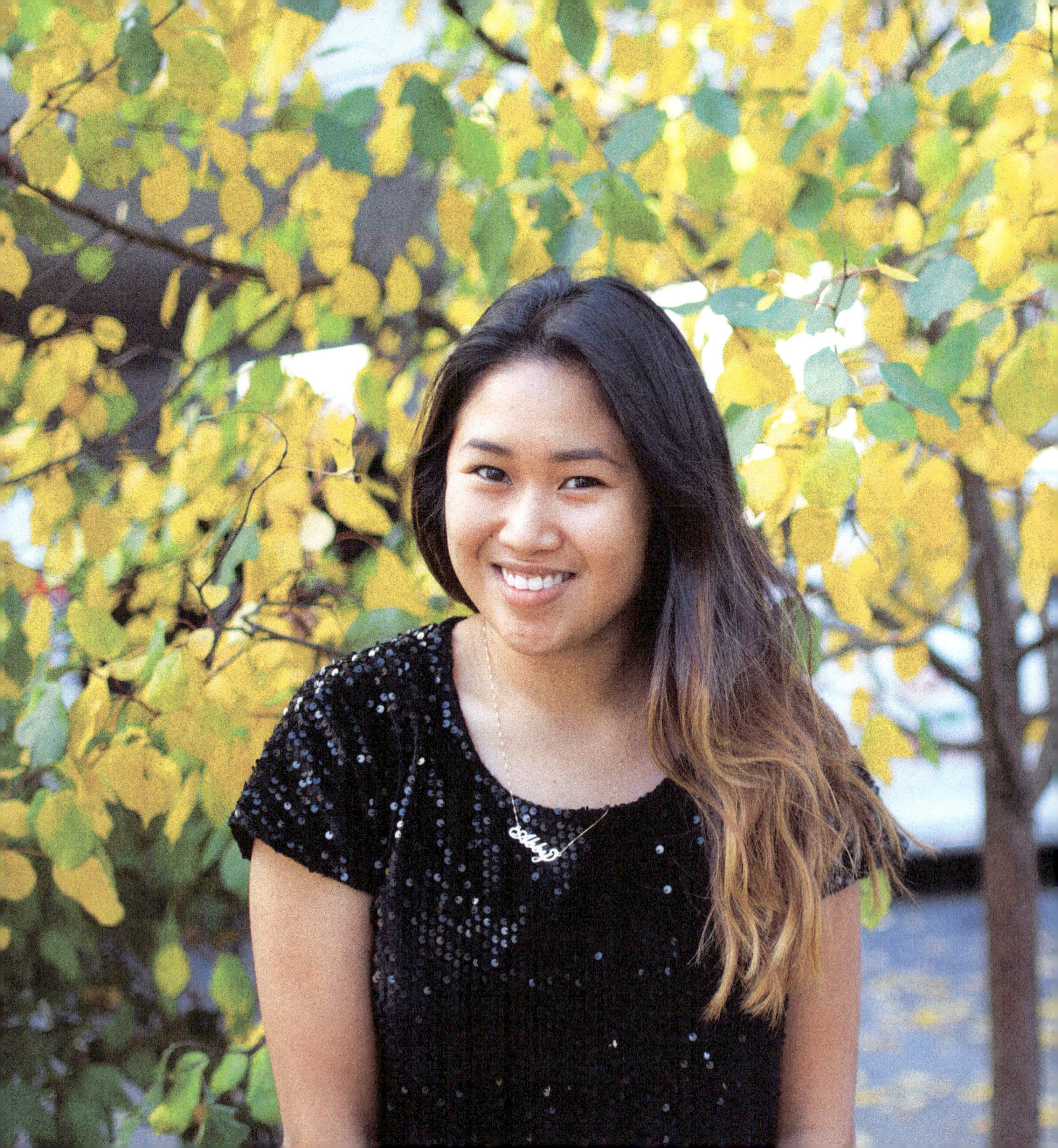
Abby

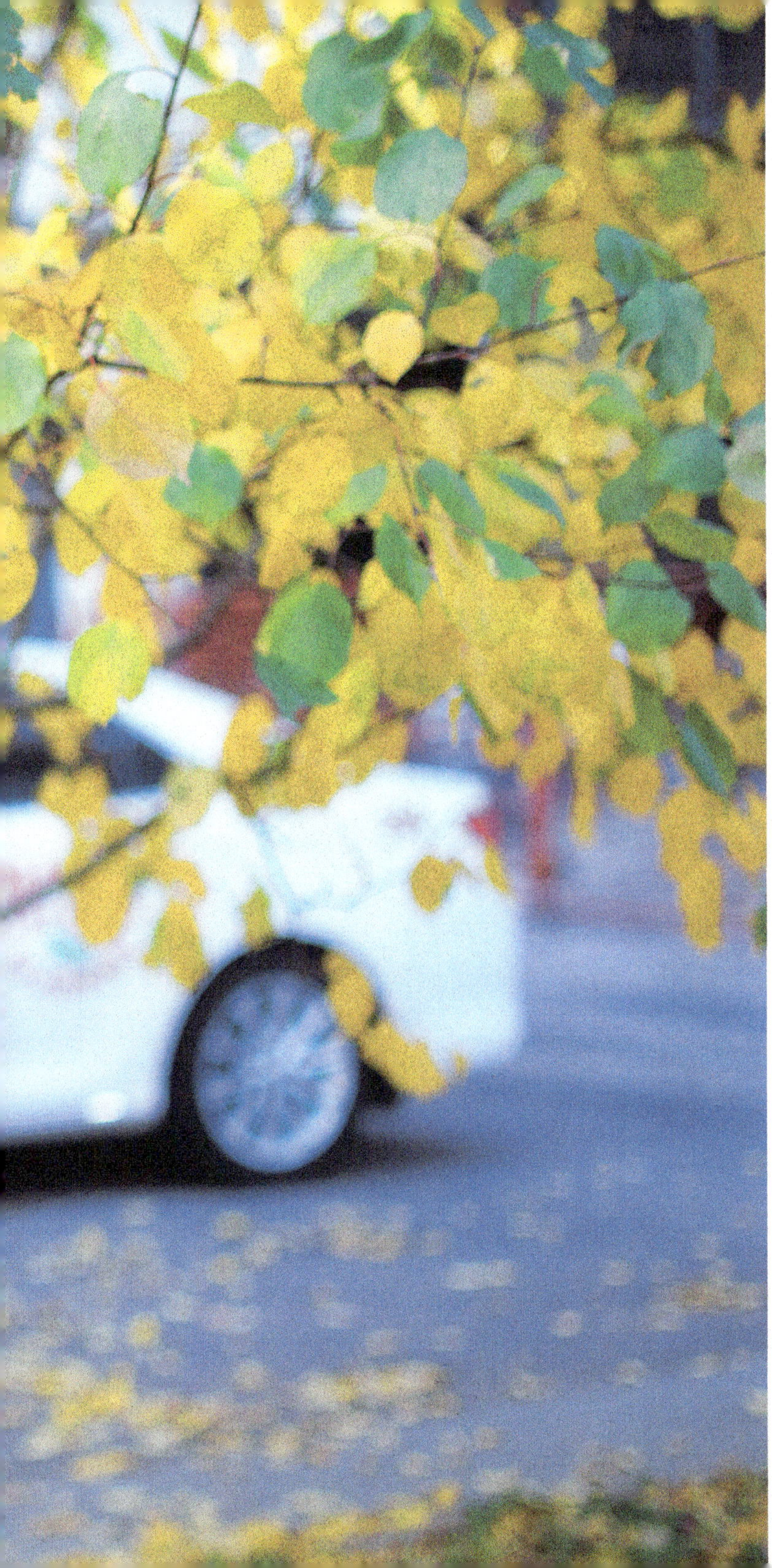

The leaves crunch under her feet as she walks down the sidewalk.

"What is something nice that a stranger has done for you?"

"One time I was going home and I had lost my bus pass. I didn't have any money and only had my debit card. A man gave me one of his bus tickets. That was really nice. I was so happy because I didn't know how I was going to get home."

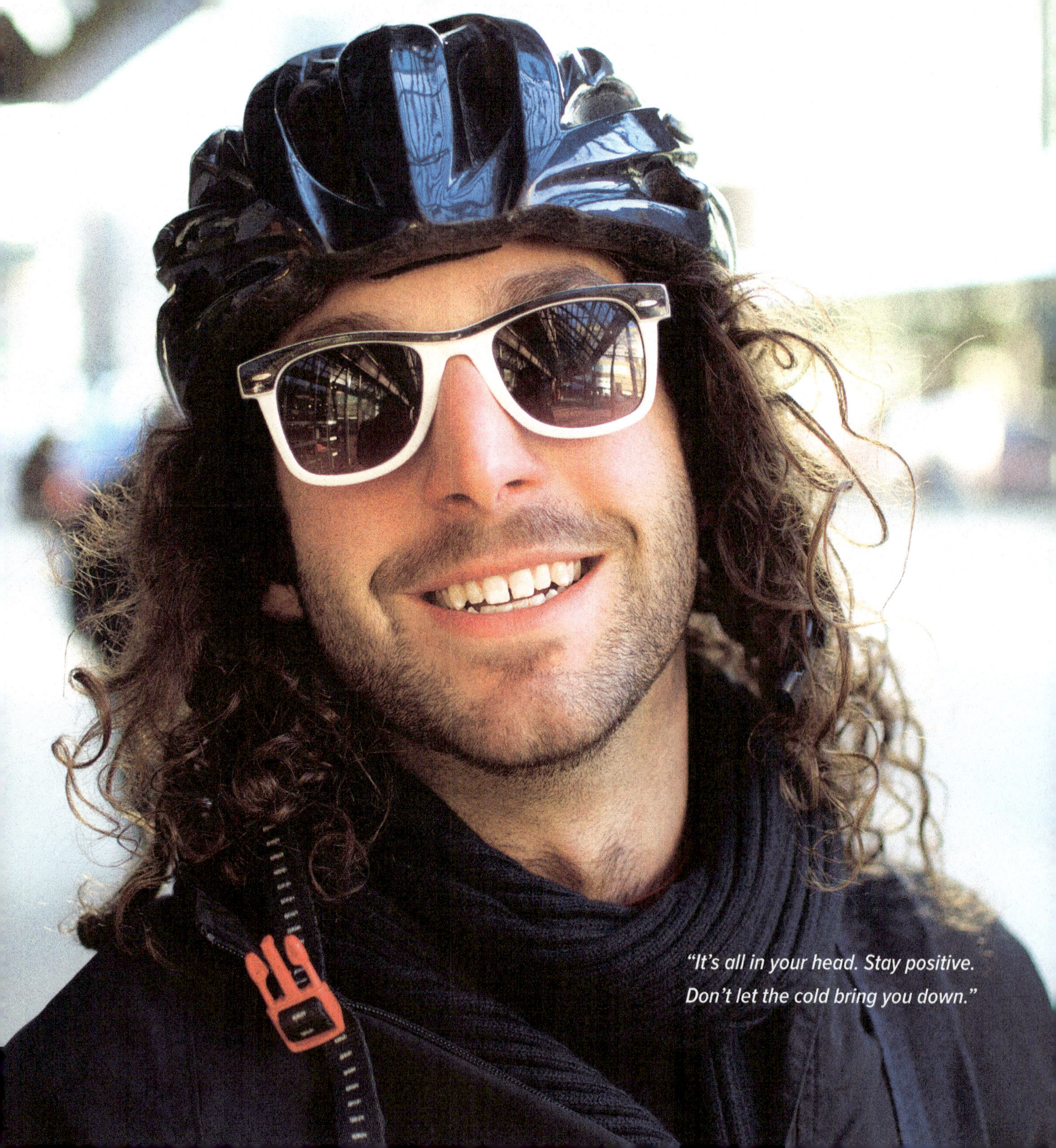

*"It's all in your head. Stay positive.
Don't let the cold bring you down."*

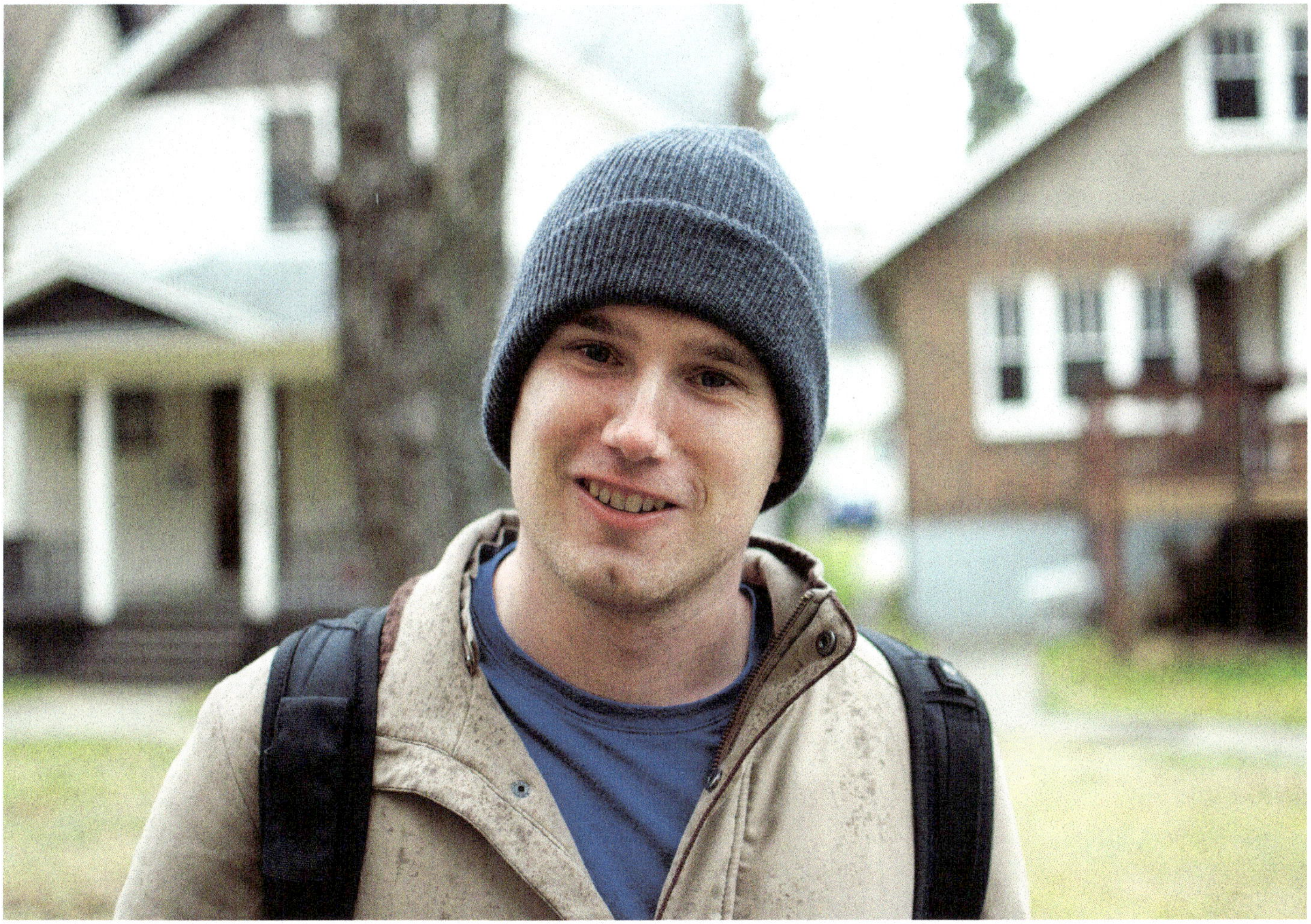

“I grew up in Vancouver and moved here two years ago. I live just on the edge of the river valley and love taking my bike out. I love the fact that Edmonton has trails that go on for such a long time. Vancouver doesn’t have that.”

“Do you have any regrets?”

“I don’t know. We’ll see. This will be my third university degree, so we’ll see how the job hunt goes after this. I have a Bachelors of Business and a Masters in Latin American Studies, and now I’m in law school. I’m trying to situate myself in a certain niche. We’ll see how it goes.”

“Do you have lots of debt from the degrees?”

“Oh, yeah,” he says, laughing. “It’s there. It’ll get paid off eventually.”

“I wanted to be a veterinarian when I was a kid. I love animals. Mostly cats. I’m a cat person. My cat has monster feet. He’s got seven toes on the back and six toes on the front.”

“What brings you hope?”

“My son. It’s cool to be learning what he’s learning. Everything he’s learning is so past tense for us. We learned it forever ago. But for him to learn new things, teaching him stuff, brings me hope.”

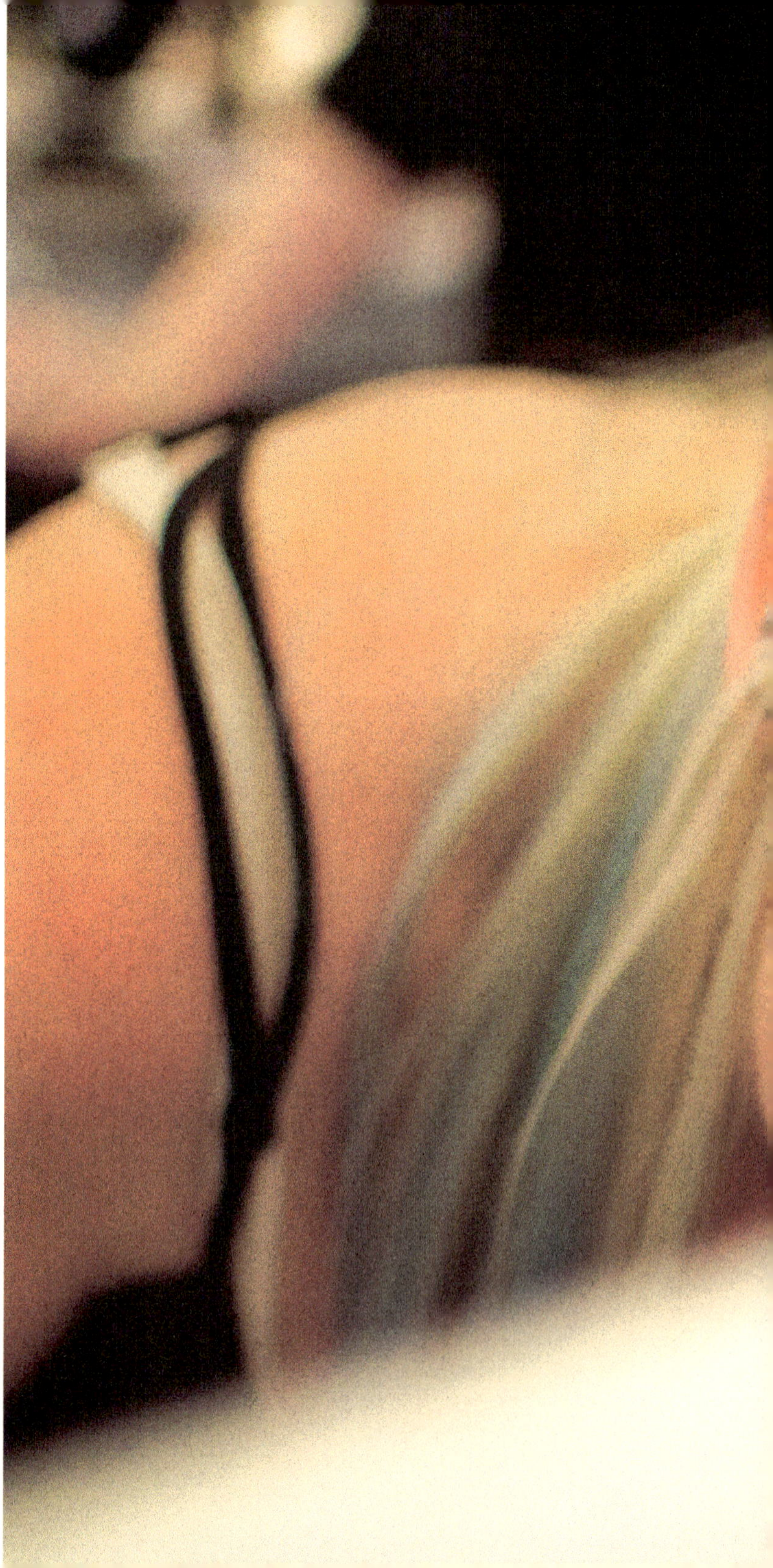

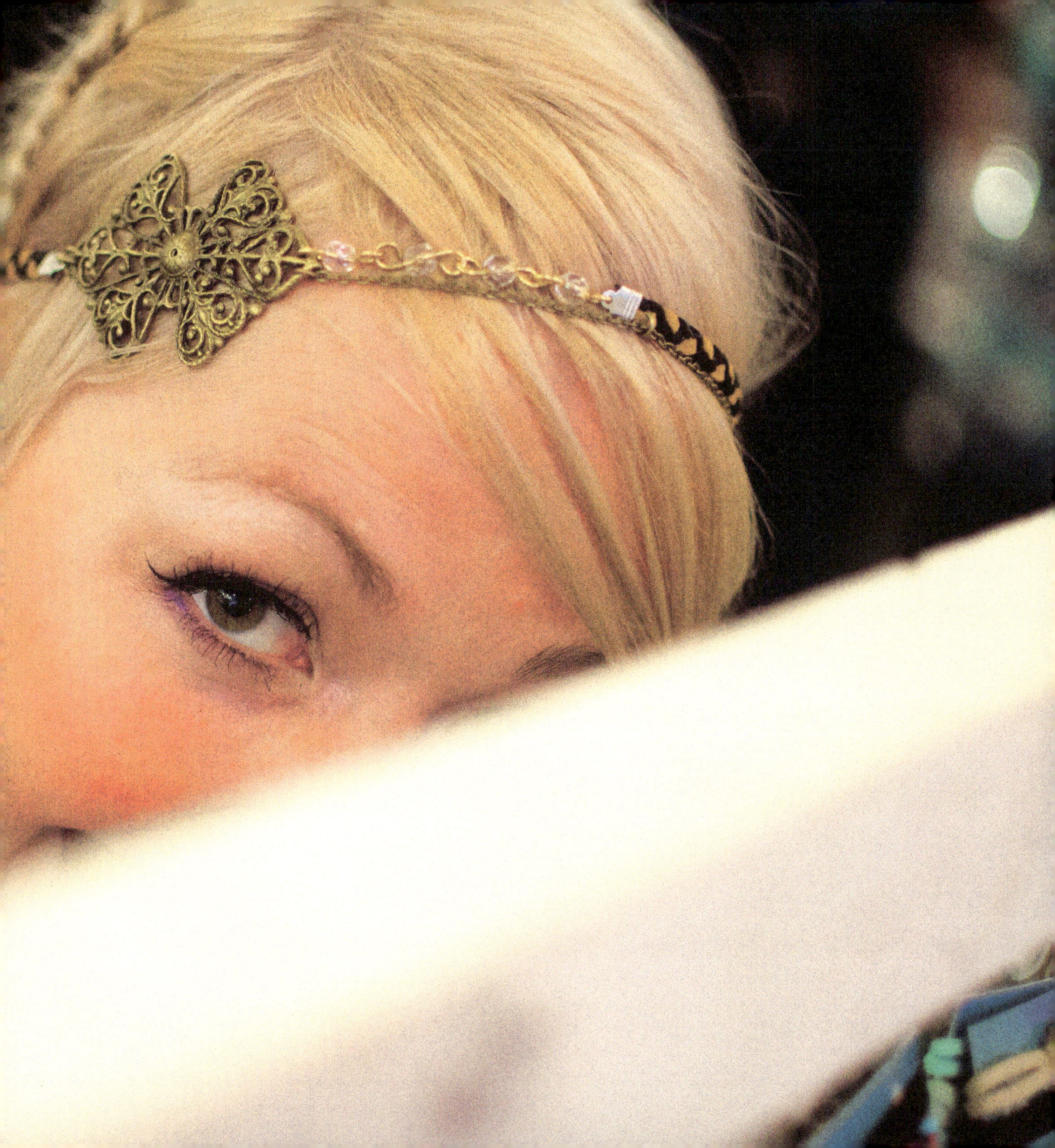

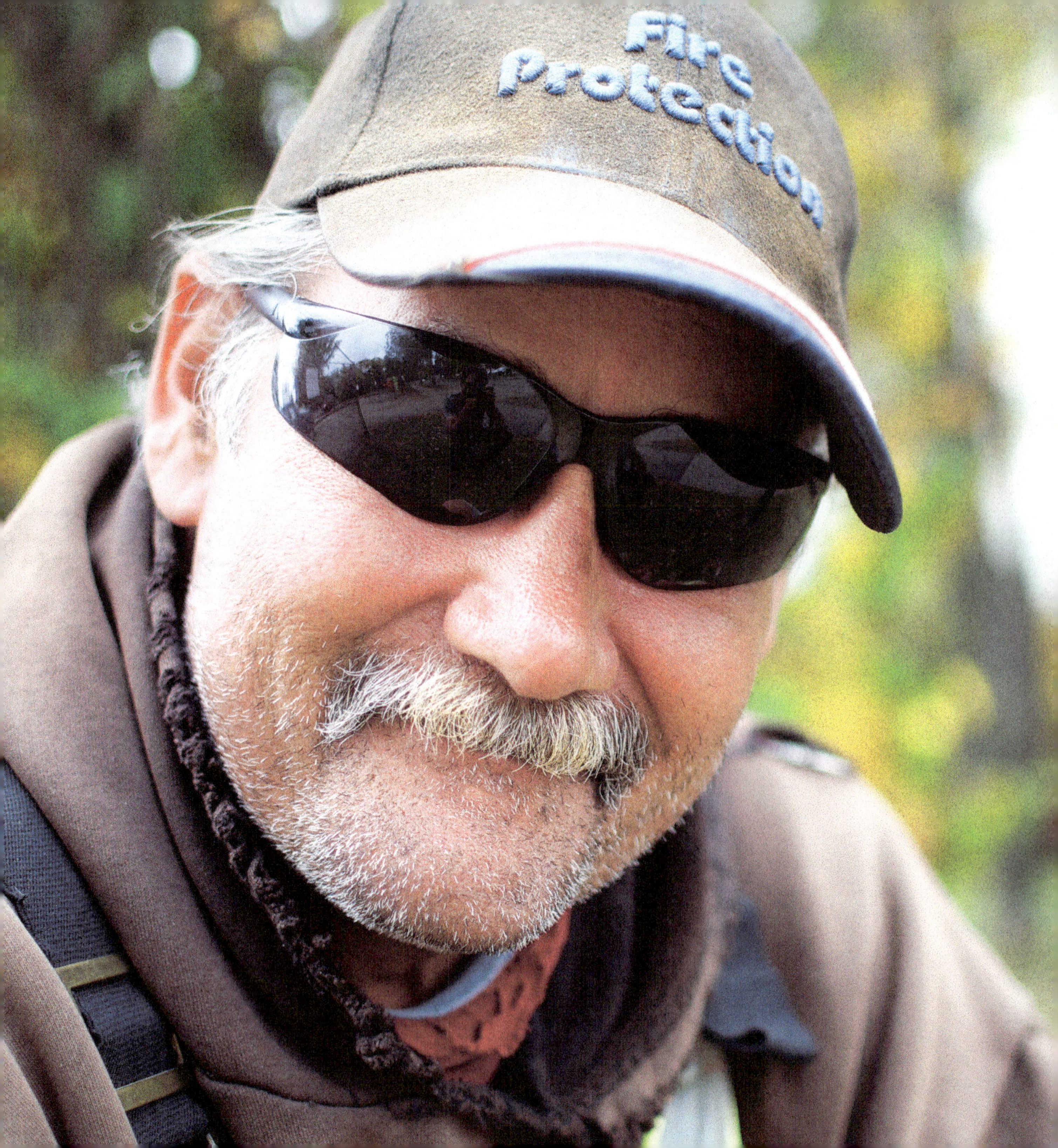
Fire
Protection

DO YOU HAVE A FAVOURITE MEMORY?

"I don't know if you'll like this or not but I used to be quite the hunter at one time. The first moose I shot, I was fourteen."

"Were you with anyone?"

"My dad. He was pretty damn proud."

"Was your dad a good hunter?"

"Oh yeah. He actually had his picture in the Edmonton Journal. Monster Moose. It ah, huge rack of horns. That was back in the late sixties."

"What did you do with the moose you shot?"

"We ate it. Gutted it and all that kind of stuff. We grew up on a farm so all that stuff was just second nature for us. A lot of people don't like that kind of stuff but for a lot of people that's how they made it through life. That's just how it was. I never tasted beef until I was twelve years old. We were raised on moose. Every winter we would have three moose in the deep freeze. And it would last all winter and all summer."

"What does it taste like?"

"It's not like beef that's for sure because of what it eats. It's richer, leaner, very lean in fact. Back then it's all we had. We didn't know anything else."

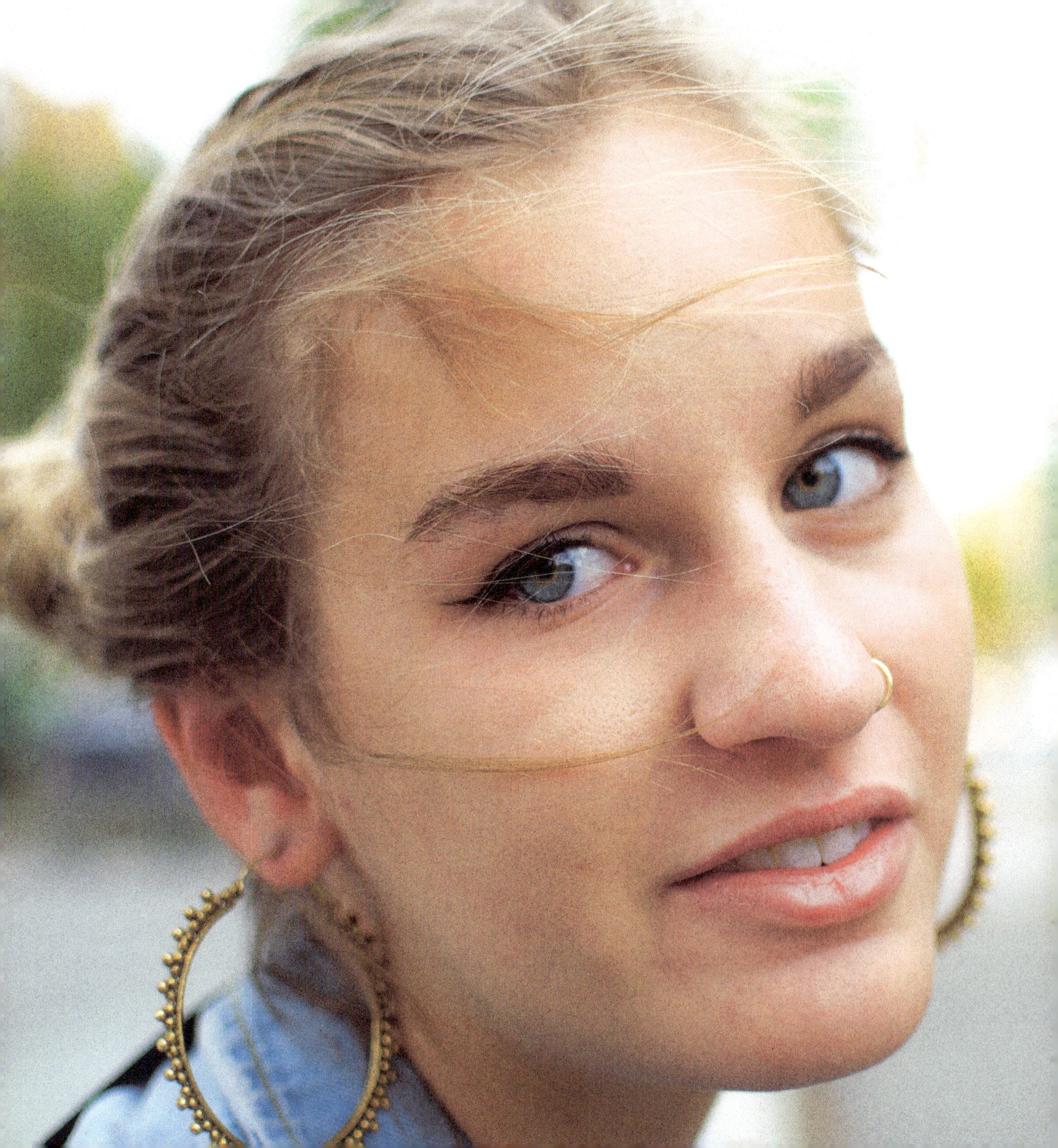

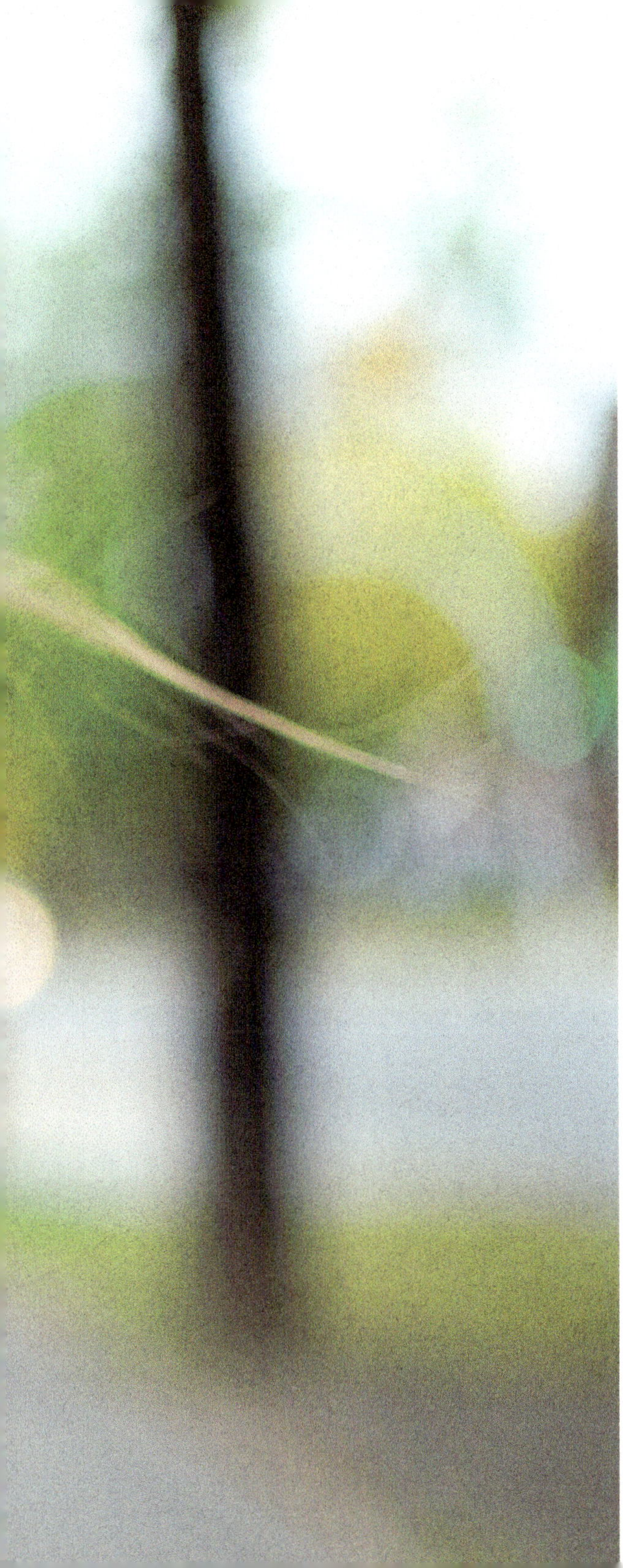

"What are you most passionate about?"

"Probably photography. I mean, I'm not that great at it but ..." her voice trails off. I snap a couple photos. "I'm really bad in front of the camera," she says. "I feel that I know what I like and I love photographing people but then when I'm on the other side of it, I'm just so awkward."

"I don't think you're awkward," I say. "What do you really want to do in life?"

"I started a clothing slash jewellery company. It's called Shop Crystal Myth. That's my website. So it's kind of a funny play on words. I just started that with my sister. She and I both own the business together. We started it in the summer. So eventually I just want to work for myself. I don't really want to work for anyone." She smiles and snickers.

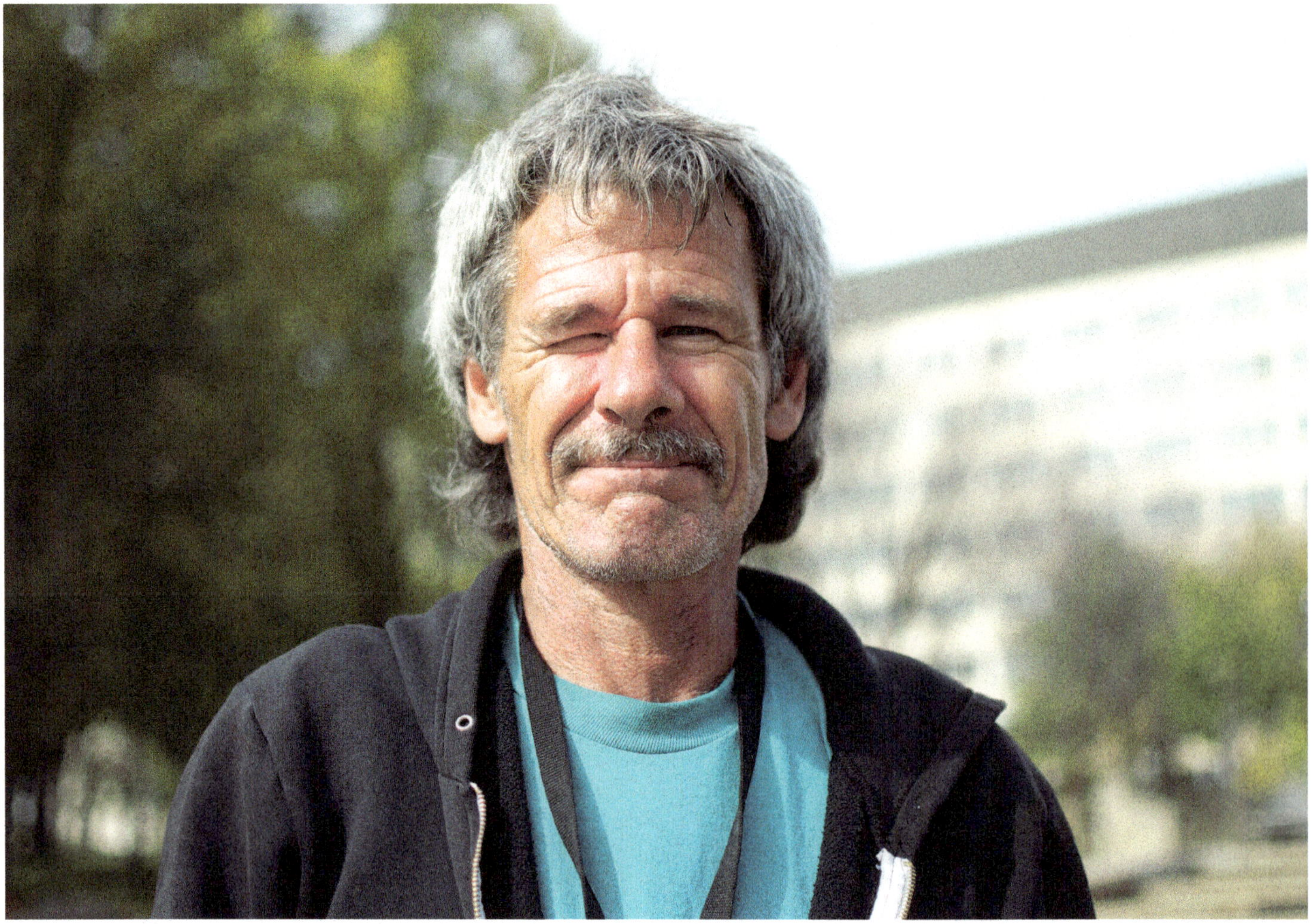

“When am I happiest? When I’m left alone with peace and quiet, like at work and all that. No one to bug me, I just go about doing my work. I think about nothing else. Just easygoing. I don’t enjoy working with others because it’s all, ‘What do you have to do? What do you have to do?’ Working with me everyday, you should know. And then asking the same question, I get frustrated. I like people when they catch onto the job.”

He goes back to work cleaning the leaves out of the fountain. “Have a good afternoon,” he says. “My day’s nearly done.”

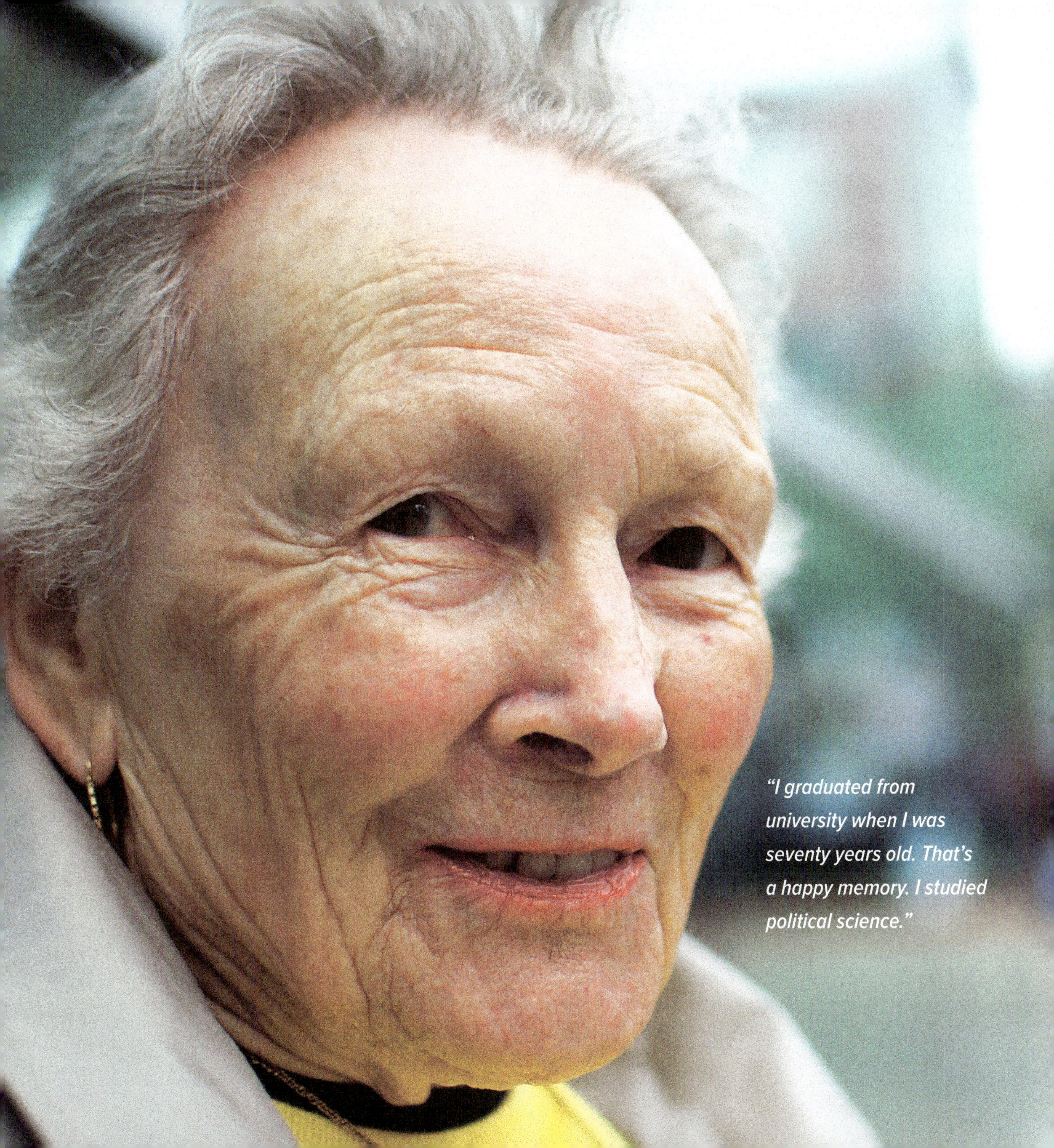

"I graduated from university when I was seventy years old. That's a happy memory. I studied political science."

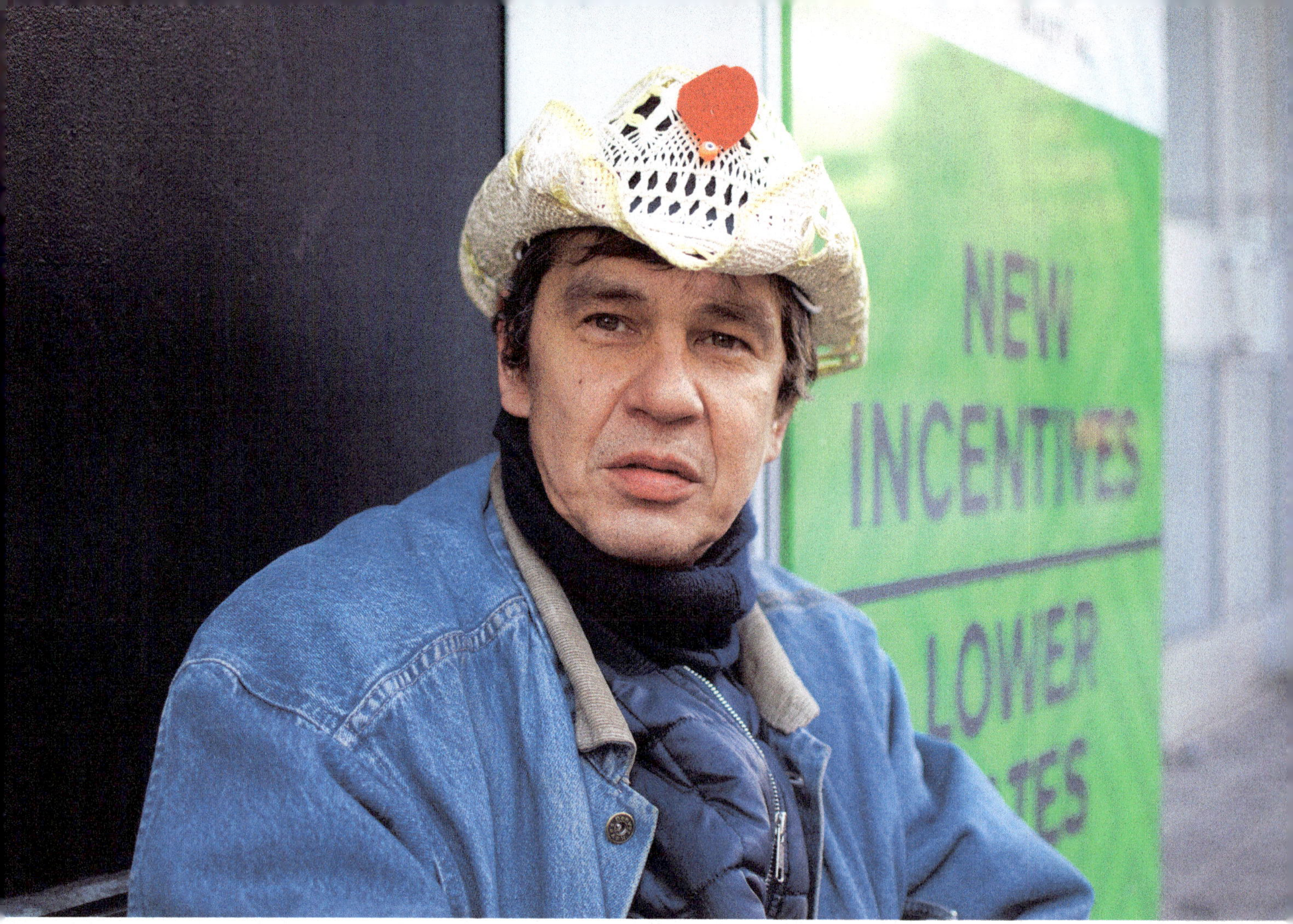

“I play the harmonica each day and try to make a living. Get off the booze and the drugs. Get a little older and get a little wiser. I’m trying to appreciate life and people. It’s surprising how much time goes by. I’ve been here … must be eight, nine hours on and off. I go and take a few breaks, come back and play a little more. I blow ‘em hard. I could crack glass. I got four different types of harmonicas. I’m into them. You buy ‘em from Sweden. This one,” he says, holding up the one in his hand, “is made in Germany. It’s a Hohner special. You gotta blow lightly in the morning to get ‘em warm. I was thinking of getting into building Canadian-made harmonicas myself. Might as well make them in Canada, here in Edmonton, eh. Get a little money, get a little shop, and turn out different harmonicas. But with no money and when you’re a halfbreed … you’re limited and you don’t got the ins. I think we all have chances in this country though. We all have chances in Canada. We can drink, we can be dysfunctional, or we can achieve. That’s what I tried to do every day.”

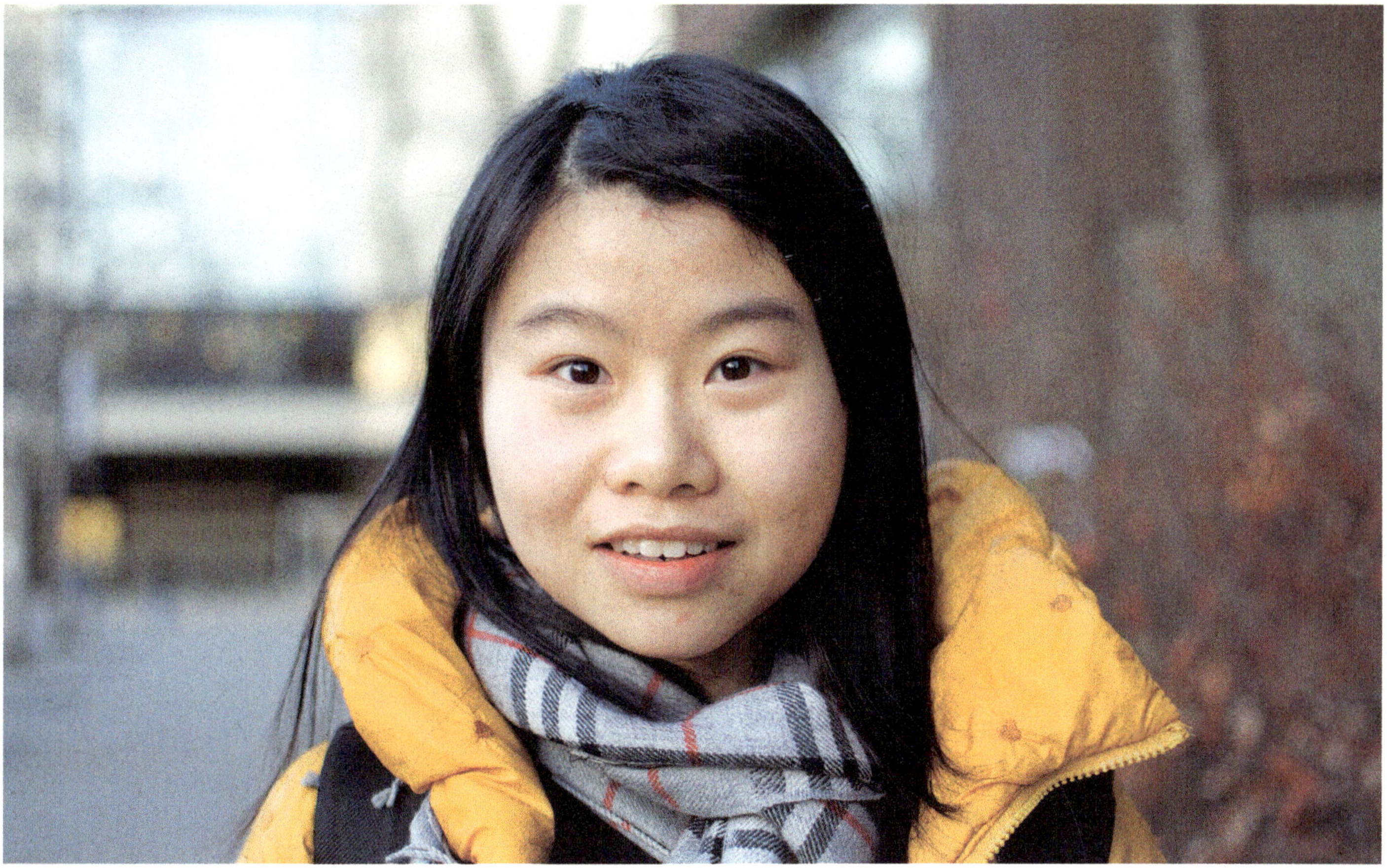

"Every day is very happy. The temperature, seeing the sky. Everything is beautiful and it makes me very happy."

"So you're always happy?"

"Yeah, because everything is just there, and if you are not happy, it won't change anything. So why not be happy. I want to chase my dream."

"What's your dream?"

"I don't know yet," she says, giggling. "That's the problem. I want to do my best to chase one thing and I think this is the most important."

"I live here at the YMCA. I play the piano. I'm not working right now. I'm on AISH. I don't really do a lot. I've got schizophrenia and bipolar. I'm not a very social person."

"What's your life like?"

"You kind of get nervous being around people. You don't know what people are thinking. Sometimes you think people are after you. Stuff like that. It's just a disease I guess. Some people, you look at them and you think, 'That guy doesn't have anything wrong with him.' But it's a lot deeper than what most people think. You can't see it."

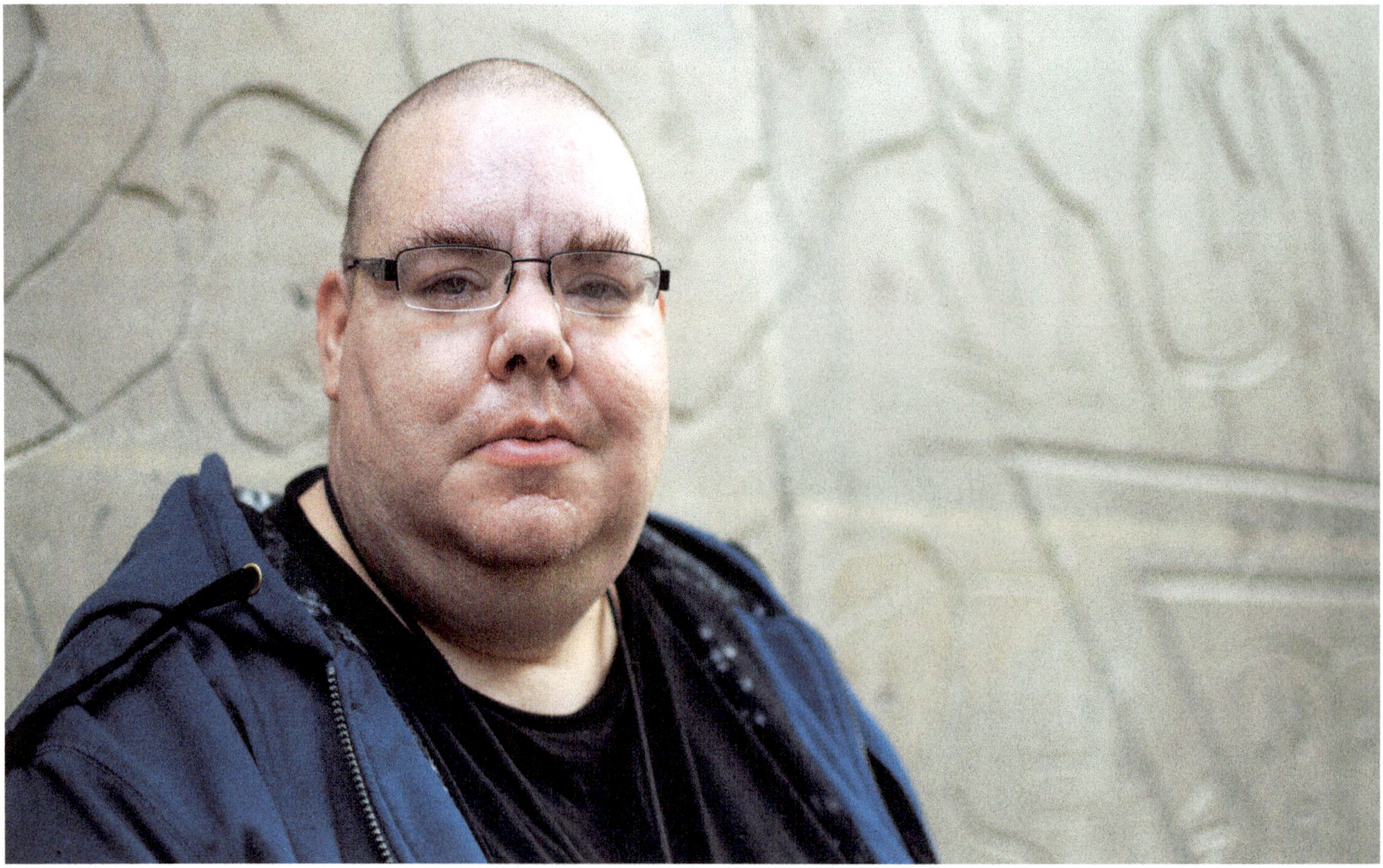

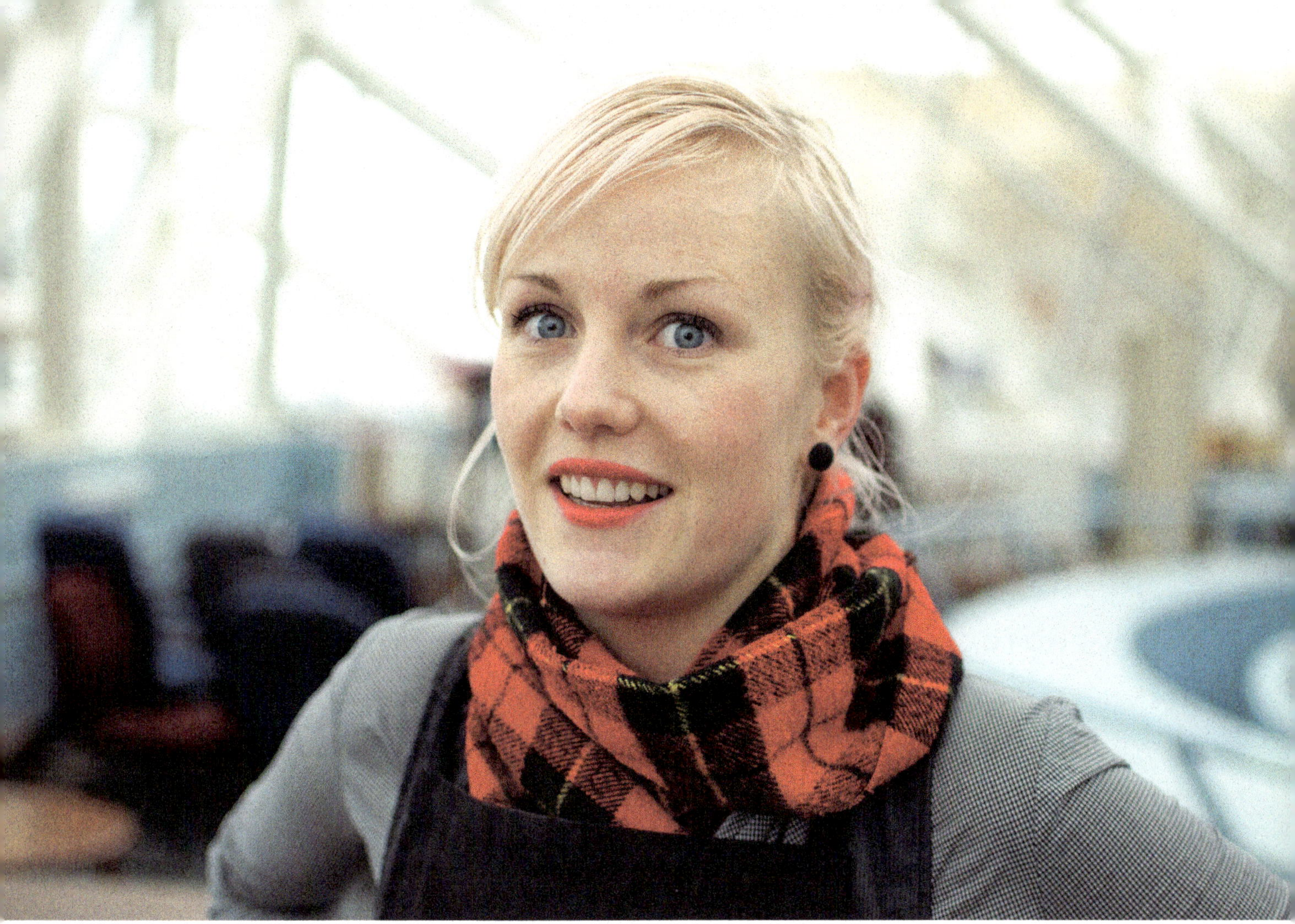

Her studio is in City Hall, inside the glass pyramid overlooking the council chambers.

“I started by painting people who work for the city and then moved into a couple things like Treaty Six, the chambers, the councillors. It’s been really interesting. I feel like I’m just starting to get the hang of it, and they just gave me an extension. It’s really exciting.”

“What’s the best thing that happened to you this year?”

“There’s a lot this year. I just got engaged, so that’s super exciting. I booked a two month trip to Thailand. And this job getting extended. It’s been a really awesome year for me.” She smiles and laughs. “I feel good.”

I'M PHOTOGENIC

"Meaning that people take pictures. That's what people have always told me. I don't believe if that's true or not."

I show him the pictures I've taken.

"Oh yeah. Oh yeah. Yeah, I'm waiting for a bus. Fifty-two to Southgate. I live up by Southgate."

"What's your favourite thing to do?"

"Watch TV, bowling. As long as the balls are not too heavy. Like West Edmonton Mall balls are heavy; they can break your arm. I nearly dropped a ball on my foot once. The ball slipped out of my hand, and I moved my foot, and it went—CRACK—against the floor. Would've broken my whole foot."

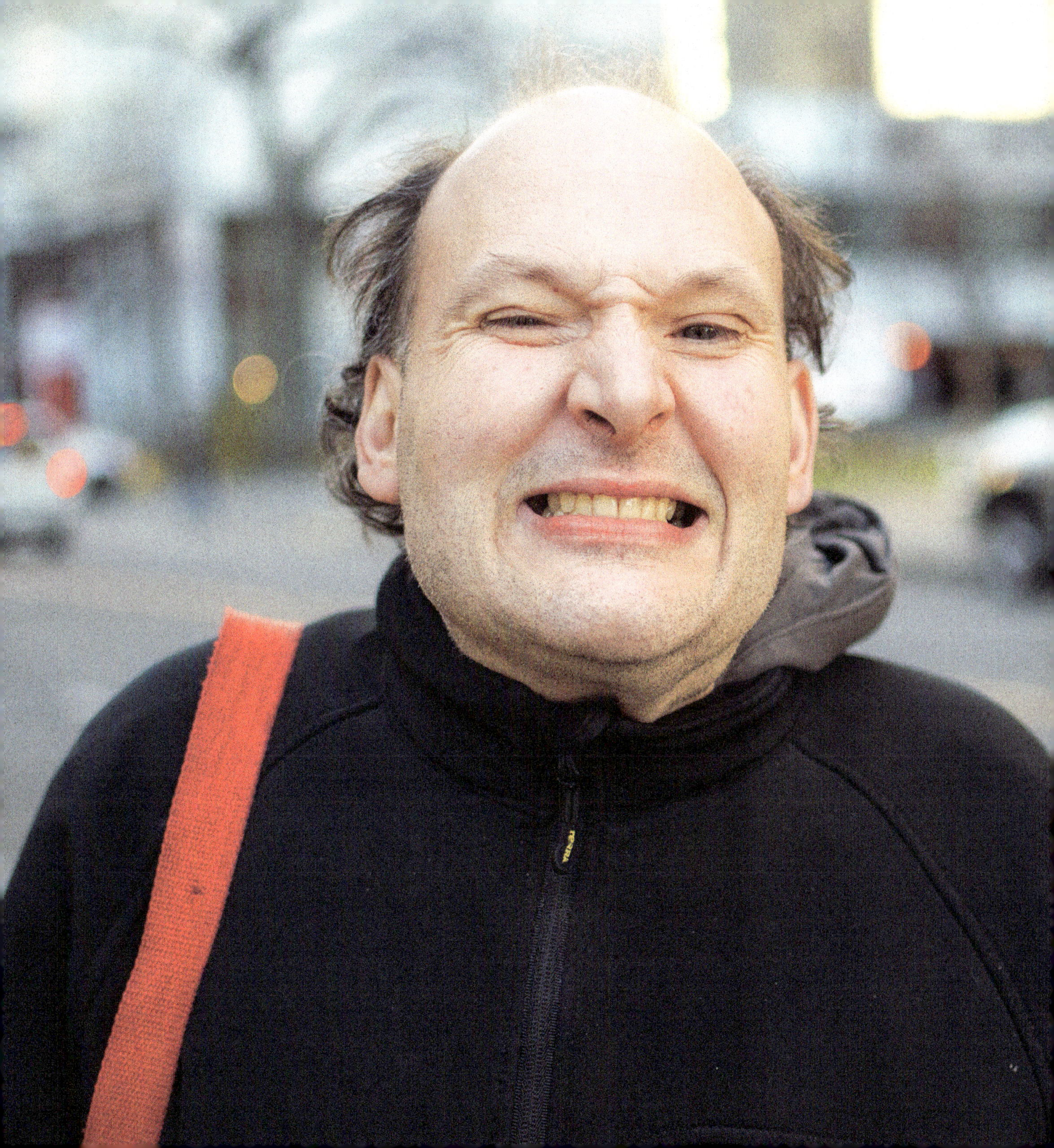

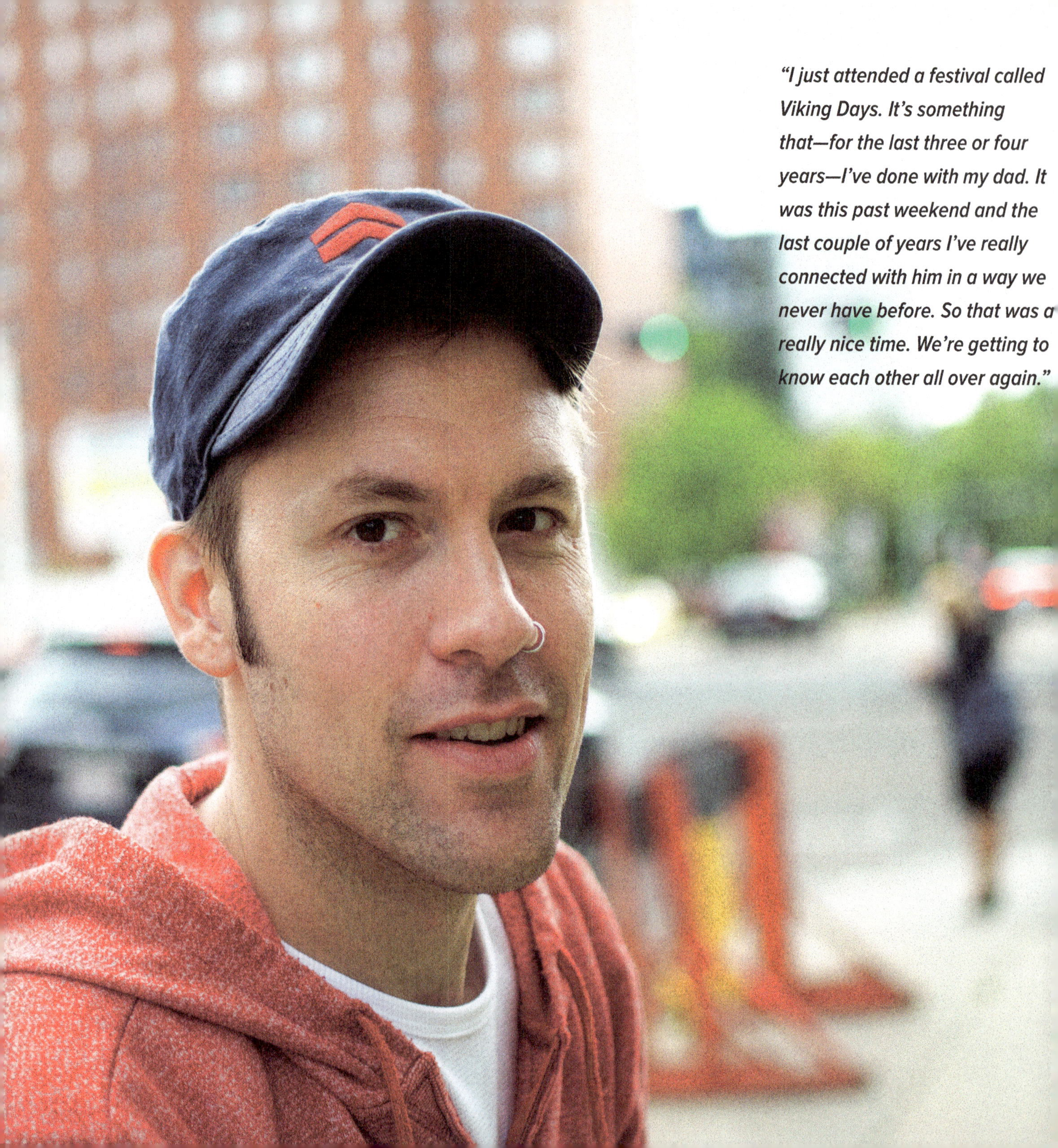

"I just attended a festival called Viking Days. It's something that—for the last three or four years—I've done with my dad. It was this past weekend and the last couple of years I've really connected with him in a way we never have before. So that was a really nice time. We're getting to know each other all over again."

"Back in 2008, that's when I became an Oilers fan, that's when I moved here. I started watching hockey and I just became attached to the team, you know. You go through the ups and the downs, the wins and the losses. You basically become part of the team. That's what it feels like anyway. You're not standing in the locker room but ... we're all on the same page. We're all there for the Oilers to win."

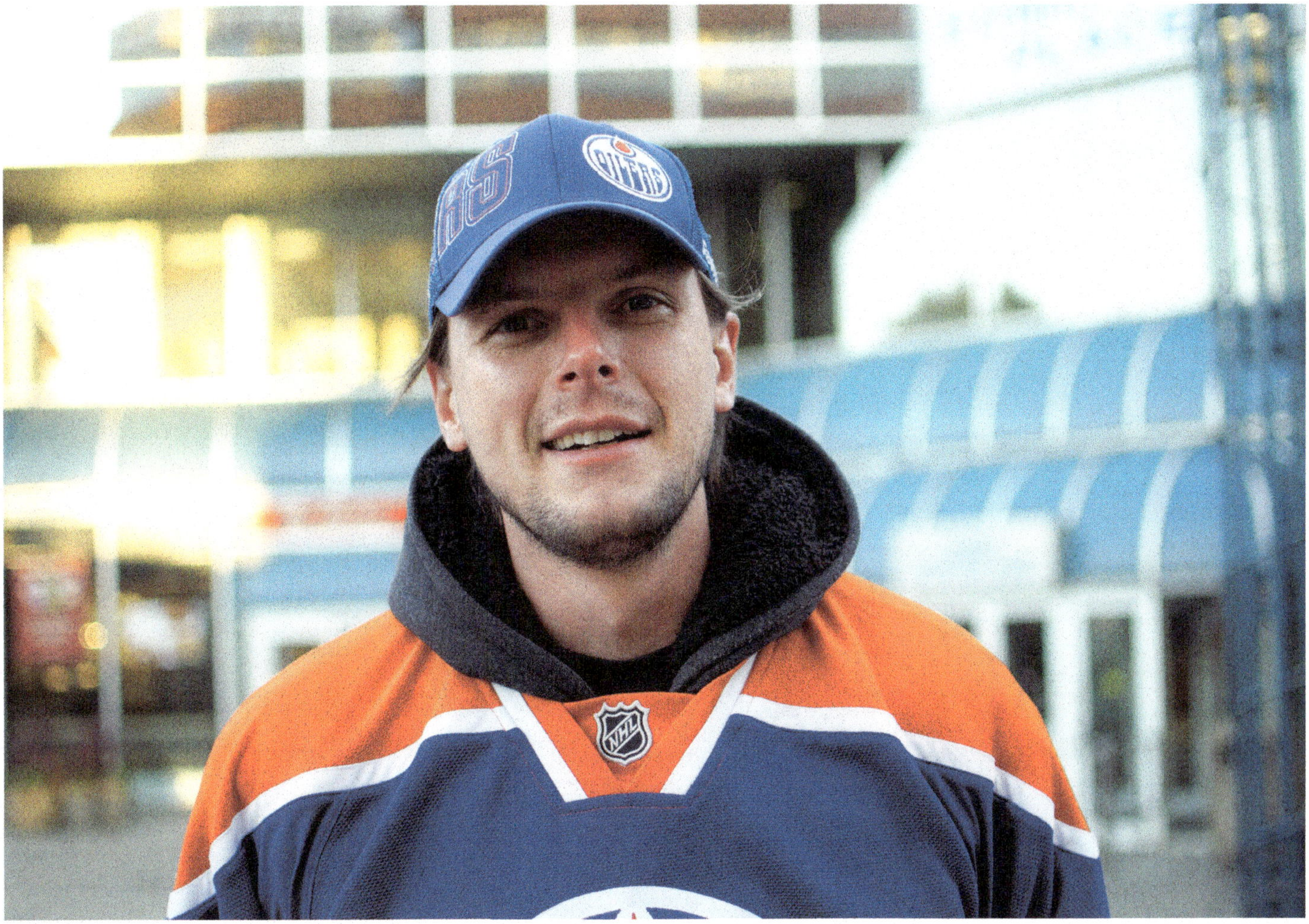

"Everyday is a new day. I'm so grateful that I'm up and about. I'm grateful for the day. I have a place in Edmonton, my own space. I love that. Everywhere you go in Edmonton, it's so spacious. I had my own house where I was living before and the first thing I did was to buy a home for my family here because what they needed most was security, so I felt that a house would give them some security."

"Where were you living before?"

"In Kenya. It is very different there. Now they are suffering growing pains. The country is progressing so rapidly and, of course, it's an old country. Let's hope ... that in time things settle down."

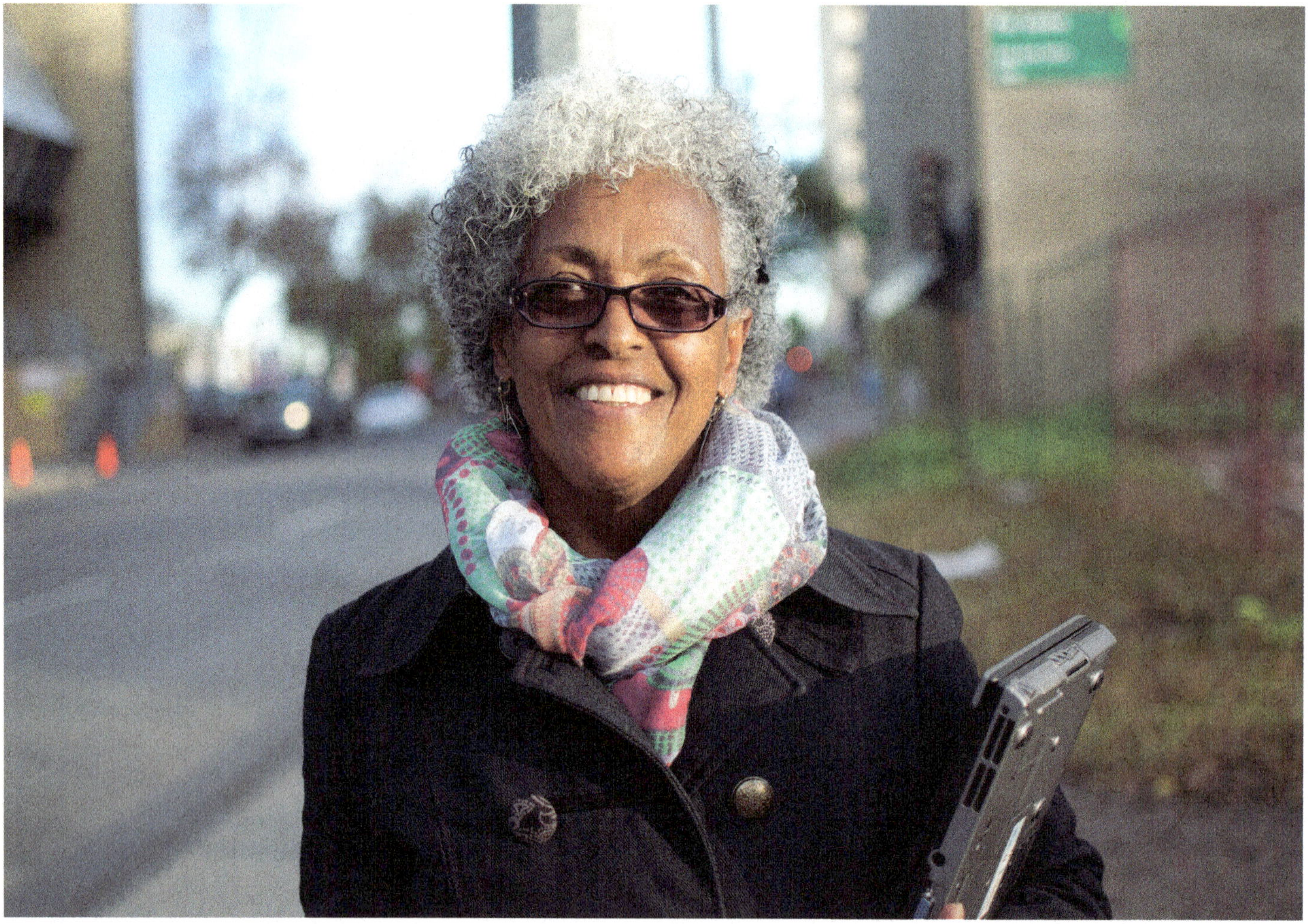

"This is my favourite place. I love coming here with my friends and just enjoying it. It's art materialized."

"What are you writing?"

"I'm actually writing a paper on creation. So looking at it ... if it's a cosmic accident or if it's creation. I pretty much talked about, like, looking at a flower and seeing how all the different aspects just kind of ... each are pretty by themselves, and then together they're, with purpose, pretty. And then also altogether, all the flowers, they're pretty. And then blowing that up to a bee and the bee pollinating it. That interaction, how complex it is, but it's so important. Then blowing it up to the park and everything."

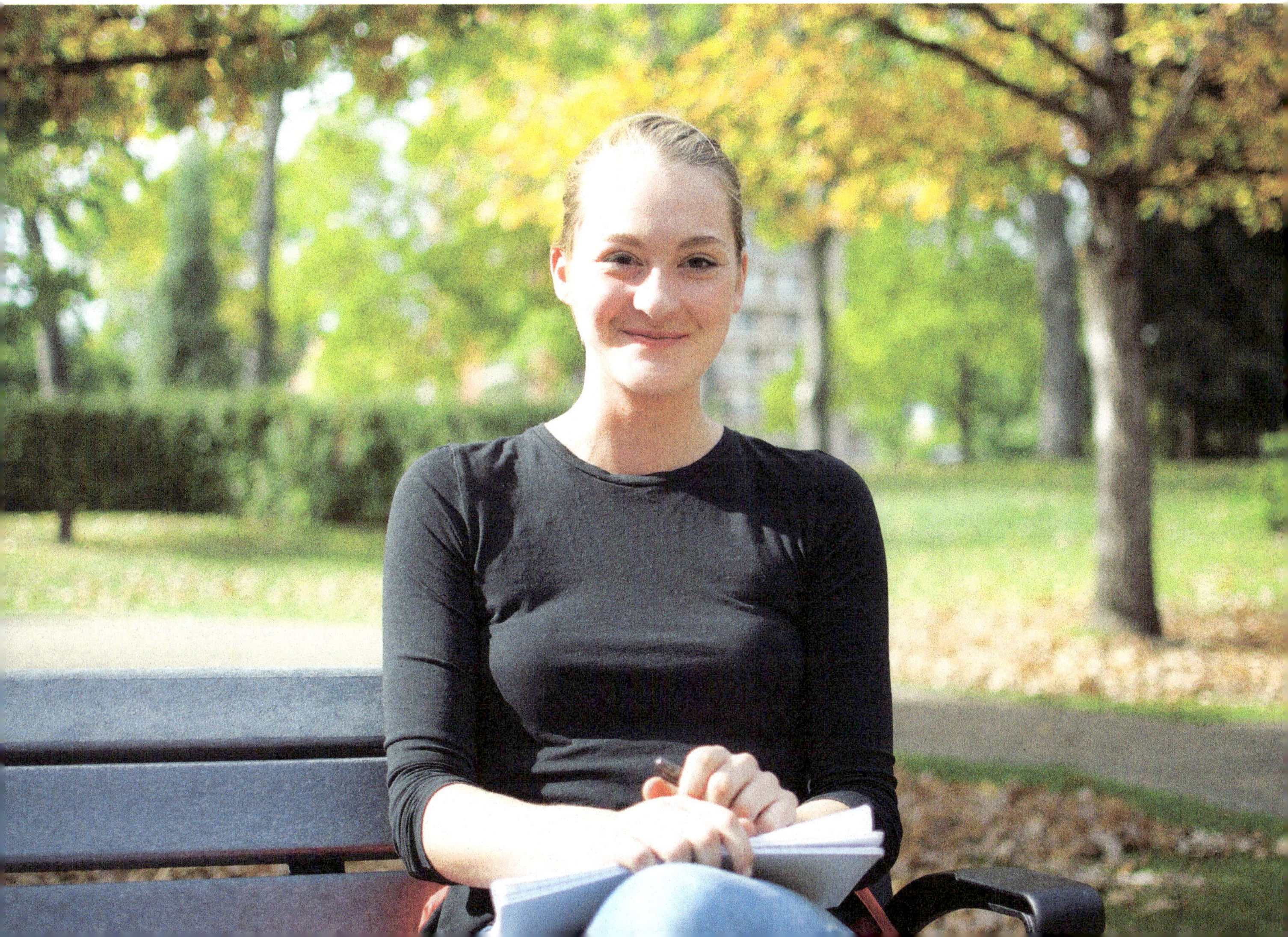

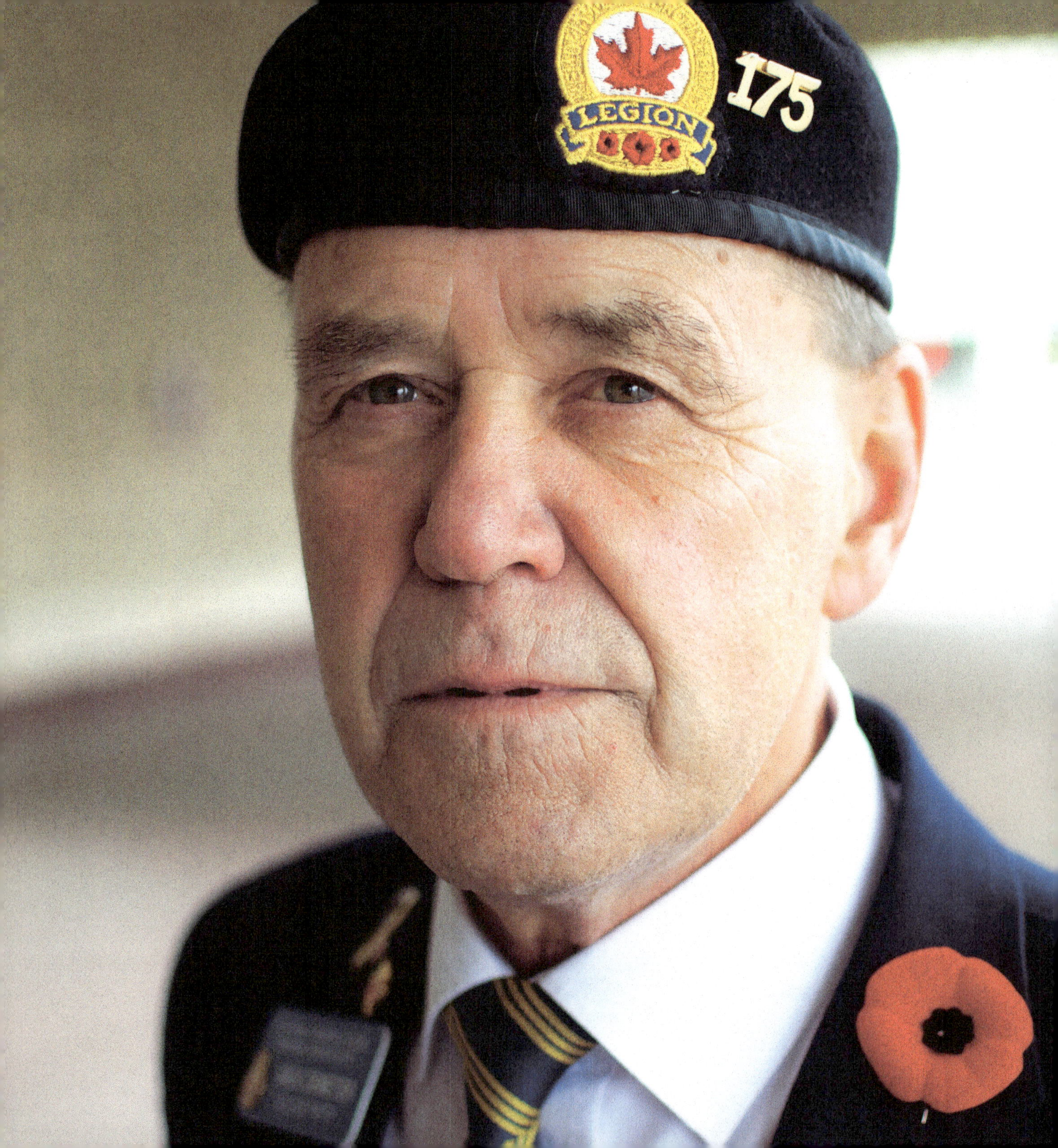
LEGION
175

I WAS IN THAT WAR IN CYPRUS IN 1974 WHEN THE TURKS DECLARED WAR ON GREECE

"We were there with the UN. This is a UN pin," he says, pointing to the metal on his jacket. "This one here is for peacekeeping."

He takes a drag from his cigarette.

"It was really kind of weird. I was outside at about five thirty in the morning, doing my pushups, getting ready for the day. A Hercules aircraft flew over top. It looked like one of ours because it was camouflaged, and we were about a mile from the airport, we could see the airport. I look up, paratroopers coming in. I'm a paratrooper also. I said, 'It's gotta be the Brits.' They were there too as peacekeepers. Next thing I know, a jet flies over and drops a five hundred pound bomb on the airport. Then the red alert siren goes off. War is declared. That scared us. There were seven contingents over there: the Brits, the Danes, the Aussies, Canadians. We were the only ones that had our first round of ammunition. The other guys didn't have anything. Not a damn thing. So, of course, we had the first round of ammunition and had to do everything. And my worst experience was going to a school where they dropped a bomb and having to pick up dead bodies, little kids."

He lifts is cigarette to his mouth again.

"I get back here ... I just couldn't ... I couldn't ... I was looking for a fight all the time. It takes a long while to get it out of your system, if you can at all. But as they say, my friend, life goes on."

WALKING THE CAMINO IN SPAIN ...

"It was maybe two weeks of walking, and I was just very discouraged and very ... remembering every dark thing, like every dark thing in my life was on my back. I was wondering if I'd ever feel well, if I'd ever feel free again. Thinking, 'How could I feel amazing half an hour ago and so overburdened now.' And then I noticed this bush on the side of the road that was unremarkable, and I decided that I would remember how good I had felt, the bush in my line of vision when I made that decision. I made a commitment that whenever I felt this dark again, this overburdened with sadness and depression, discouragement, I would remember that it's possible to feel good and well and that life can be remarkable or unremarkable but it's still a miracle. Every little thing and every grand thing is equally miraculous."

"And all this came to you while looking at the bush?"

"From the bush or it came to me and that's what I was looking at in the moment. But the bush became the hallmark of that realization."

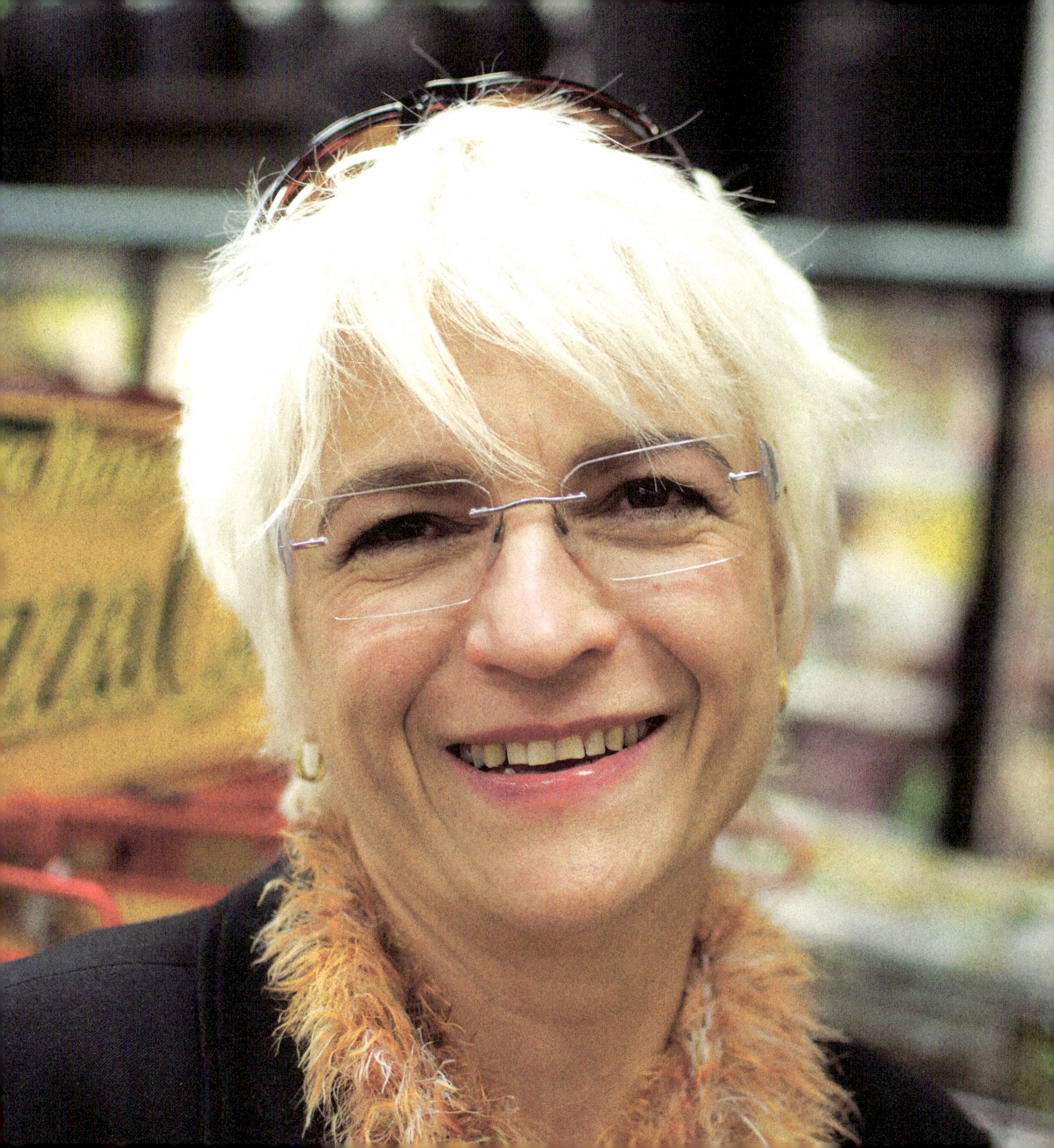

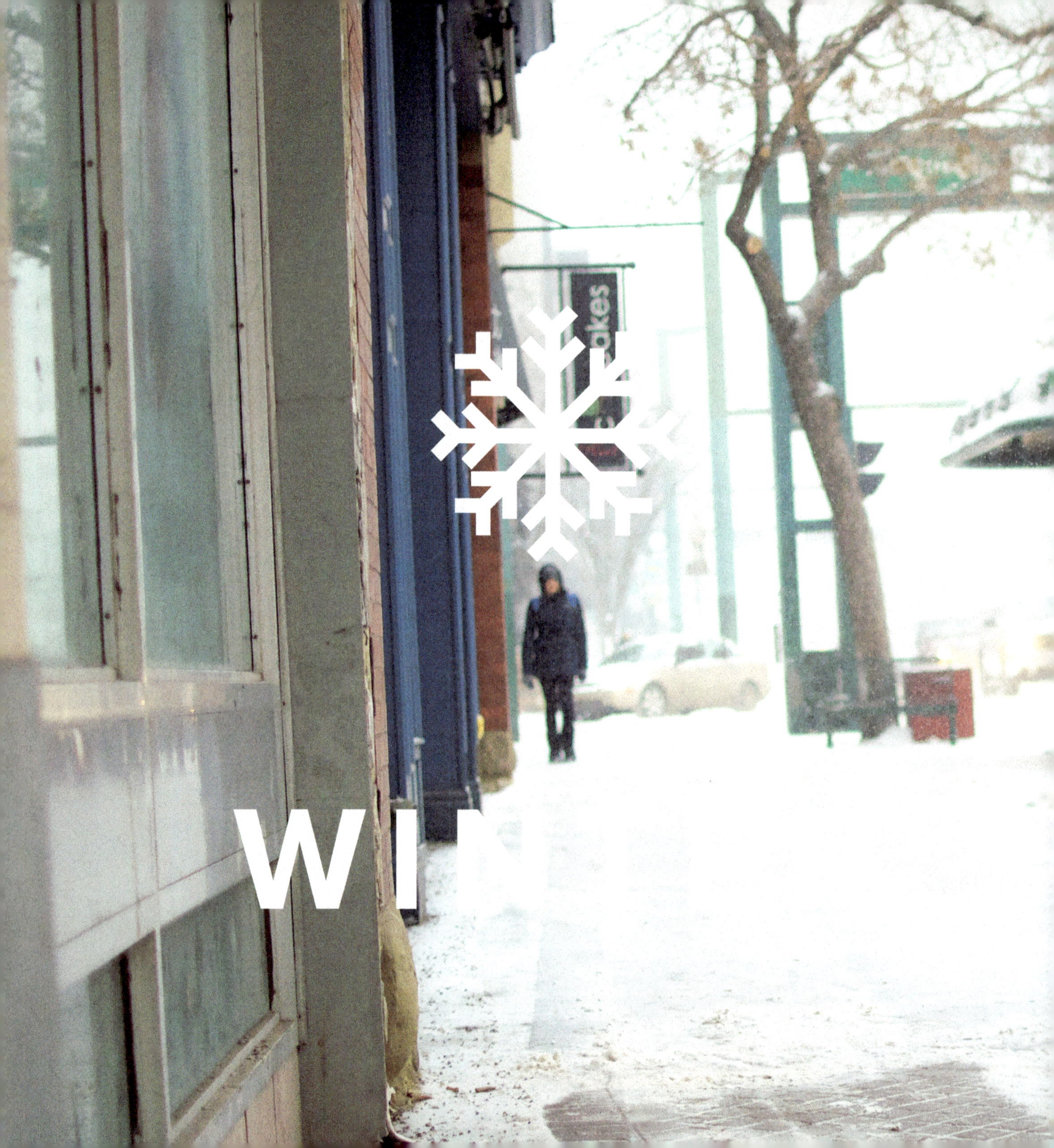
WIN

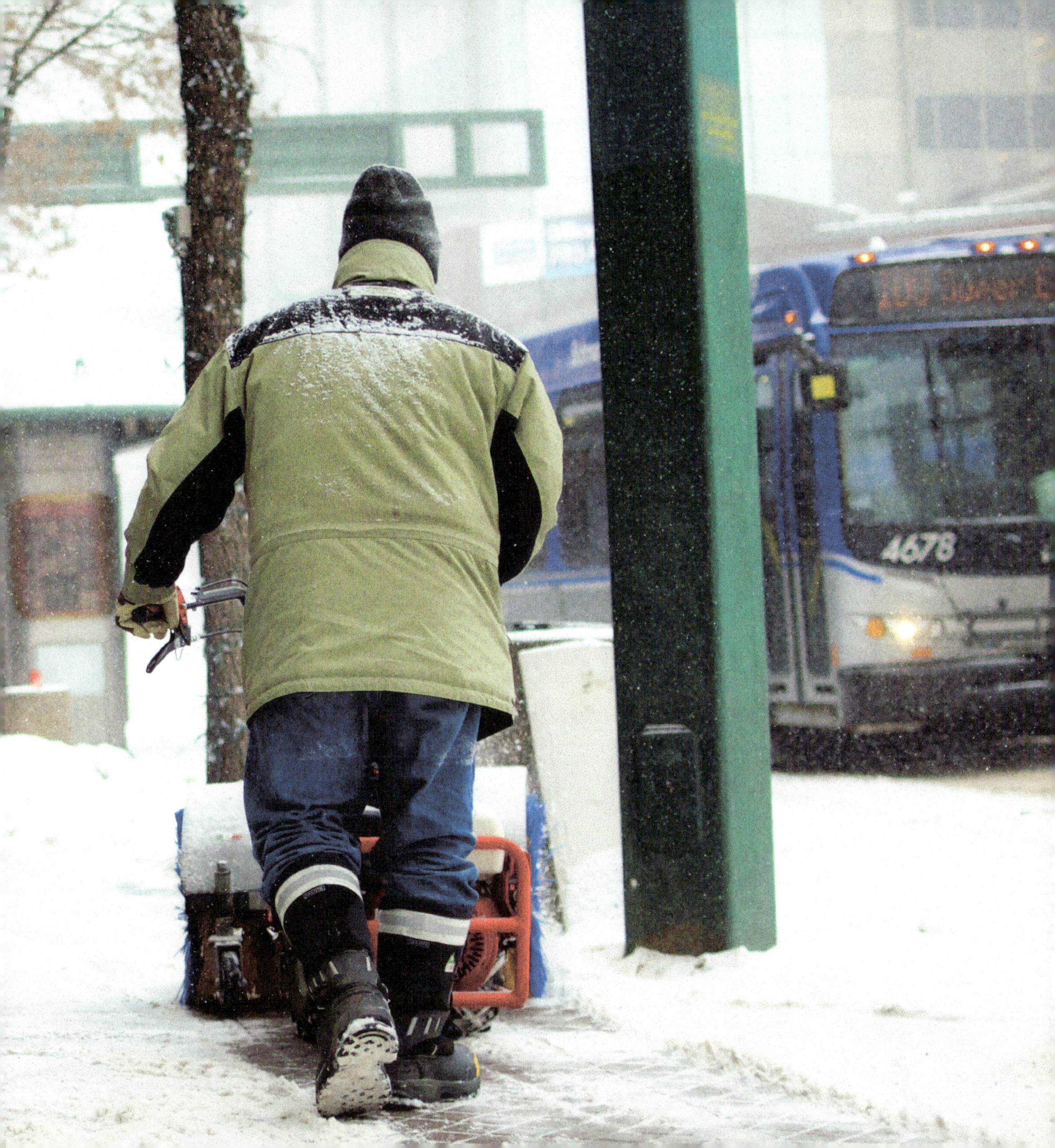
4678

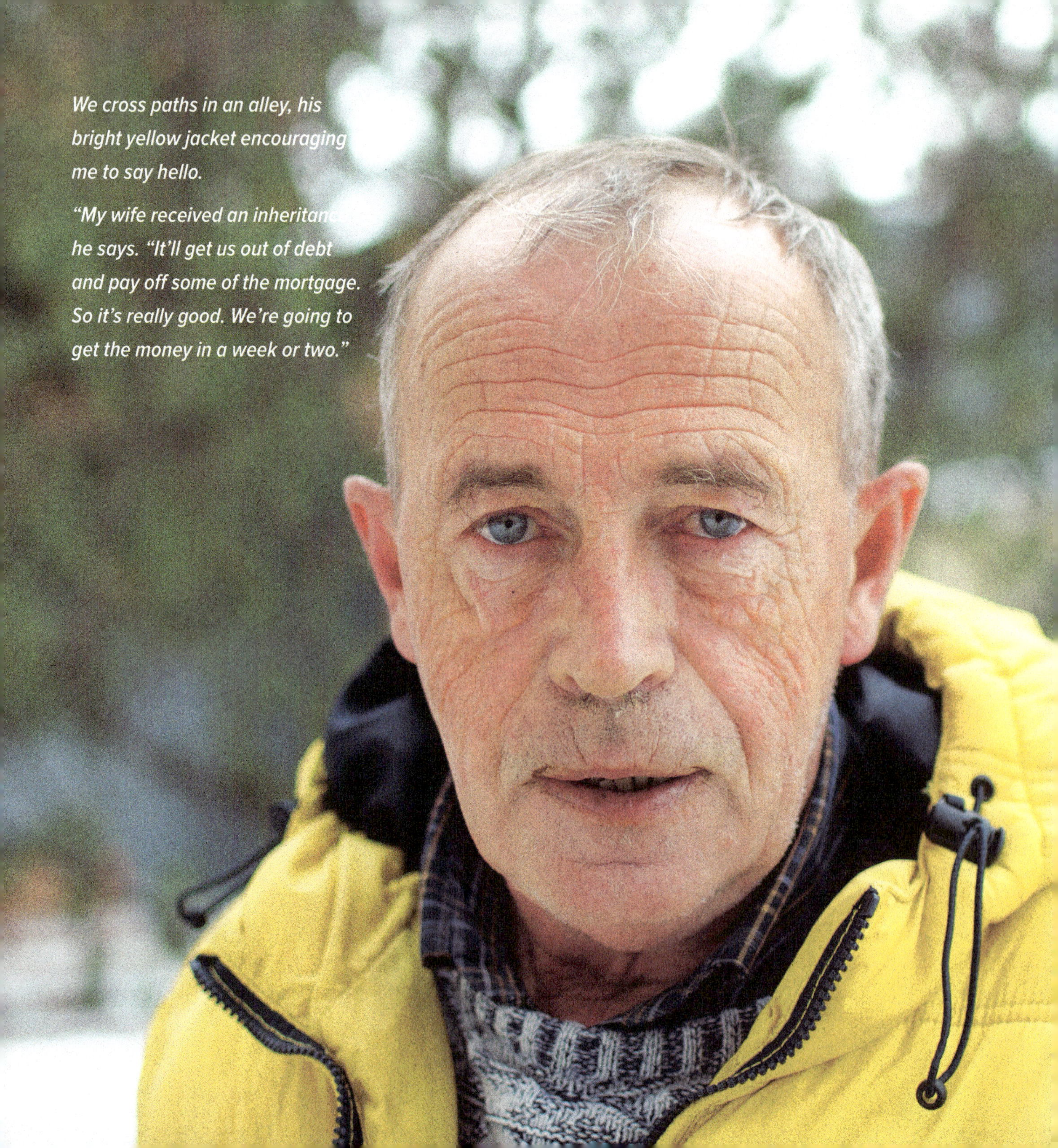

We cross paths in an alley, his bright yellow jacket encouraging me to say hello.

"My wife received an inheritance," he says. "It'll get us out of debt and pay off some of the mortgage. So it's really good. We're going to get the money in a week or two."

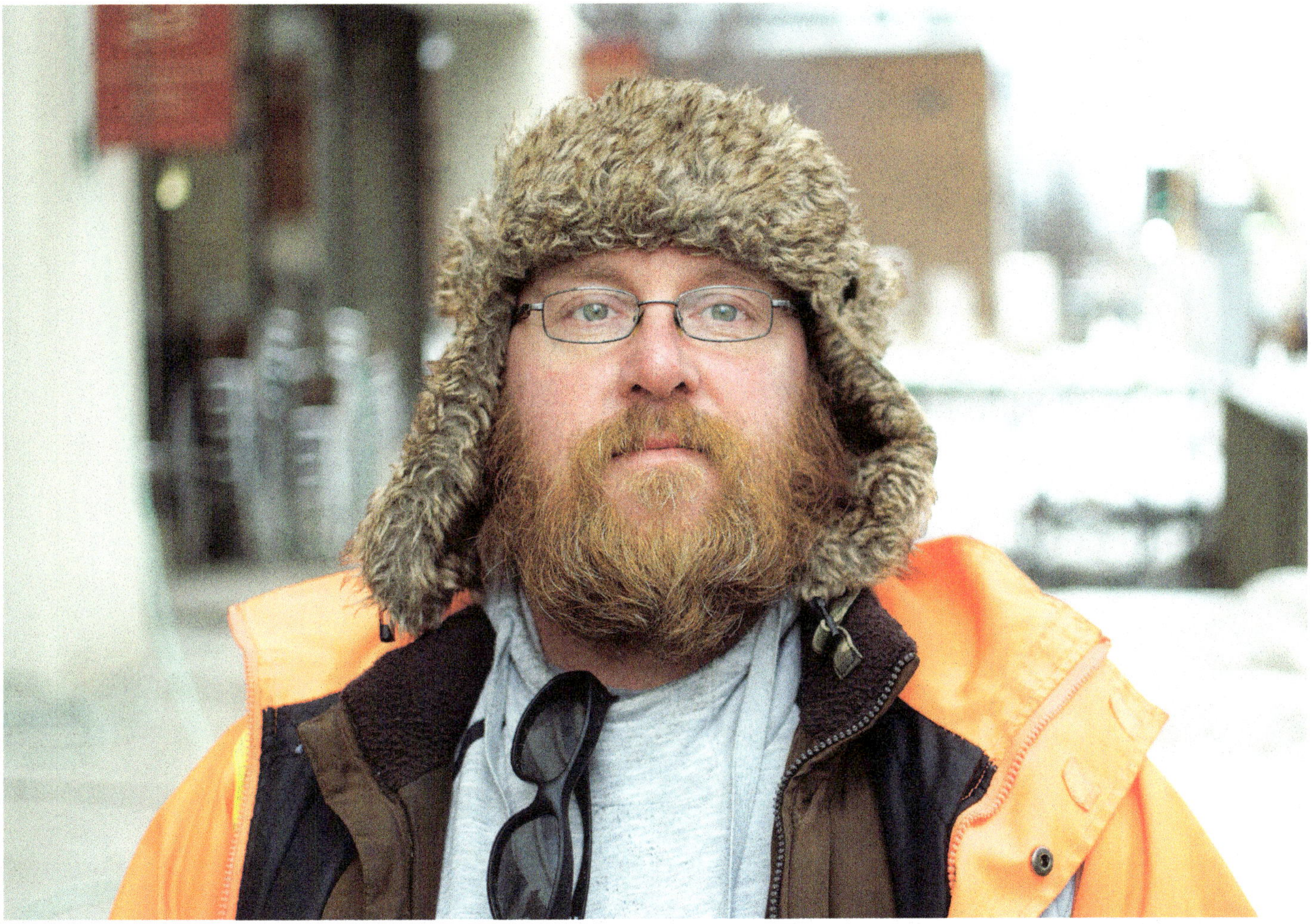

He stands beside the entrance to a high-rise, staring up at three window washers high above.

“I’m spotting them,” he says, “because they’re using an acid up there to clean the windows. There are a lot of stains on them right. So …”

“If you could time travel, where would you go and what would you do?”

“I’d go to Scotland. Yeah, ‘cause my ancestors were the first ones to settle Scotland. I would love to go back to Scotland in the sixteen hundreds.

MY NAME'S RANDY FAITHFUL. YEAH, THAT'S MY LAST NAME, FAITHFUL.

"I have no home. I just wander around, collecting bottles as I usually do. I'm from Lloydminster. Frog Lake it's called. It's a reservation northwest of Lloydminster. I don't have a home out there so I spend my nights at George Spady or ... the Remand Centre."

"What's your biggest challenge these days?"

"Oh, alcohol. Yeah. It's kind of ... I can't really ... I have tried looking for a place but I just kind of forgot about it, drinking all the time that's why. So, I don't know. I figure I'll live anyways. Try anyways. I had a wife. Three and a half years ago she died out on me. After fifteen years."

"What happened?"

"She died of a massive heart attack. I come home one day, I thought she was sleeping on the couch, she was dead. I tried waking her up, but she was dead. For two days she was dead. Fifteen years. So I've been on my own ever since. Fifteen years. Fifteen years with the same woman and then, all of a sudden she's gone. Her son's in that house now. I can't stay there. Too many memories."

"Actually, you know, tomorrow I get my oil money. I have to send my daughter some money. She's in foster care right now. So I usually send her money every month. Even though I don't get too much money, five hundred bucks I get, I send her a hundred bucks every month. For one year now. She just turned thirteen years old. And my son, well he's all grown up now, he's twenty-five. He's got a wife. No kids though. I'm not a grandfather yet. In time I will be."

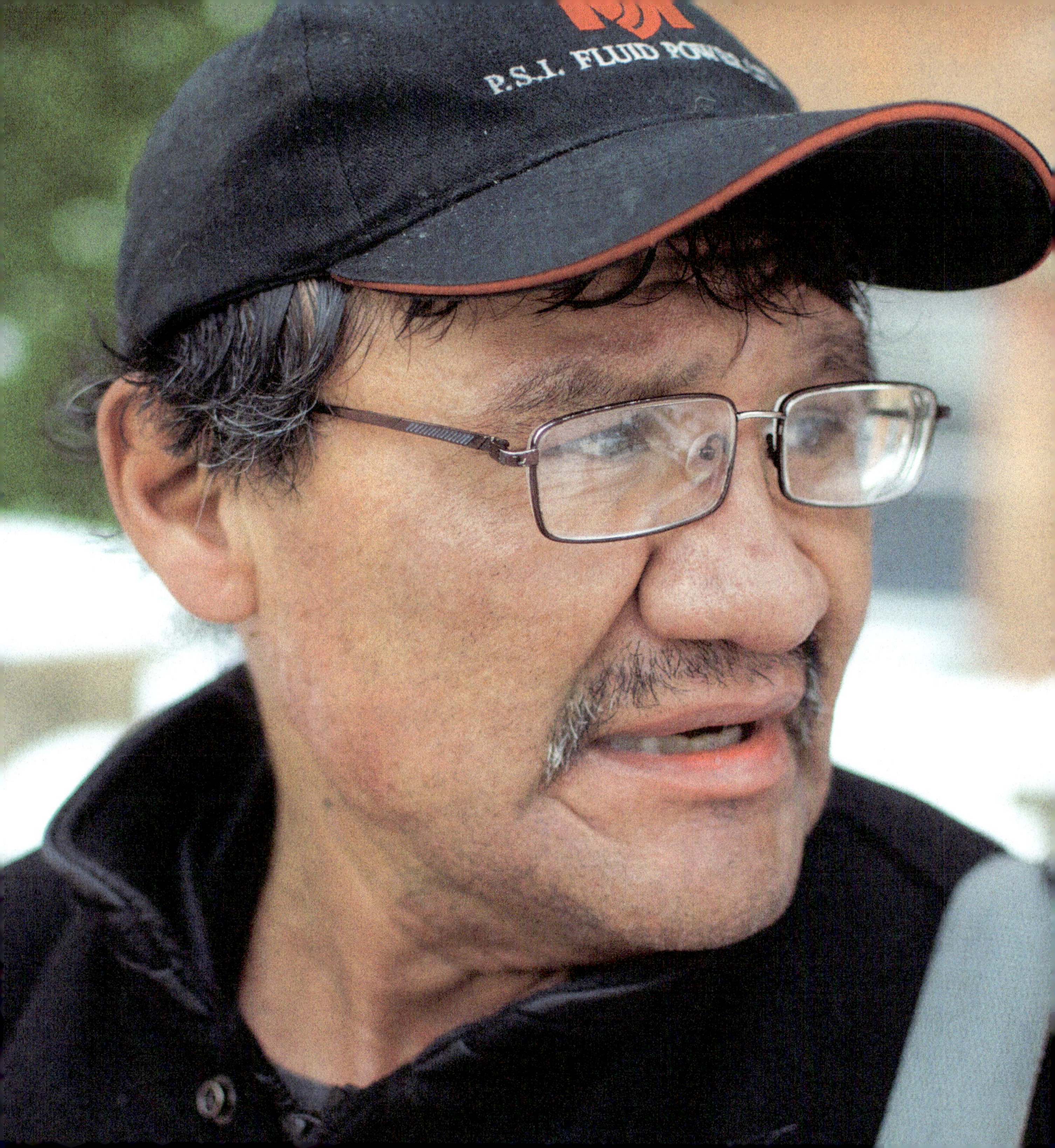

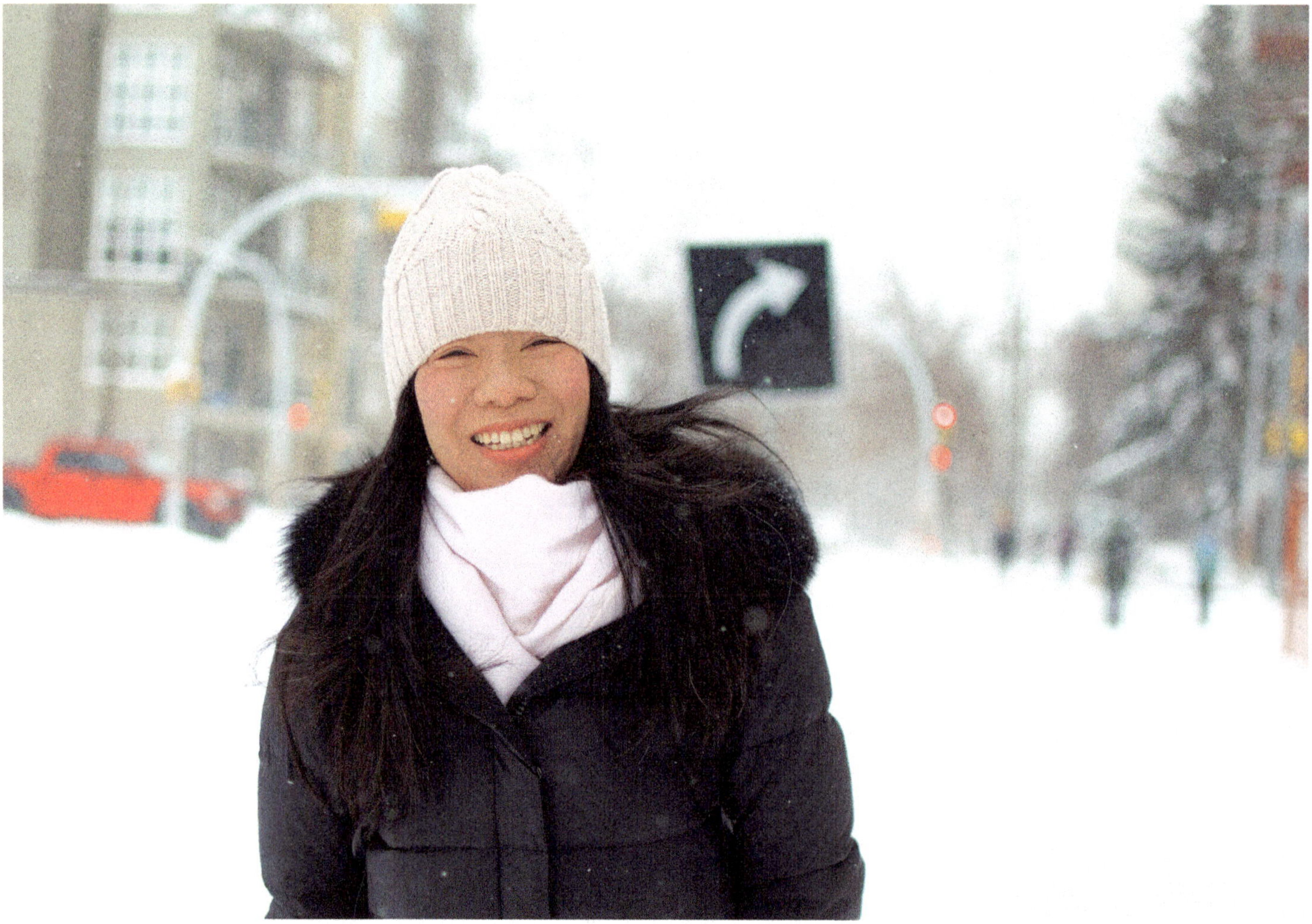

As she walks, she snaps photos of the snow blanketed city with her phone.

“It’s just too cold,” she says. “This year I came to the U of A as an MBA student. I’m from China.”

“How do you like it here?”

“Everything is wonderful except for the weather.”

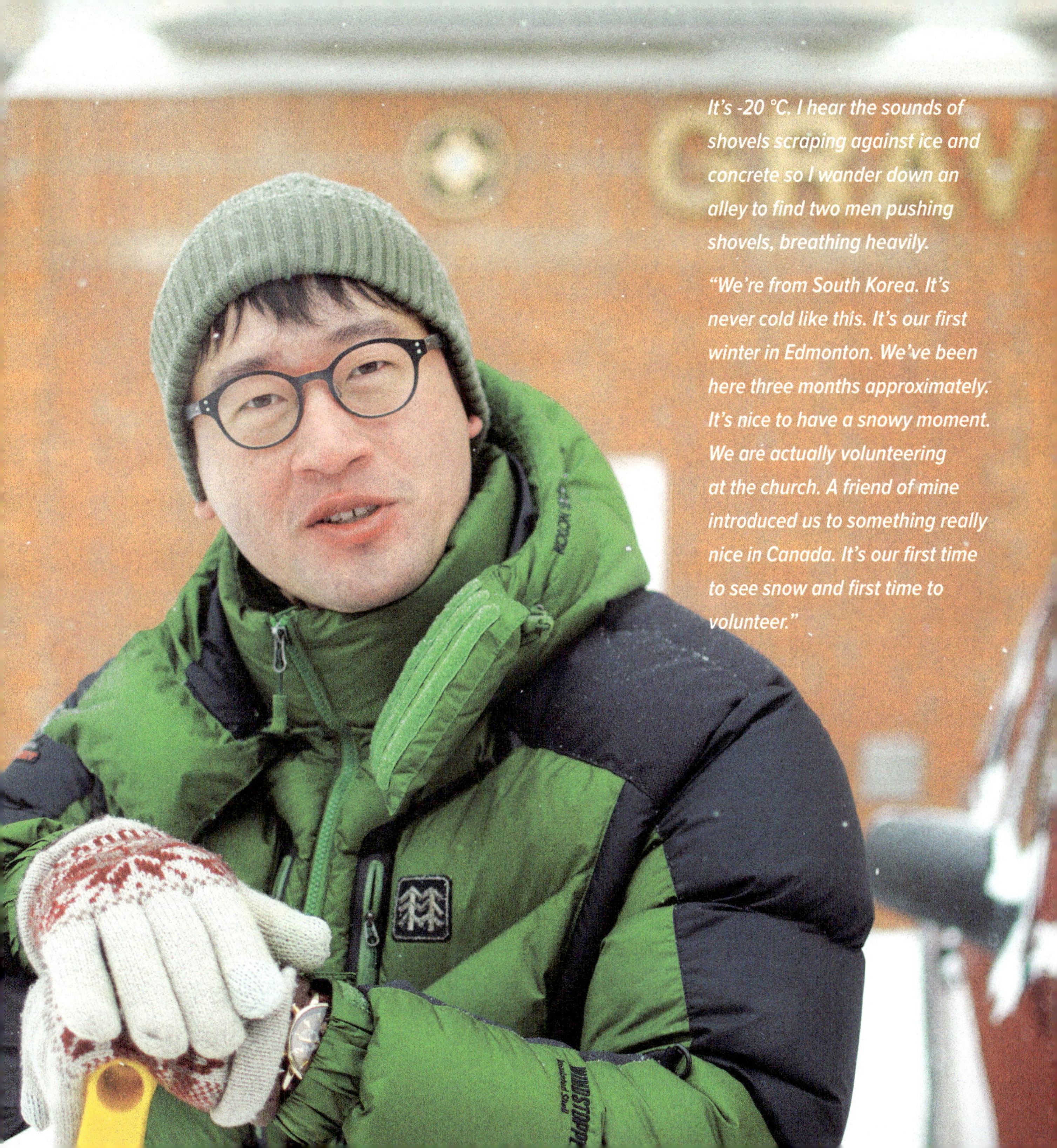

It's -20 °C. I hear the sounds of shovels scraping against ice and concrete so I wander down an alley to find two men pushing shovels, breathing heavily.

"We're from South Korea. It's never cold like this. It's our first winter in Edmonton. We've been here three months approximately. It's nice to have a snowy moment. We are actually volunteering at the church. A friend of mine introduced us to something really nice in Canada. It's our first time to see snow and first time to volunteer."

"What's the best thing that happened to you last year?"

"Nothin'."

"Really? What was your year like?"

"It was all right. Been keeping busy, workin'."

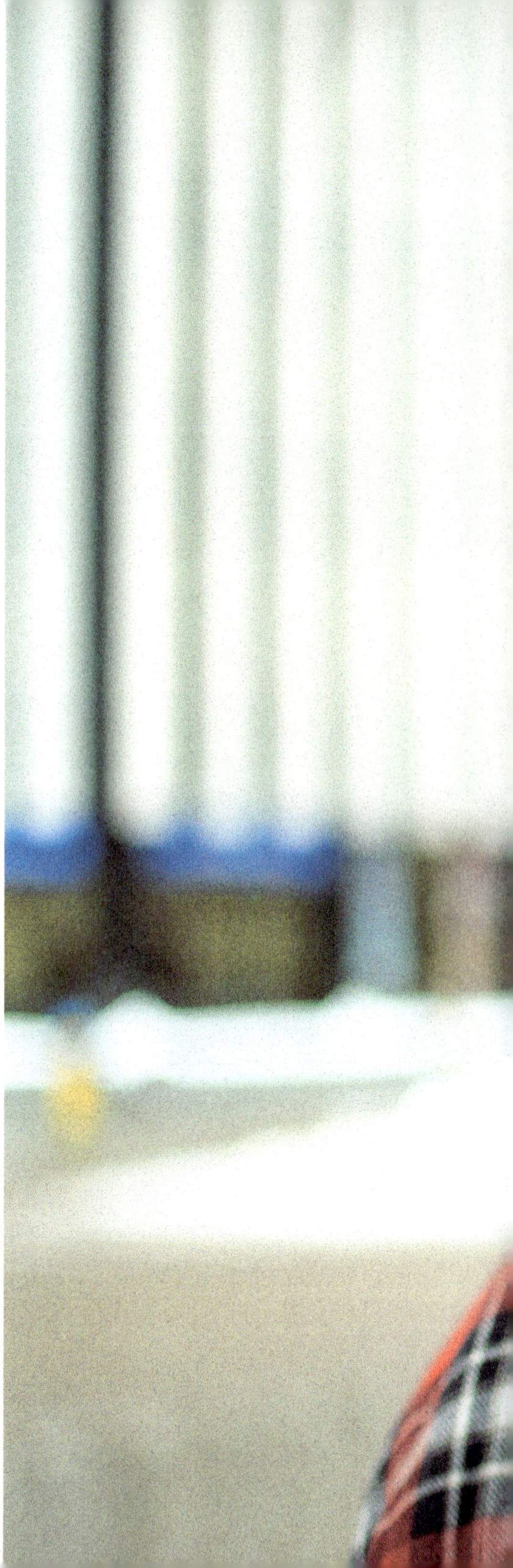

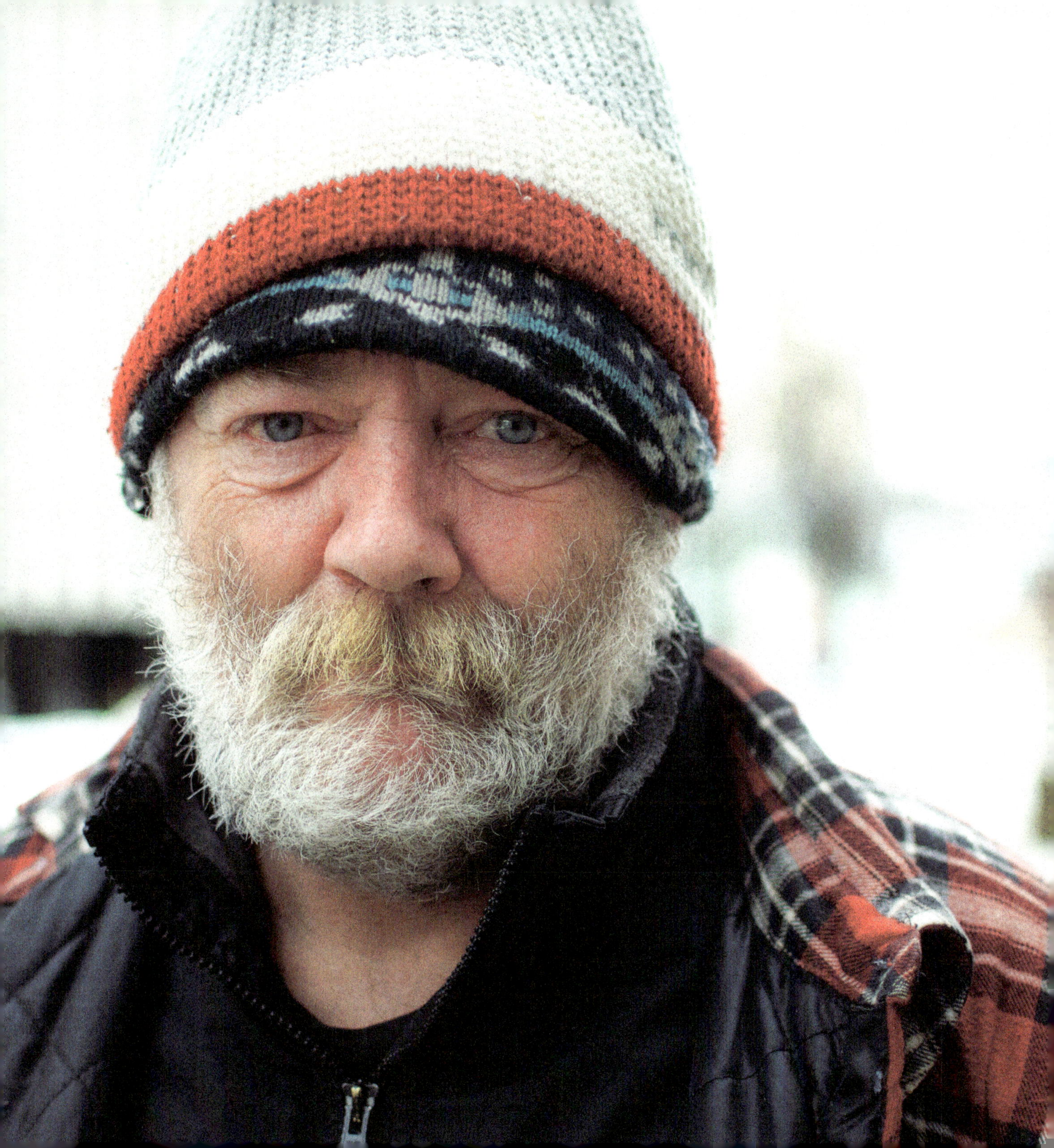

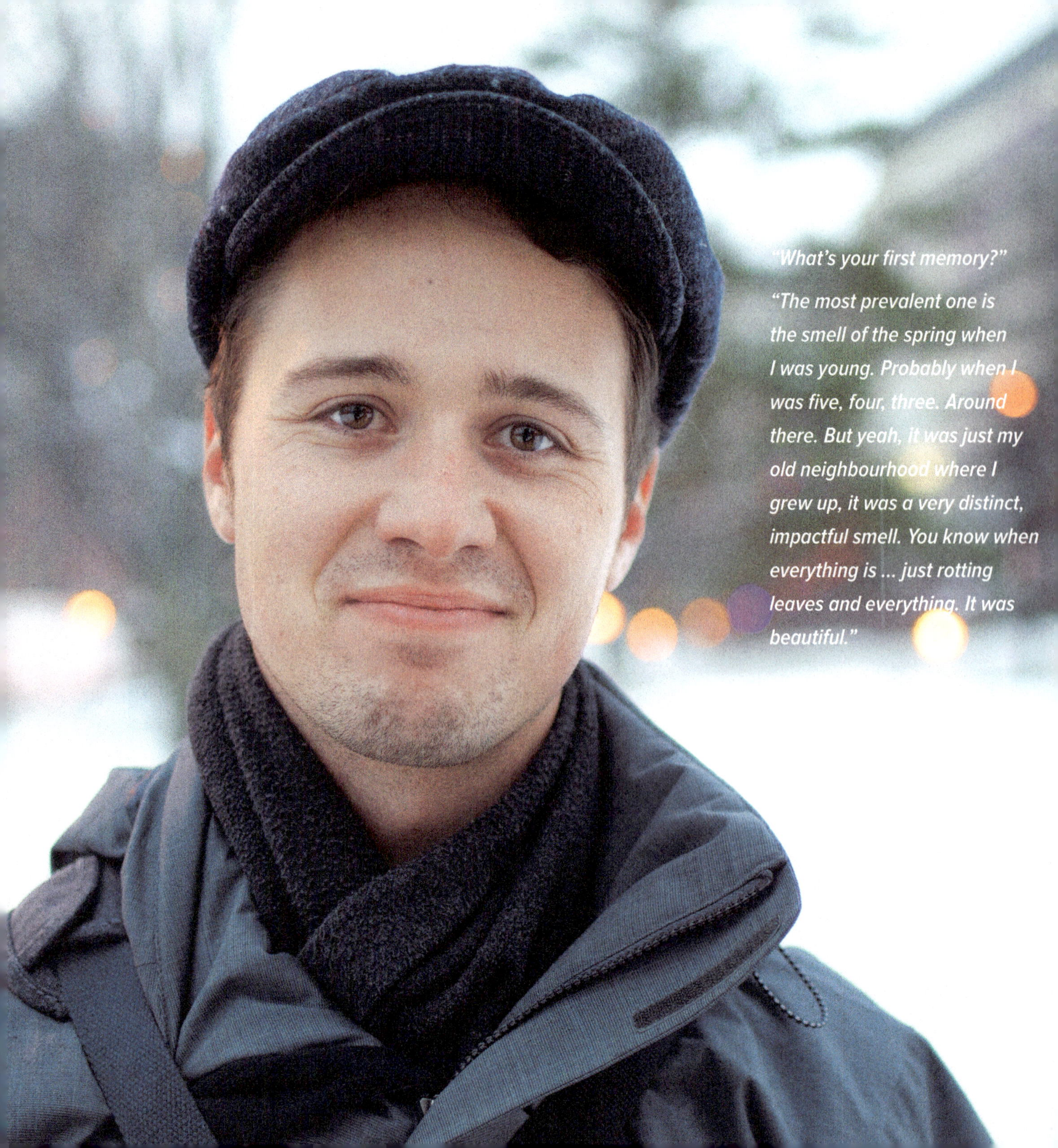

"What's your first memory?"

"The most prevalent one is the smell of the spring when I was young. Probably when I was five, four, three. Around there. But yeah, it was just my old neighbourhood where I grew up, it was a very distinct, impactful smell. You know when everything is ... just rotting leaves and everything. It was beautiful."

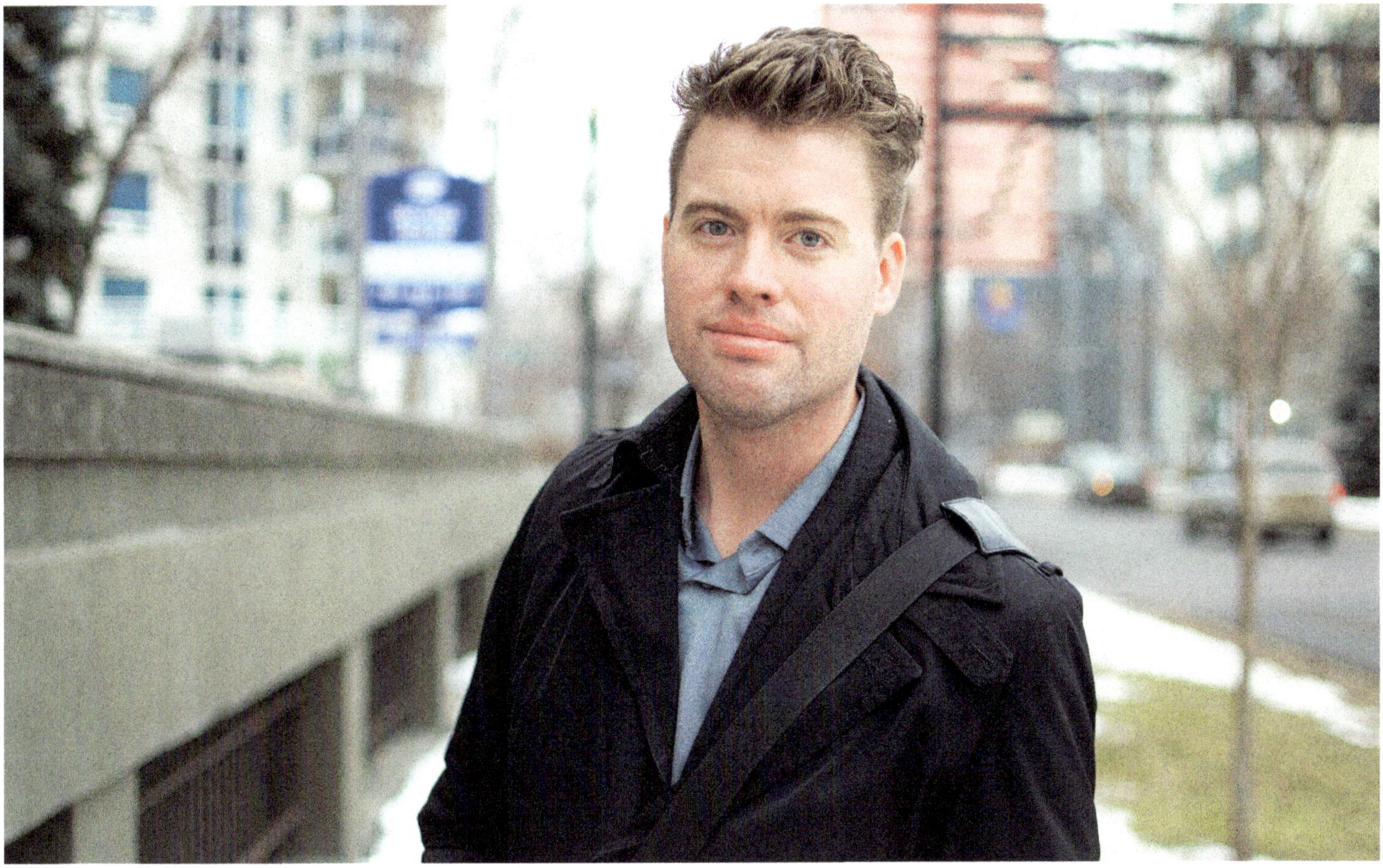

"My challenge these days is trying to afford a house in Edmonton. Prices go up every year so ..."

"What did you want to be when you were a kid?"

"A professional snowboarder. I used to snowboard with the other kids all the time. I still snowboard but not the same way I did back then. You gotta have something to look forward to in the winter, right."

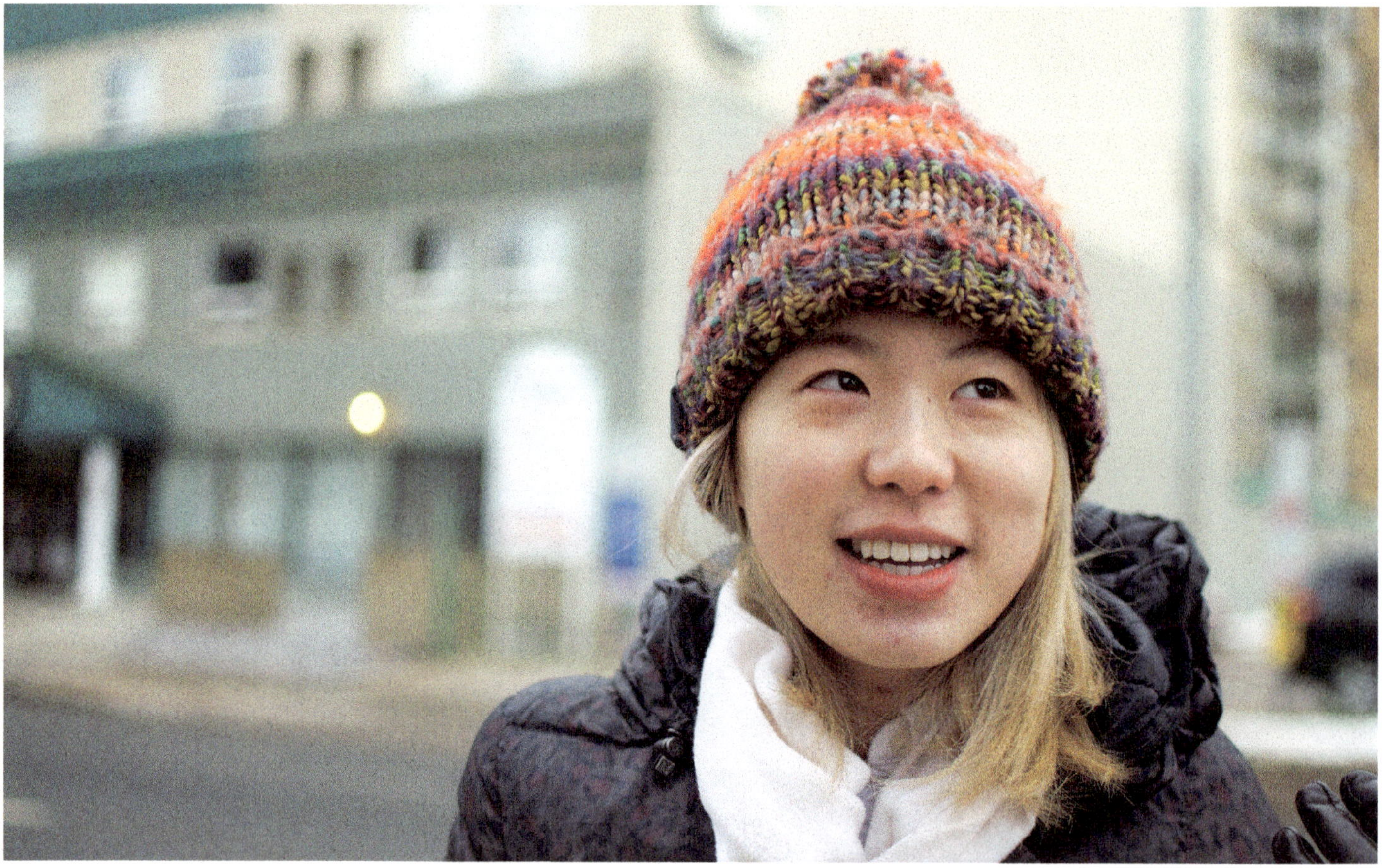

“What’s your biggest challenge these days?”

“Finding a direction. I’m twenty-five right now so I’m at that quarter-life crisis stage. I think a lot of people feel the same way as me. A lot of people have something that they’re working towards but they are just living day to day.”

“What are you working towards?”

“I am working towards something but I don’t think I want to say it out loud because when you say it, you really really have to commit. So I want to be sure of myself first.”

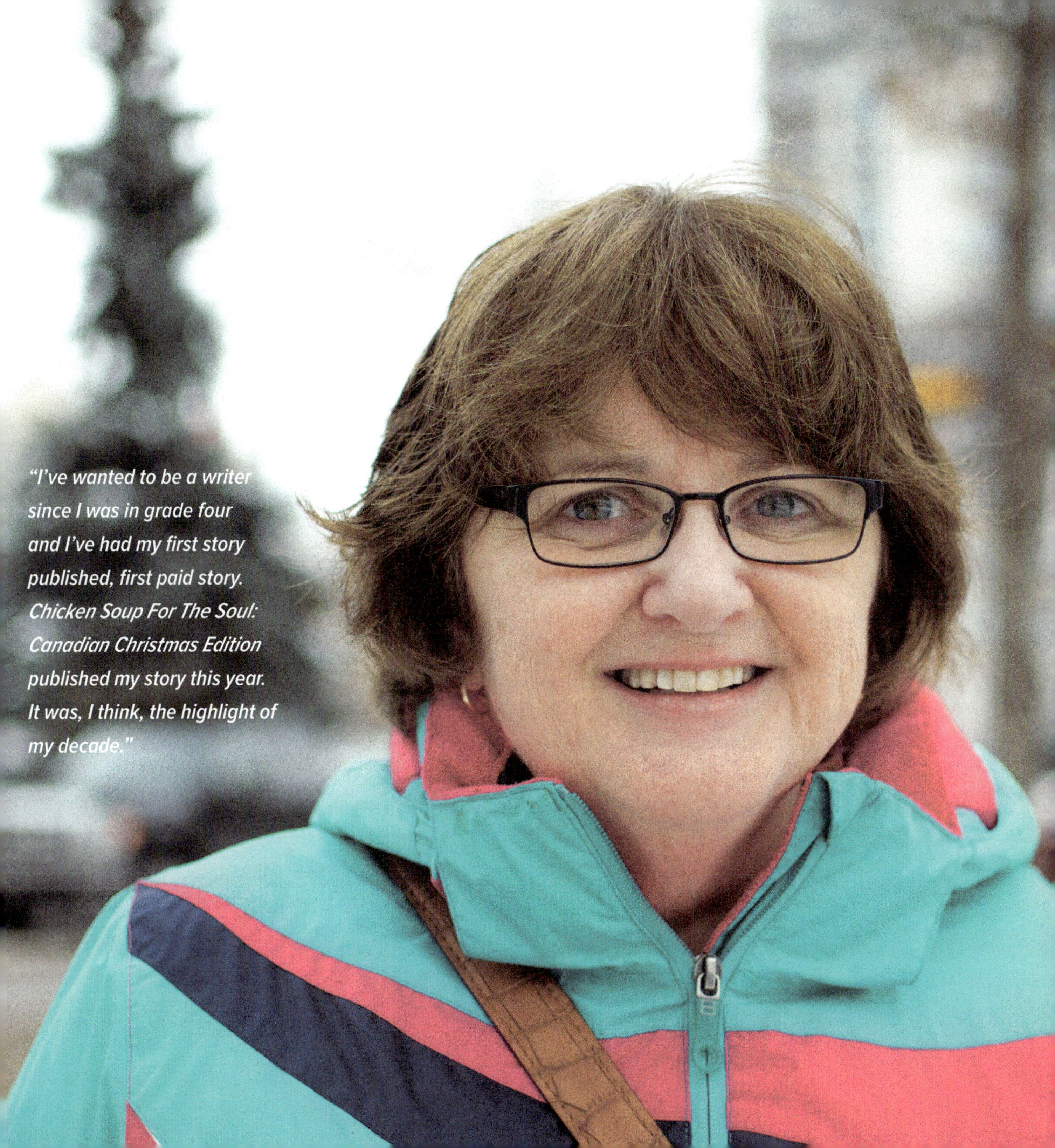

"I've wanted to be a writer since I was in grade four and I've had my first story published, first paid story. Chicken Soup For The Soul: Canadian Christmas Edition published my story this year. It was, I think, the highlight of my decade."

WHAT'S ONE OF THE HARDEST THINGS YOU'VE EVER HAD TO DO?

"I would say my father's eulogy. That was tough. It was February. Less than a year ago. That was tough because he was a young man. That would probably be the toughest. After that, I would say seeing my friend, who's still living, struggle with ALS. A lot of bad things happen in life. I run a company so I've had to let people go. And that's tough, having to fire somebody, that's tough. But there are always other things. There are always other opportunities. And as tough as that is, people always bounce when it comes to career. But when you've got a disease that's as debilitating as ALS—and he's like a little Stephen Hawking—the average life expectancy is about four years, eighty percent don't make four years after being diagnosed. So this guy is going on year six or seven. The humility of it—your mind is one hundred percent but you lose all your motor skills and there's atrophy in your muscles. Anyways, I was his best man; he was my best man. His kids were pretty young when he was diagnosed, so one is still in high school. The last six years for them have been a different world. It kinda sucks."

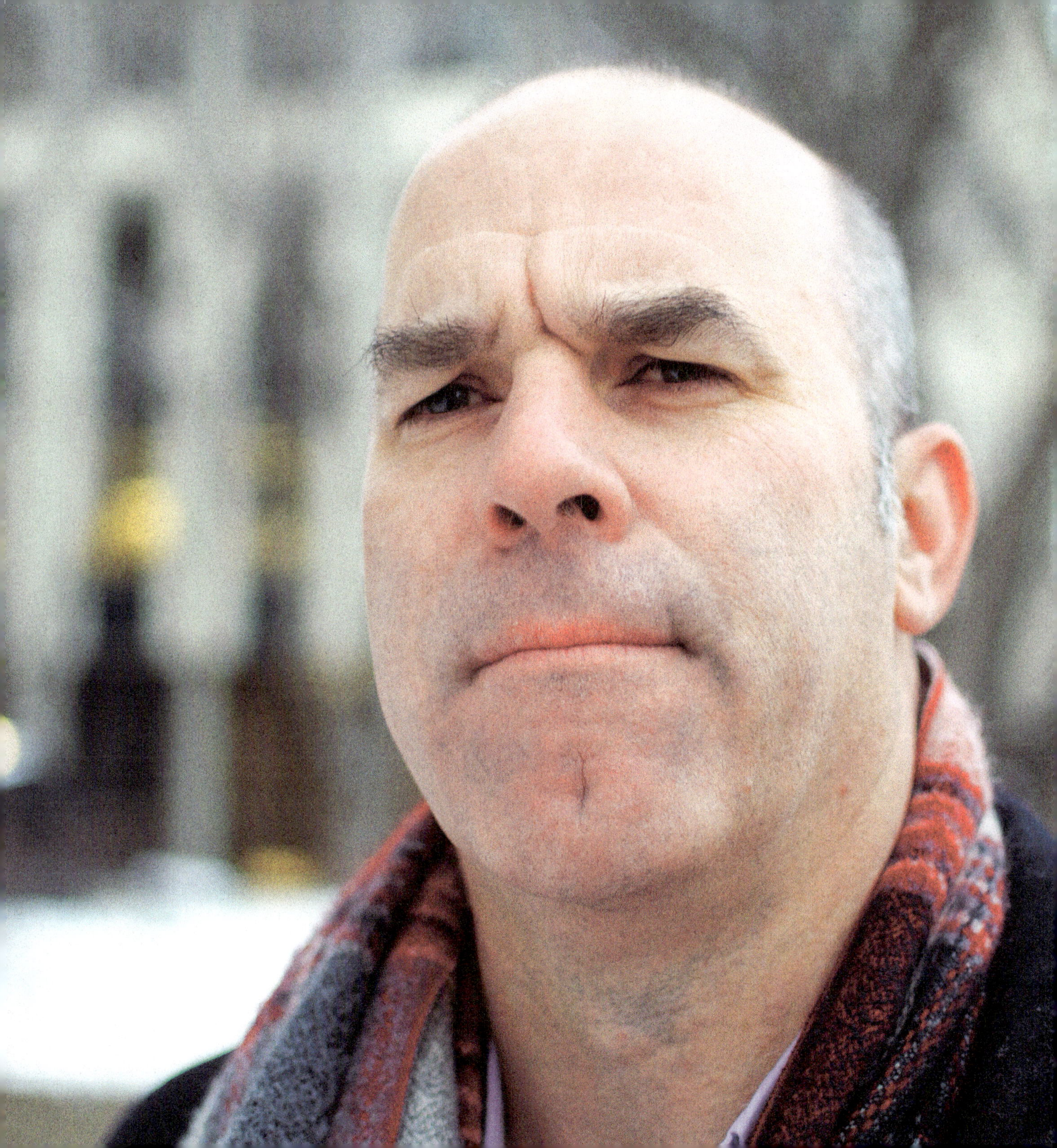

BRODY

Coming from the hospital, he cradles his left arm, which is in a cast and hidden beneath his fuzzy blue blanket.

“What makes you happy?”

“Christmas.”

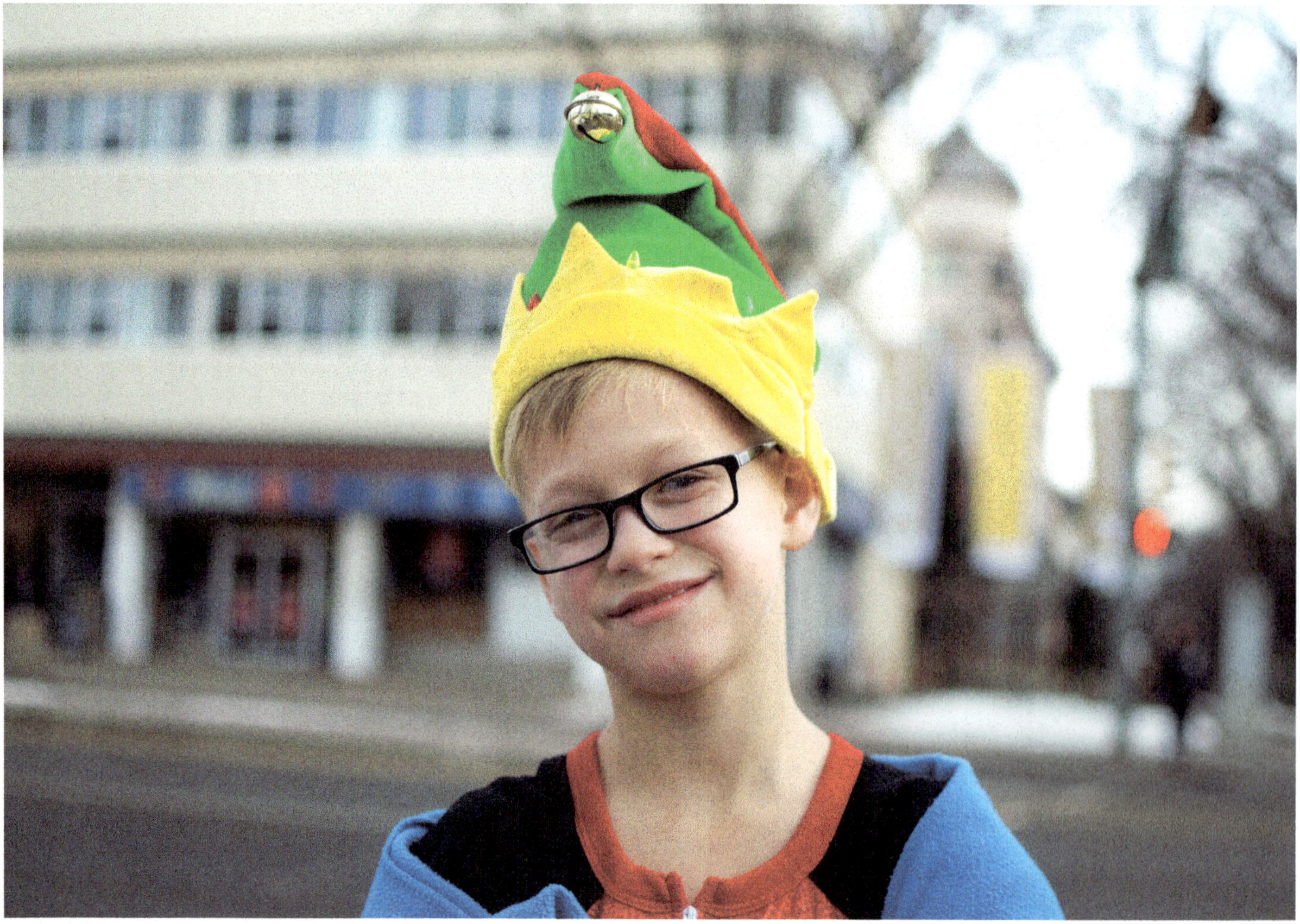

SANTA

"Being Santa is an awesome thing. Being as old as I am, it starts to wear on the knees. So I am looking for an apprentice."

"What would you like for Christmas?"

"I'd like a puppy for Christmas. Actually, an old puppy, a rescue dog. Mine passed away."

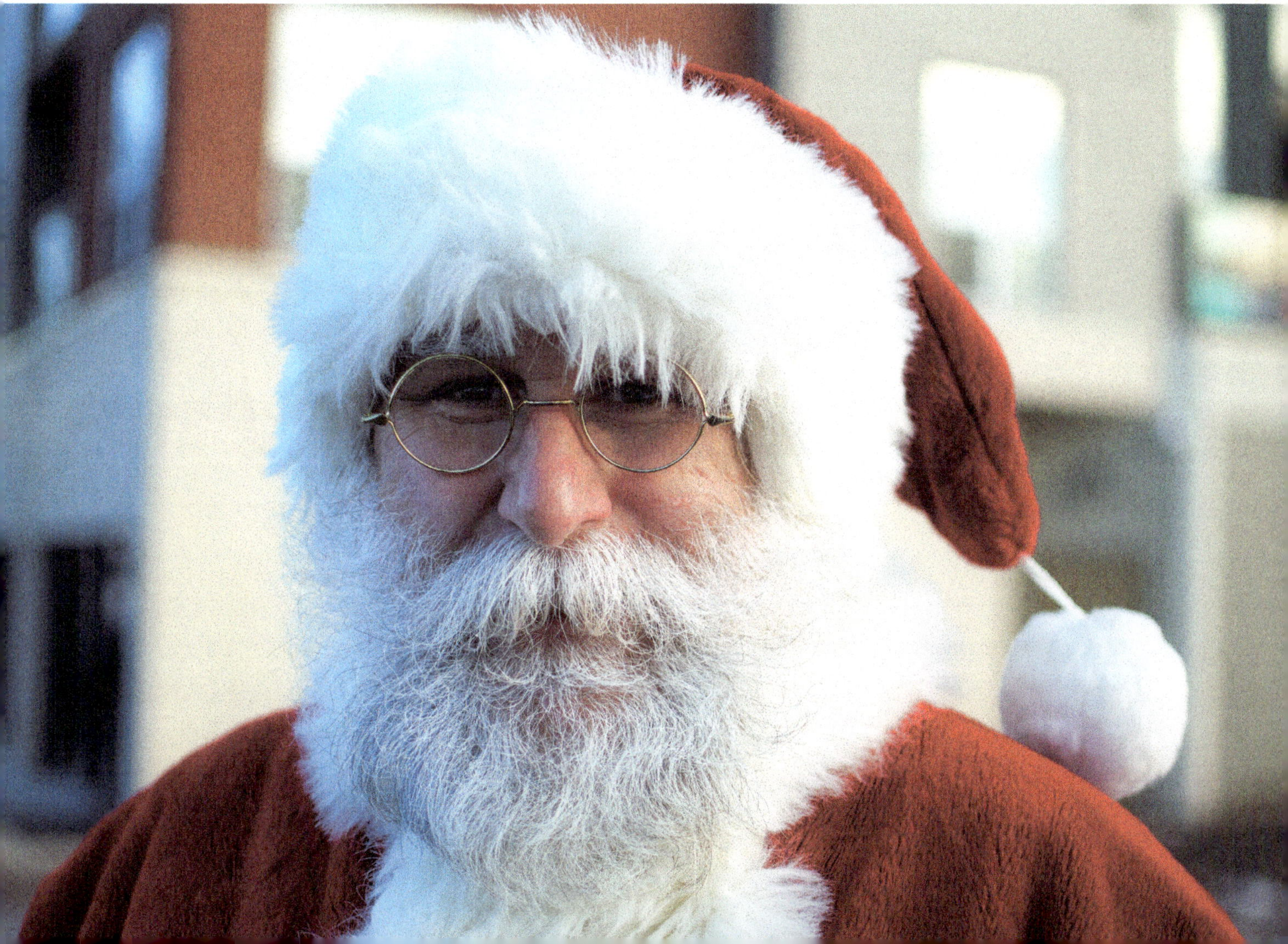

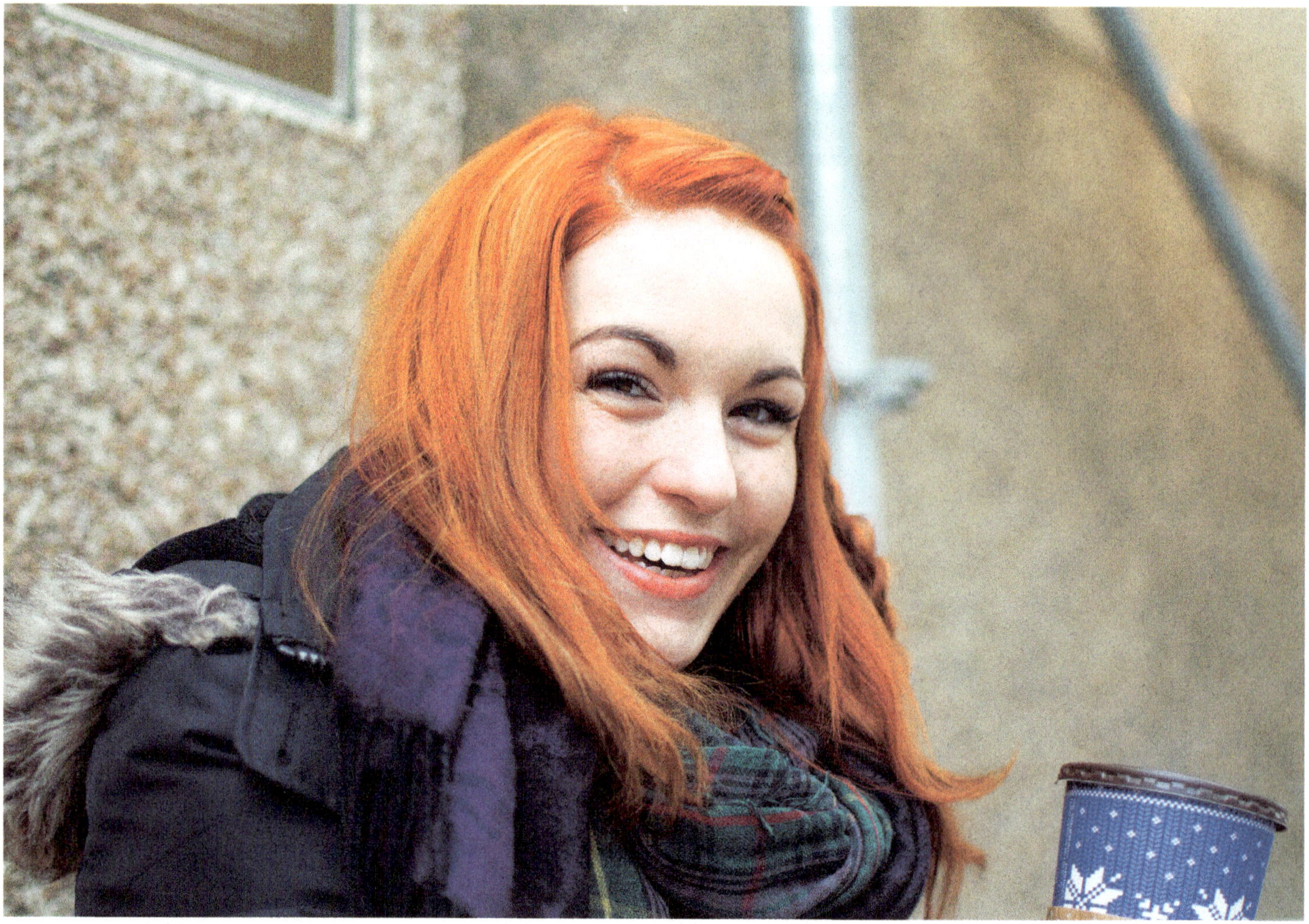

“Every day is a new adventure,” she says, taking a sip from the to-go cup in her hand.

“If I could grant you one wish right now, what would it be?”

“For people to have realistic expectations. And for people to have happier attitudes. This city can be a little grumpy at times. A smile goes a long way. The city is definitely rebuilding and looking nice though. I live close to one eighteenth so there’s been a transformation for sure. It’s looking a little friendlier down there, not so scary to walk down the street.”

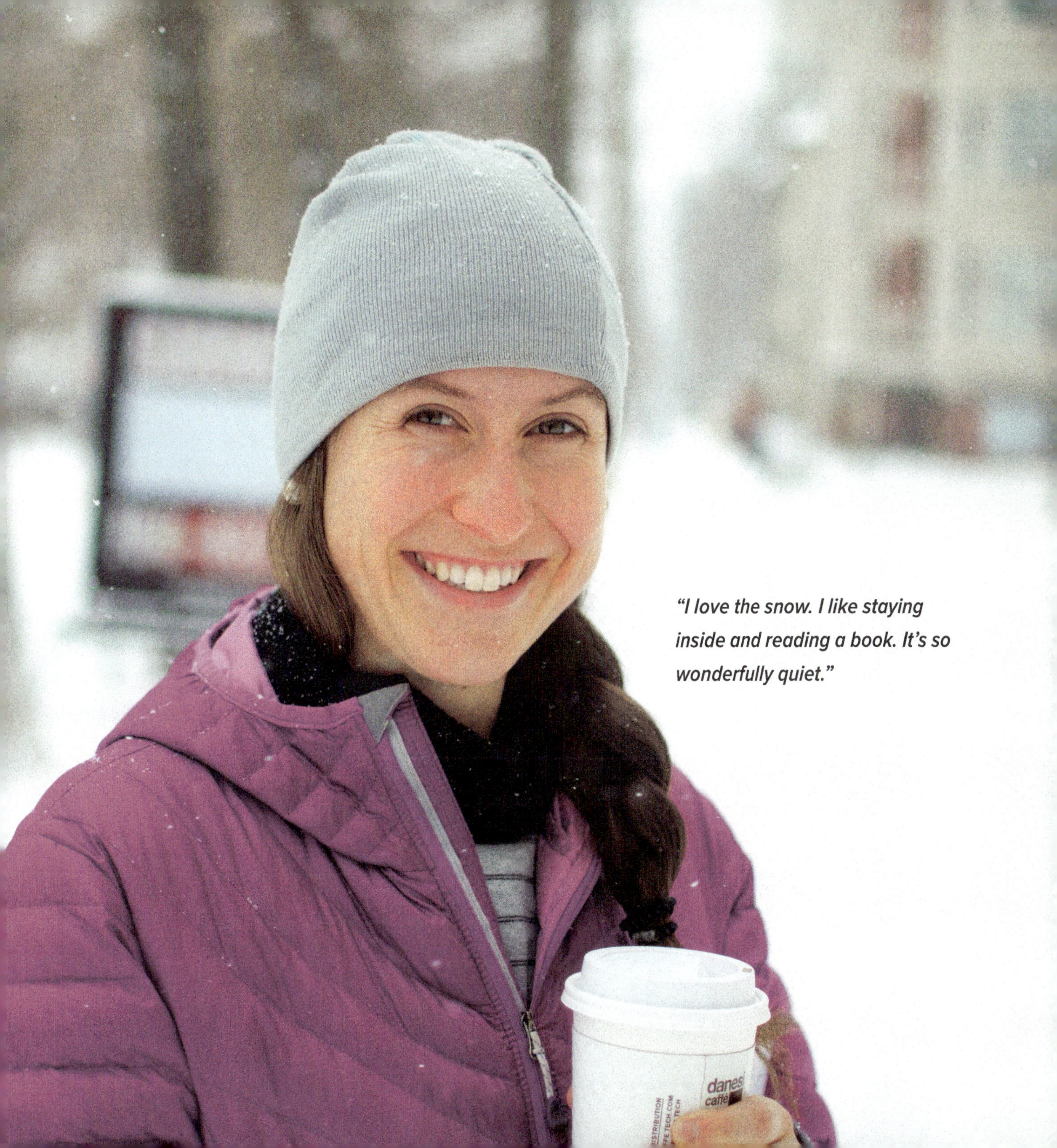

"I love the snow. I like staying inside and reading a book. It's so wonderfully quiet."

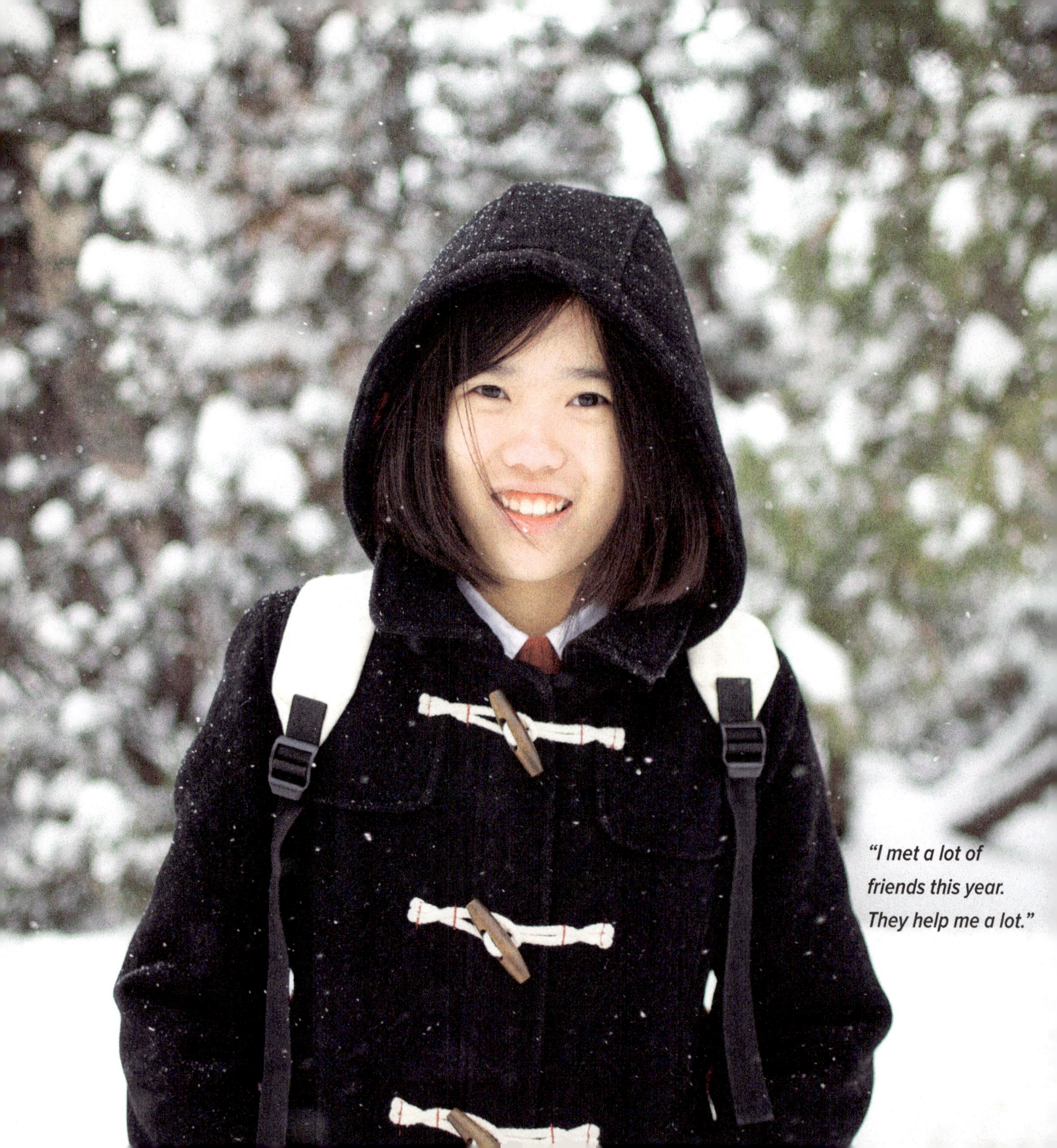

"I met a lot of friends this year. They help me a lot."

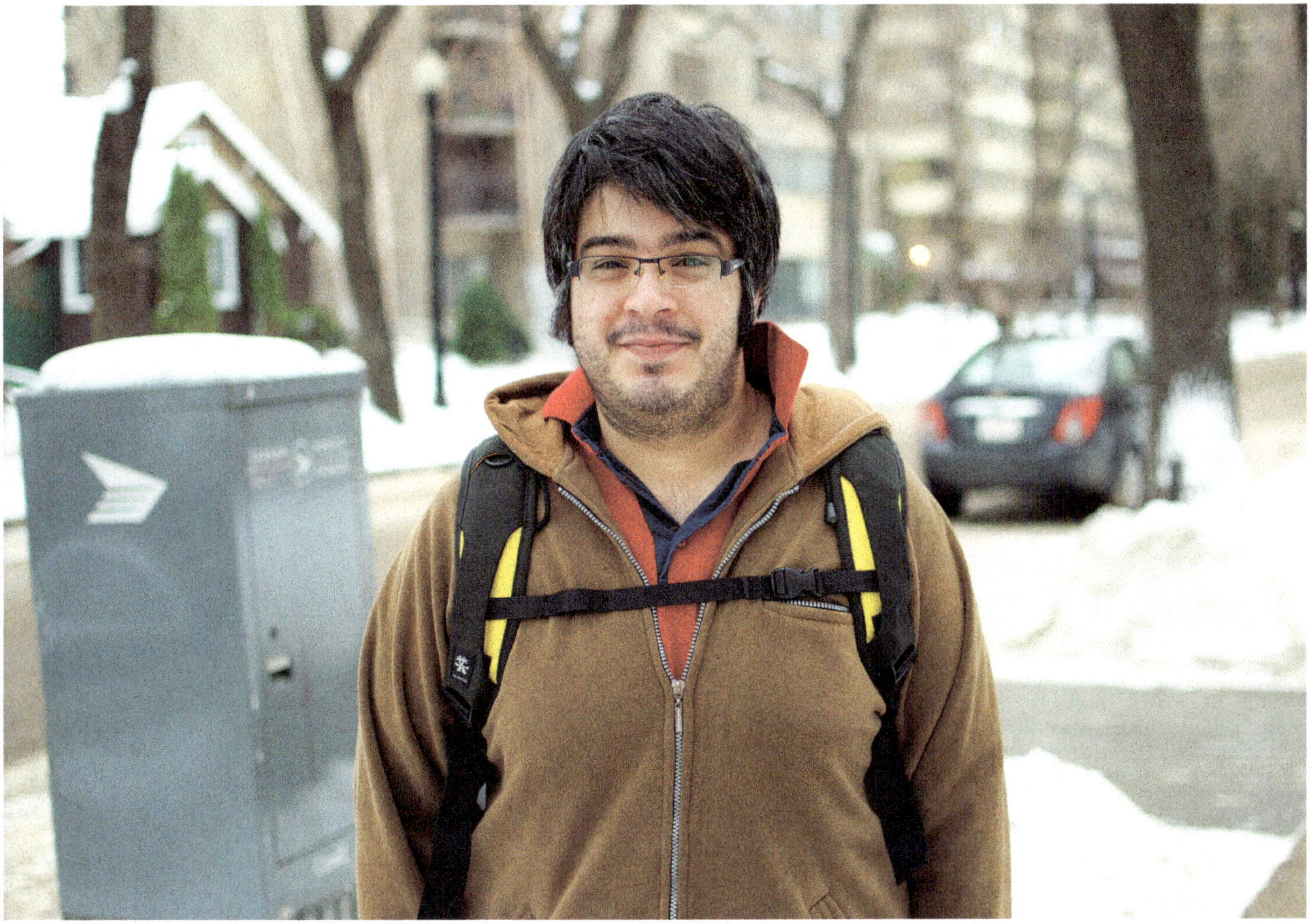

"What's the best thing that's happened to you this year?"

"I graduated for the University of Alberta. Back home, in my country, I studied Mechanical Engineering and here I studied Chemical Engineering."

"What's the biggest challenge in your life right now after graduating?"

"I live thirty thousand kilometres away from my family and friends. You cannot hug people through the Internet."

He stands on a corner, selling copies of Alberta Street News.

"I stick around here for five days. Then on Saturday I go to the Farmers' Market on the south side. Sunday I go to Sacred Heart Church; sometimes I go in, sometimes I stay out."

"What do you do when it's really cold?"

"Survive," he says, laughing, his laugh deep and hoarse. "It hasn't been that cold yet. But when I stand here, I can go inside there," he says, gesturing to the building behind him. "Warm up and use the bathroom, you know. They pretty well know me. I've been here for four years.

"What's your biggest challenge these days?"

"Housing. Can't find no new housing. We're homeless. Other than that, the paper brings me the food I need. I go to the Dollarama and buy the little bit of food that I need. I go to the homeless shelter at the Remand and I snooze there."

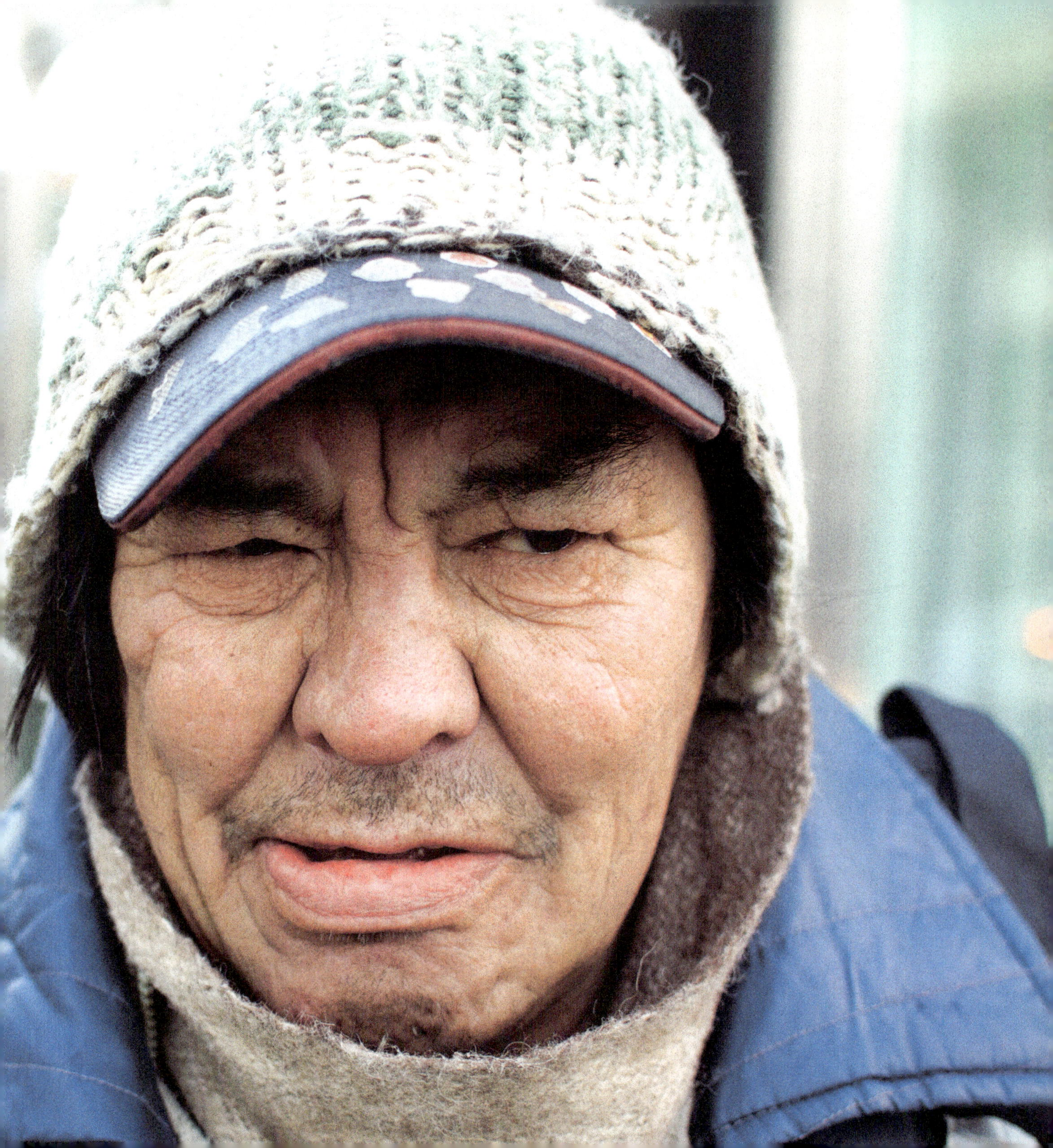

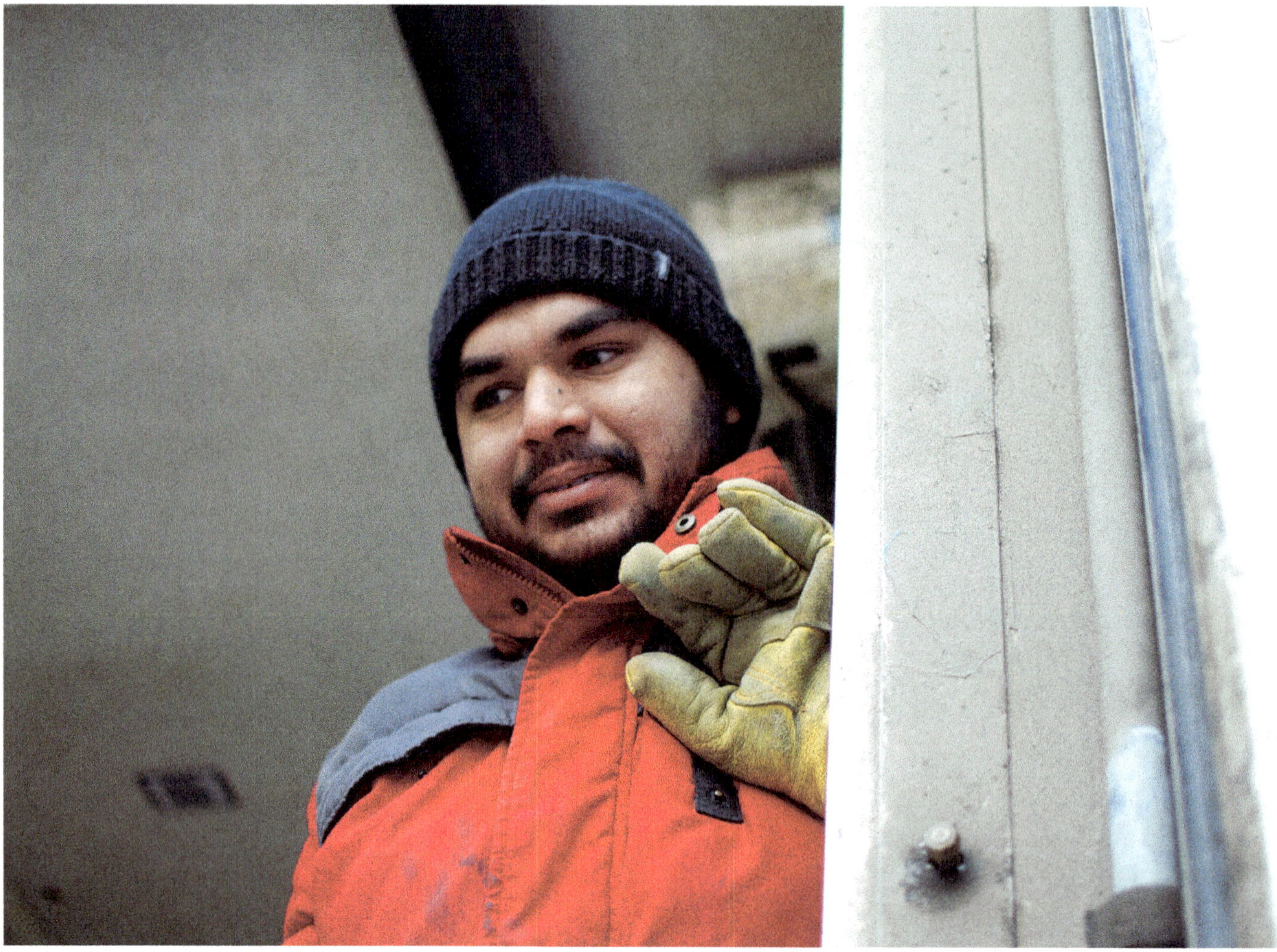

"How was your year?"

"I came to Canada this year from India."

"How has it been?"

"Good. Not good but good. School is pretty good. That's probably the best thing. I study at NAIT. Business Management."

"What was it like leaving India to come here?"

"It's hard but okay. I have to work part-time to support myself. In India I didn't have to do that. I just had to study. And I miss my family of course."

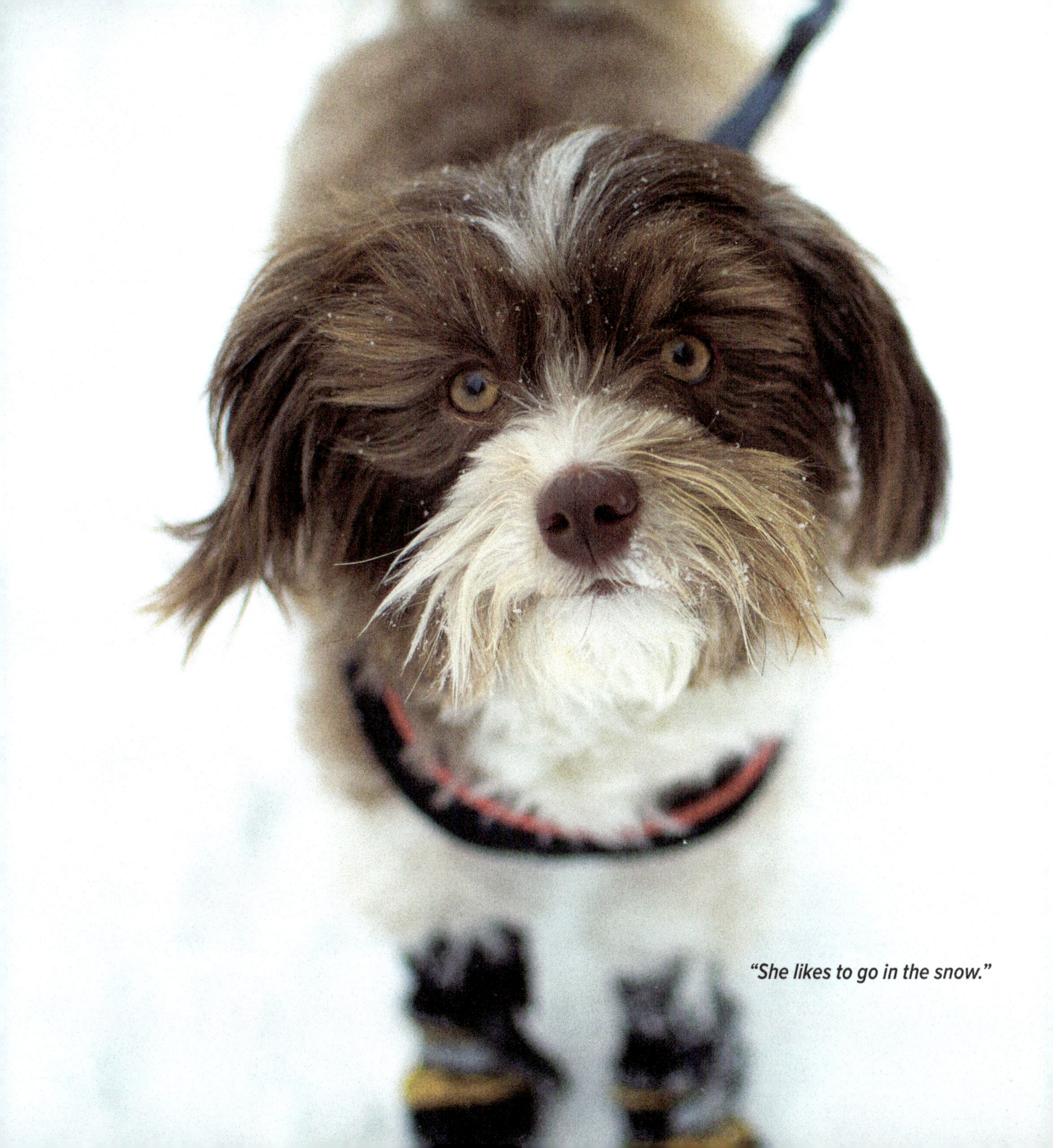

"She likes to go in the snow."

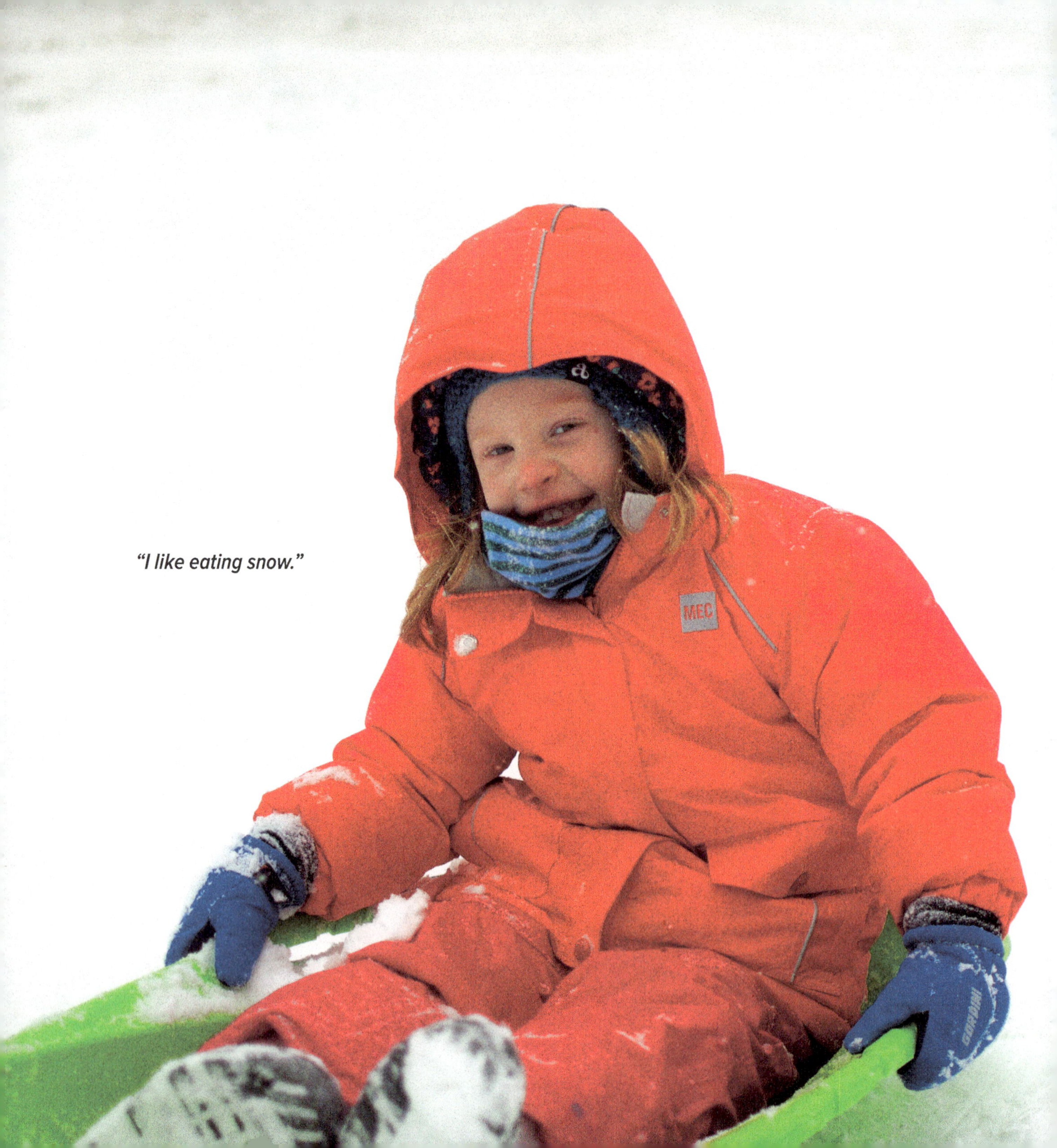

"I like eating snow."

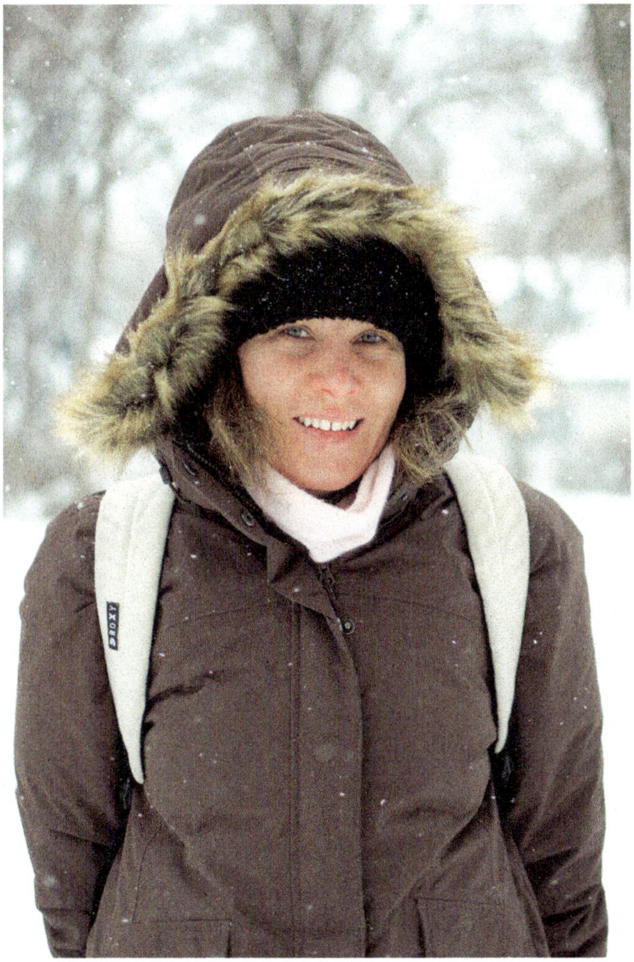

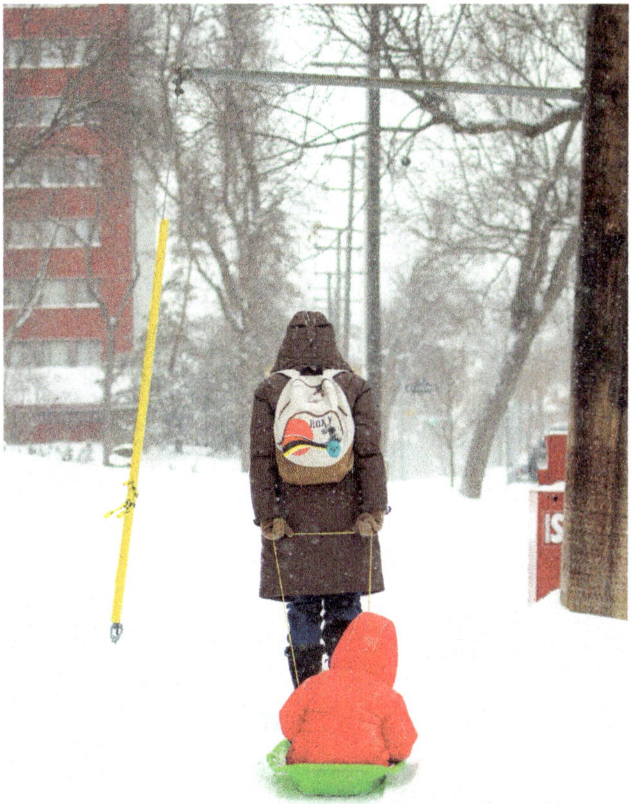

With her arms behind her back, hands gripping the rope attached to the green sled her daughter is on, she trudges through the snow, pulling her daughter behind her.

“There are so many happy moments with her. Like this morning, after I got out of the shower, she asked me if I heard a crunching sound while I was showering. I said, ‘No.’ Then she said, ‘Oh, I ate a cookie.’”

“Right now I’m upgrading at Centre High, trying to figure out a direction. I still haven’t found one though. I took the last year off just to play chess for the whole year. So I just travelled across Alberta playing chess. That’s pretty much been my life for the past year. It’s been my passion.”

“How was playing chess around Alberta?

“Really interesting. You meet all types of people. Across Alberta, chess players range from doctors and university professors to homeless people who are still just as good. It’s a very interesting experience to meet people across the entire spectrum.”

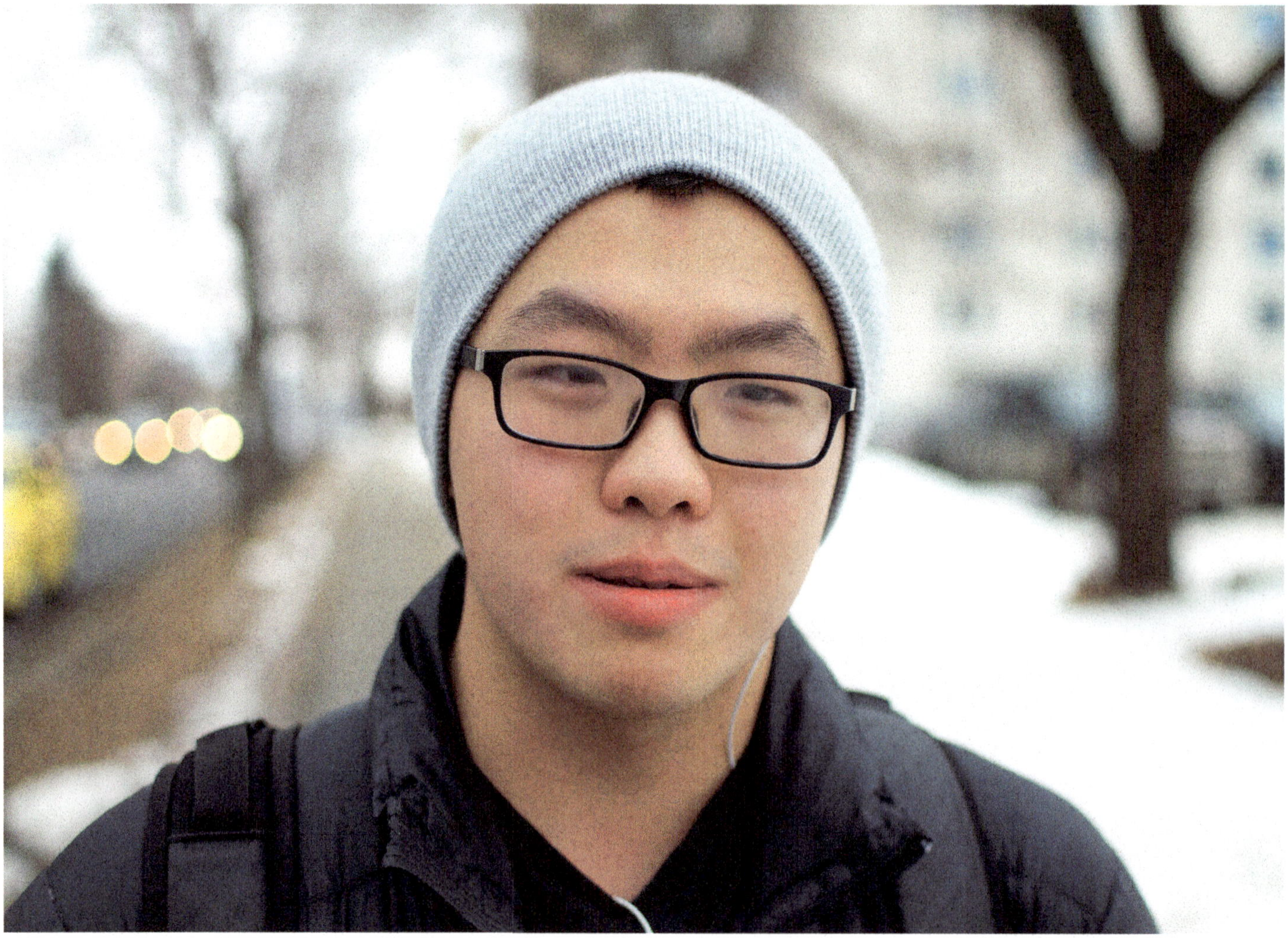

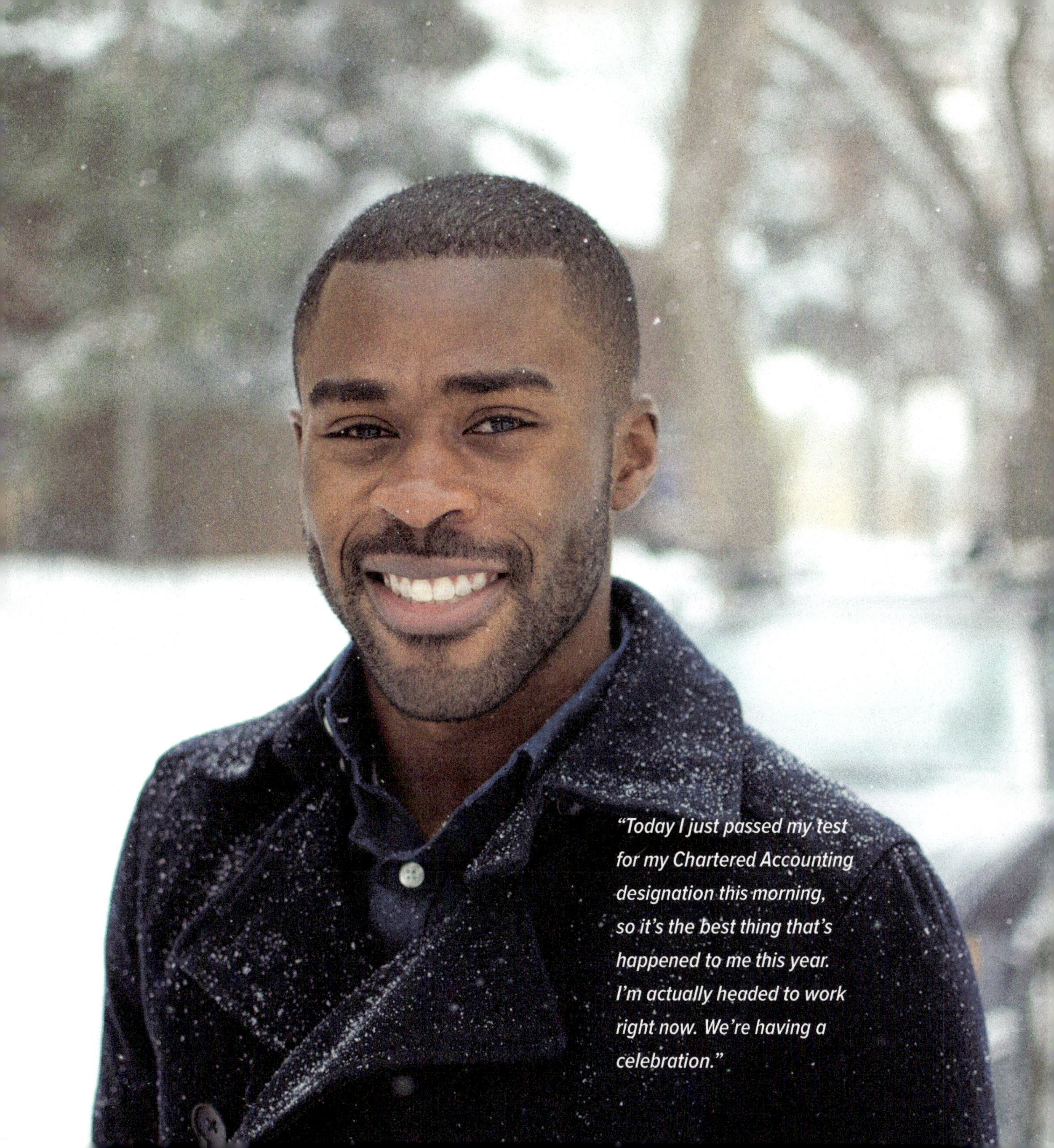

"Today I just passed my test for my Chartered Accounting designation this morning, so it's the best thing that's happened to me this year. I'm actually headed to work right now. We're having a celebration."

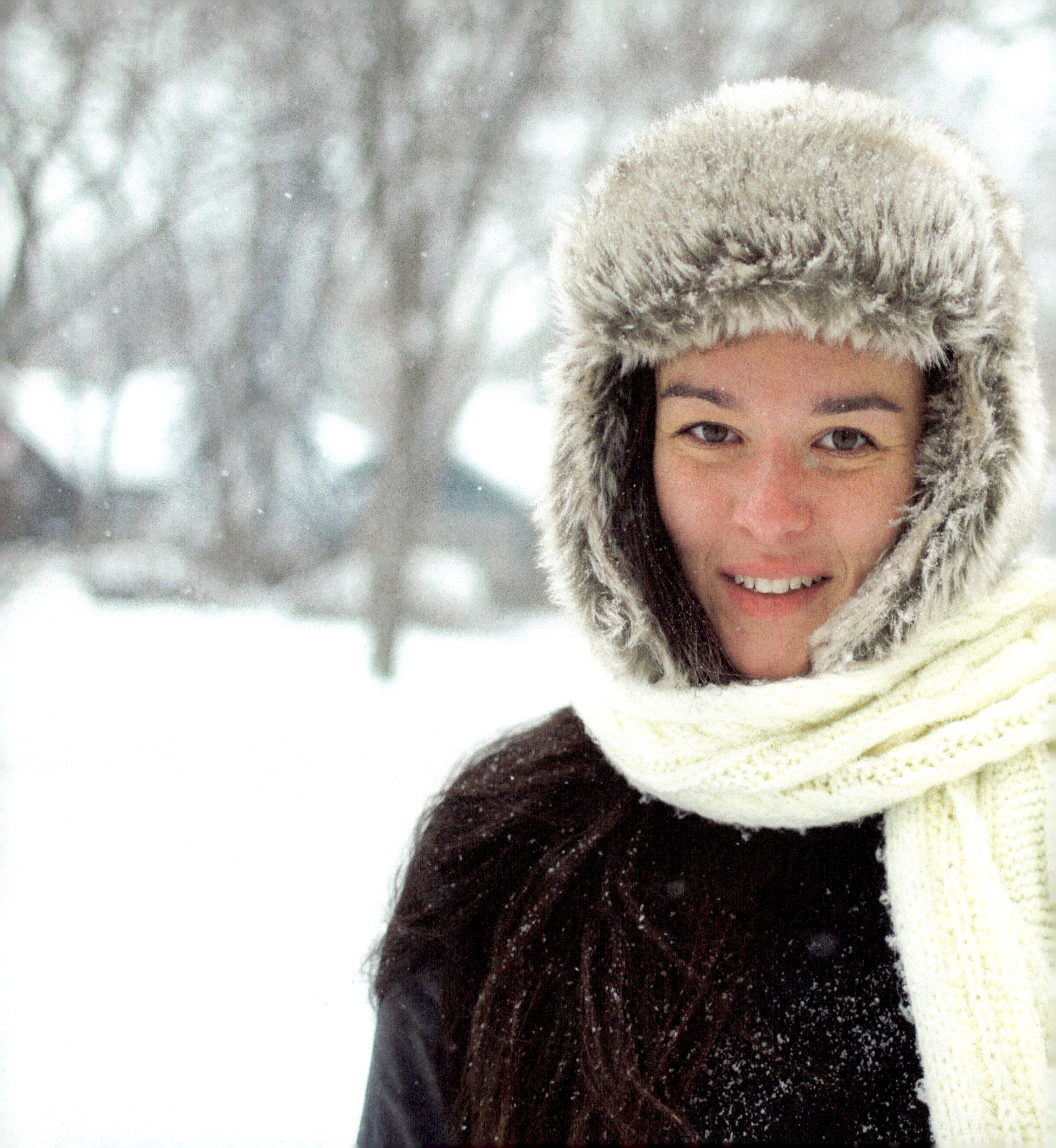

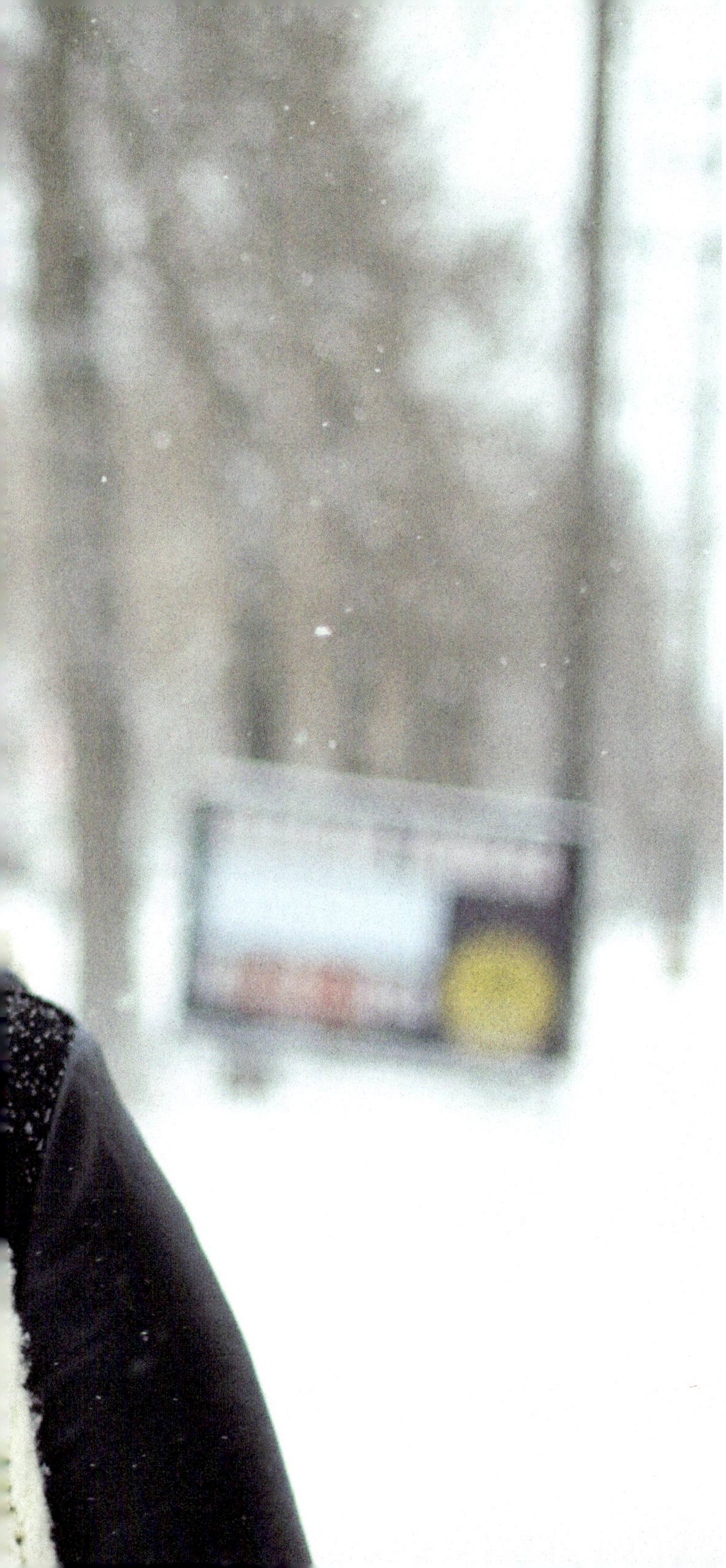

"This is a typical face of Edmonton," she says, laughing through the cold.

"I am teaching my first four hundred class at the U of A. So that's good. It's popular music."

"Are you a musician as well?"

"I sing with Pro Coro. We preform at the Winspear all the time. It's a professional choir. But I'm an academic theorist primarily. "

"One of the hardest things I've ever had to do? Bungee jumping actually. My girlfriend at the time was doing it, and I'm terrified of heights, so I just had these two days when I was trying to picture myself doing it and I wasn't able to. I was just imaging standing up there on a solid thing and then choosing to leave that thing. I wasn't sure if I was going to do it and I had sort of decided against it. Then I went into the office and she was signing up and in a moment of stupidity or bravery, or whatever it was, I decided, 'I'm going to do this.' So I agreed. I signed up. It was in Costa Rica. The highest one in Central America apparently."

"Just to make it even more terrifying," I say.

"Yeah, exactly. But you're not even standing on a ledge. You're on this little ten by ten platform that just like wheels out into the middle of this valley. So I'm shaking like crazy. And the guy's like, 'OK, so what I want you to do is, don't hesitate, don't blink. I'm gonna say, One, two, three, bungee, and then you jump. 'Cause if you don't jump, if you hesitate, you're not going to do it.' So my whole body is shaking. I'm sweating like crazy. I go to the edge and hear, 'One, two, three, bungee.' And I hesitated and then I went. I sort of flopped. You're supposed to jump and do this sort of proud eagle stance, and I did not. I flopped." He chuckles.

"Was there a moment of euphoria while you were falling?"

"There was this one beautiful moment. After the first fall, I was totally freaked out. And then you have this moment where you bounce down and come up and that's when you get that weightless moment. You're looking around and you go, 'Oh geez, I'm just floating here.' And then you go back down. I was predominately terrified but I did have this one brief moment when I thought, 'Oh, I see why people like this.'"

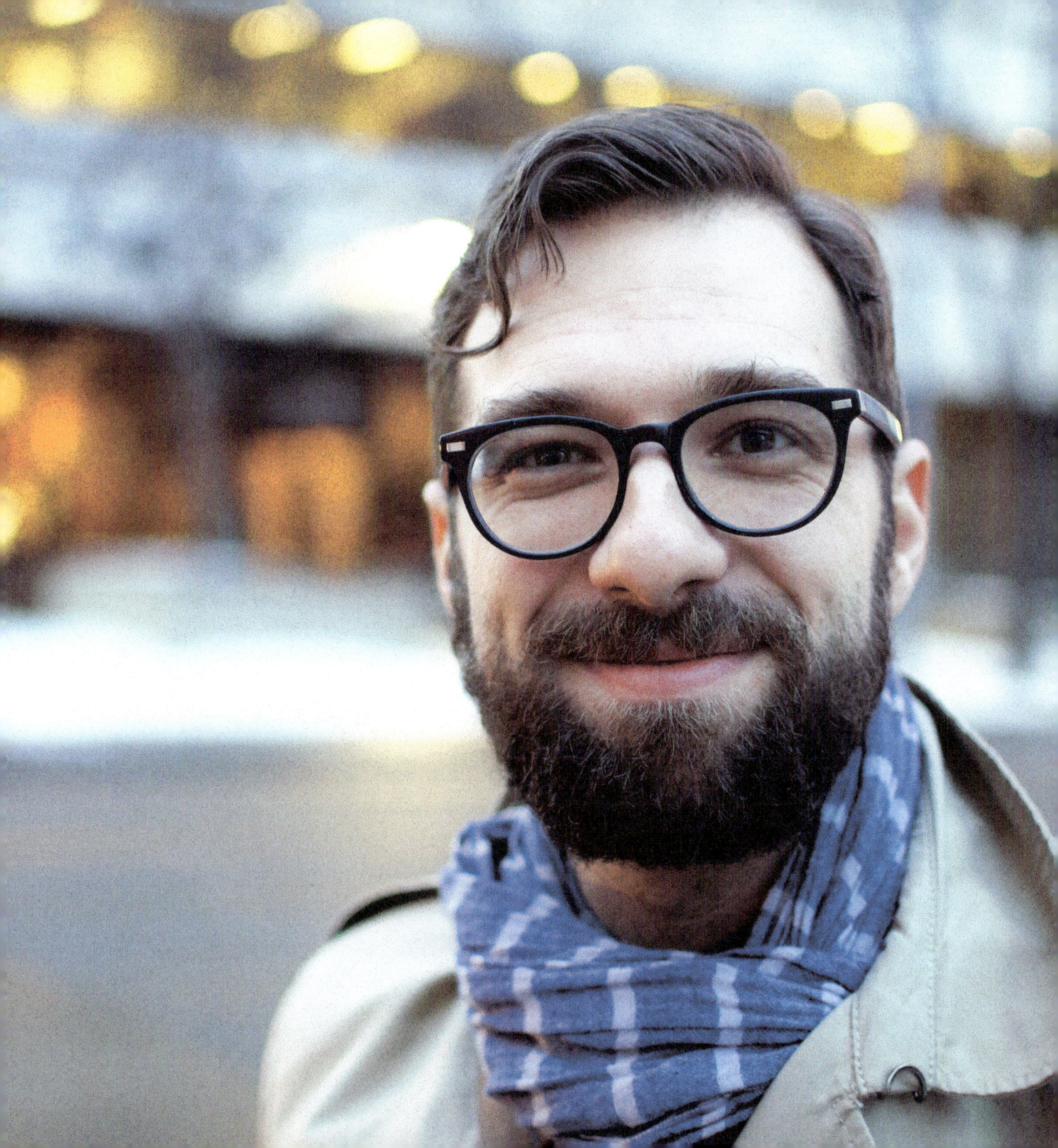

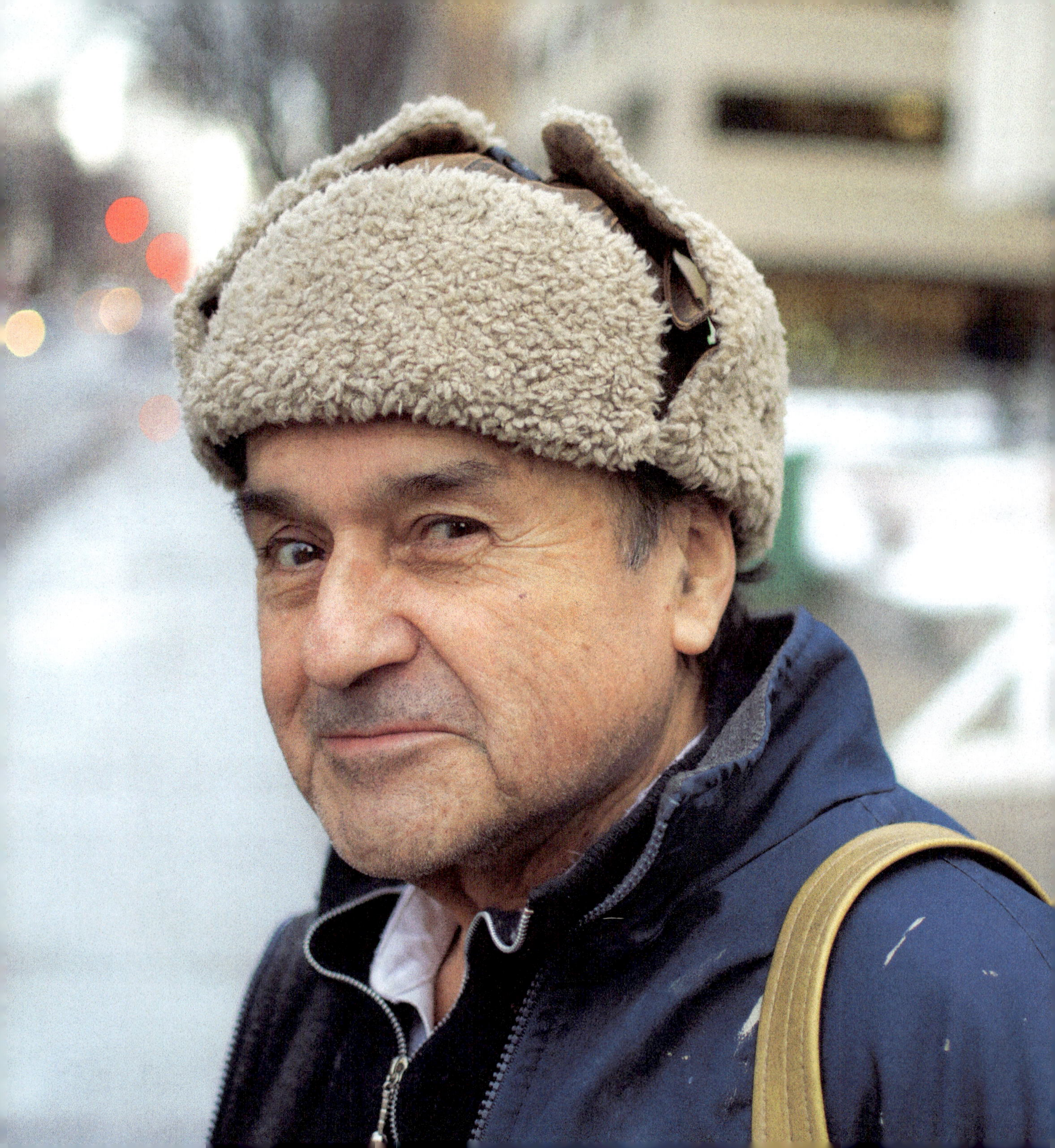

“Winning the 6/49 would be nice,” he says, chuckling. “But I’m just trying to make a living. If you weren’t born rich, you’ll never be rich.”

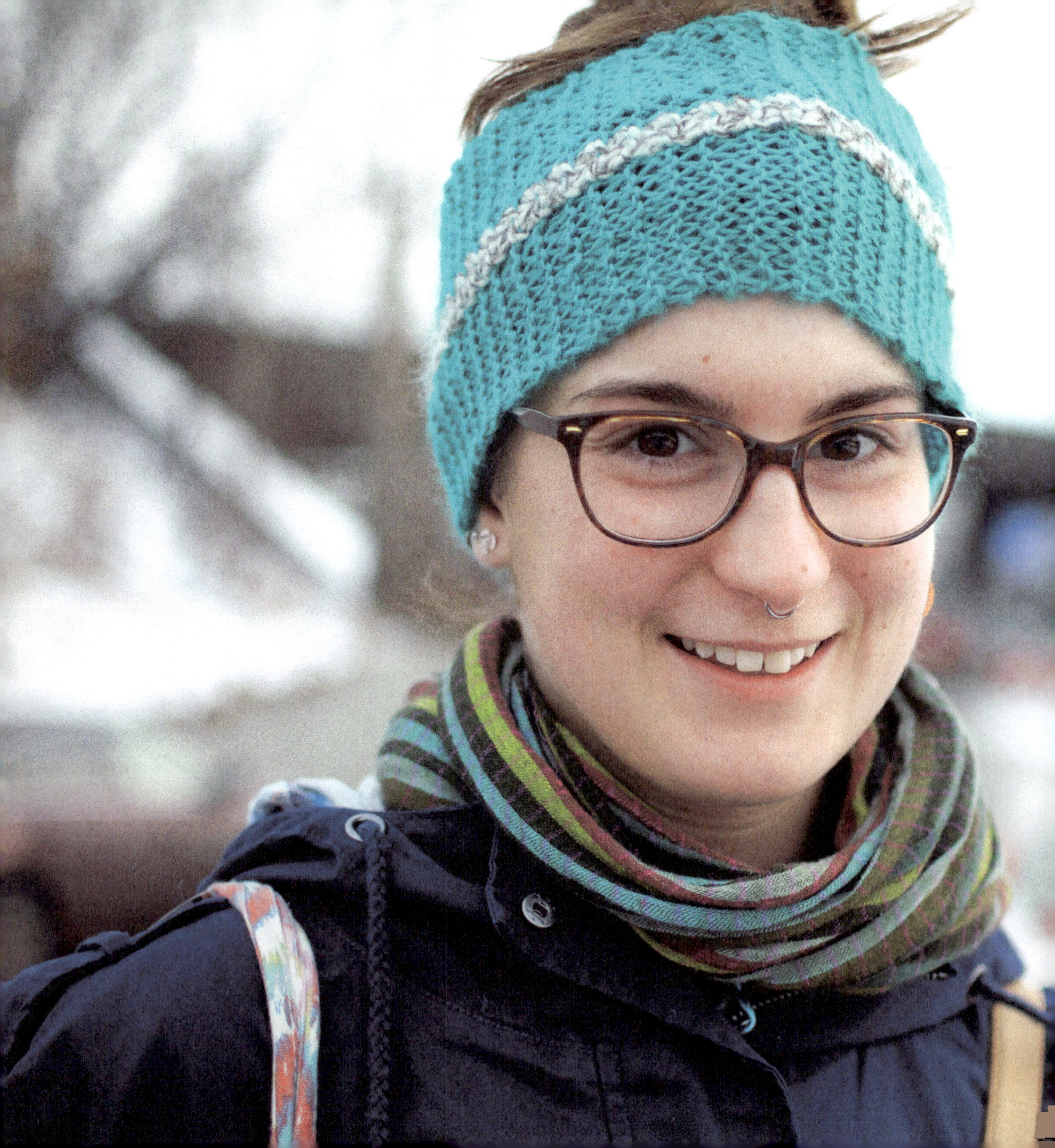

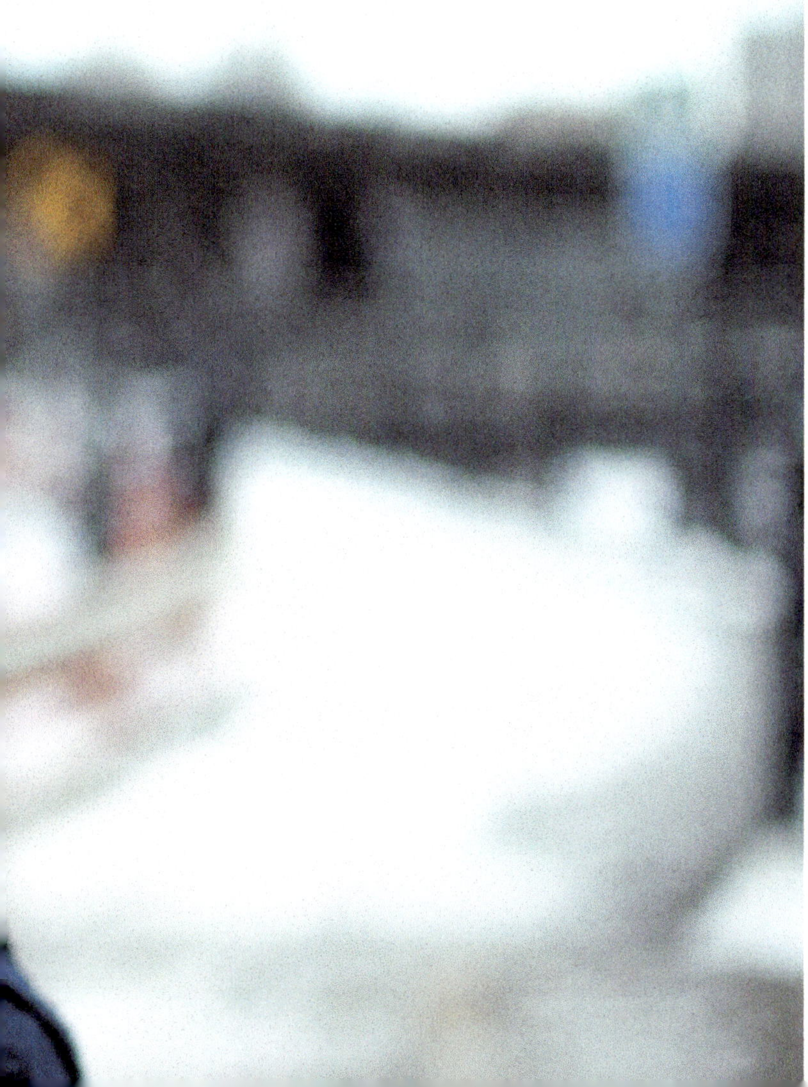

We cross paths on the High Level Bridge. She's just finishing her trek across the bridge, and I'm starting mine.

"I just came back," she says. "I was backpacking in New Zealand and Fiji. It was pretty great. I wasn't gone for that long, just for six months but it was really cool. Travelling without a plan, I ended up staying places when I wanted to and leaving when I wanted to. I wish I had more time but I had to come home. I just had a tiny backpack, so you realize that you don't need a lot of things. And then I came home and kind of cleansed all the things I didn't have any attachment to."

"What's it like being back?"

"It's pretty weird. It's always an adjustment coming back into society I guess. I was in the middle of nowhere just doing my own thing. But it's all right," she says, perking up a bit. "Today is a really good day. If you caught me another day, I may not have said this, but today is a good day. I love the winter. You don't really get a winter like this in a lot of places in the world."

ABOUT THE PHOTOGRAPHER

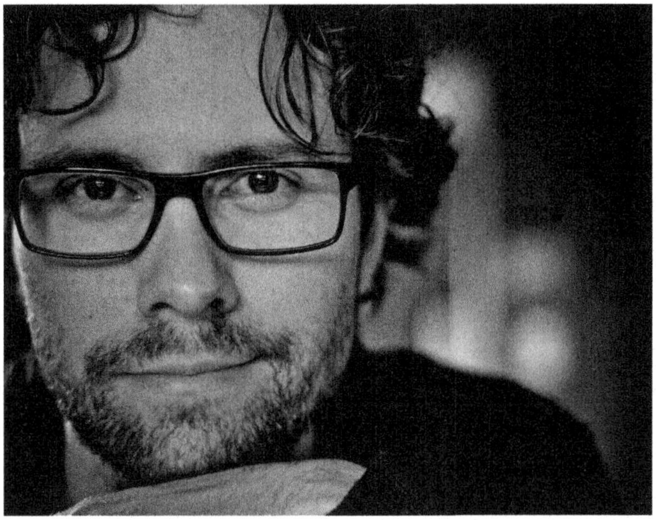

Shayne Woodsmith is a photographer and an award-winning writer. His fast-paced, thought-provoking, and at times utterly frantic, debut novel, *Twenty-Seven*, delivers a disarmingly honest portrayal of human frailty and strength while presciently casting a cold eye on our health-obsessed future. His second novel, *My Brother Mercy*, is a deeply personal, heartbreaking, and at times hilarious take on the monotony of daily life, the complexities of familial relationships, and the pursuit of meaning in the seemingly endless loop of day-to-day existence.

He is currently working on a collection of short stories and collaborating with Christian Whitty, the illustrator of the *My Brother Mercy* cover, on a graphic novel. He lives in Edmonton with his spouse Megan and their two cats, Mortimer and Tuna.

CPSIA information can be obtained at www.ICGtesting.com
Printed in the USA
LVOW05*0928080815

449360LV00020B/48/P

9 780994 810519